To Keith
from

Willi

Glue Sniffing & Out of body Experiences

William T Stead

authorHOUSE®

AuthorHouse™ UK Ltd.
500 Avebury Boulevard
Central Milton Keynes, MK9 2BE
www.authorhouse.co.uk
Phone: 08001974150

First published by AuthorHouse 5/28/2009

ISBN: 978-1-4389-7987-8 (sc)

This book is printed on acid-free paper.

There comes a time in your life when important decisions have to be taken. In my case this involved a long wait, and through a serious of circumstances I now feel the context of this story, should be expanded beyond the confines where it has remained. I started writing from a disadvantaged position, through a lack of education, and it has taken many attempts to reach this point, which has made these different ventures quite a challenge. In order to finish a project such as this, the desire has to remain strong, and the ultimate reasoning in advancing a work of this nature must override any inadequacies, or fears about confronting big issues. This is not a normal tale of drug abuse, or surviving through the hard times, it explains how a serious of events brought my consciousness into the realms of a spirit world. This information is important to those who are interested by the structures that caused the transformation.

I was born on St Valentines Day during 1959 in Glasgow. It is quite ironical, because any relevance to having a romantic personality could not be further removed. The birth itself would have caused some controversy as it resulted in an illegitimate child. The ethics of that time looked on such occurrences not with the liberal attitudes of today, but more one of disdain at its outcome. I imagine these factors would have put pressure on the woman who was my biological mother, and for whatever the reasons she sent me into children's home for adoption.

In relating this episode in my life it is necessary to rely on other peoples accounts. This would have been during the first few months of life; also to make matters a little more complicated I developed asthma and other related chest infections, which made those early years quite unpleasant. The children's home turned out to be a transitional phase, and the people who came to be my new parents were an older couple called Thomas and Sarah Stead. Before leaving the home my adopted family were told that due to these chest complaints they would be taking on a great deal of work before I improved, and this was by no means guaranteed. It certainly turned out to be the case and most of these early years were spent indoors, as going out was restricted, because of the conditions.

My new home became the industrial area of Govan, which at the time was a major ship building industry, and the setting for the television sit-com Rab C Nesbit, but unlike the portrayal which appears today it was a bustling community full of life and interest. We lived in a tenement building on the second floor, and that environment became my foundation for growing up. It would have been around the age of four when I was allowed out on my own for the first time. This experience is a clear memory from that period. One advantage with being confined to such an extent was that my mother could devote time in giving me a basic education, before attending the nursery school that was opposite our home. This was a useful preparation, before beginning the primary school.

Having the ability to read and write gave me an advantage over most of the other children who had spent their time enjoying themselves. Under normal circumstances a person makes progress at a given rate as they advance with their education, but in my case this did not happen. I have no idea why this came to be. After a few years of stunted growth it caused some concern to those who evaluate your progress. They decided that I needed an assessment to find the cause of the problem. This resulted in being sent to a special school for children with learning difficulties, for a few weeks. The end result of this entailed one afternoon each week attending a small unit that gave individual coaching. This seemed to satisfy the teaching fraternity, but in all reality it did nothing for me.

During my early years at school accompanying the learning difficulties was another restriction; only this one caused some concern. Asthma curtailed my participation in developing normally, and restricted the playing of games, because to get excited inevitably brought on an attack. In time you learn the dividing line, which initiates these events, and learned to curtail my excitement levels. It was quite a relief when this condition came to an end, and I began to experience the freedom that others took for granted around me.

It was around the same period when my father was involved in serious accident at work. He was employed in the local docks that became the areas biggest magnet for attracting people. The incident occurred whilst standing by a crane that shed its load, and one of the sleepers hit him on the back. This caused a spell of time in hospital that was intended to let him recuperate. I didn't know the extent of these injuries, but from all accounts it he should have recovered without any problems.

On the day of his release our own doctor told my mother he would have to rest at home, and in due course get better. However events did not turn out that way. He seemed to deteriorate, and although this was evident to those around him at home our doctor said it was only natural. My mother was unhappy at this prognosis and arranged for a specialist to give a second opinion. His diagnosis was cancer, that of the terminal kind. He was taken back to hospital where a transformation took place beyond all recognition in a short space of time. I saw the changes, but did not equate their inevitable outcome as the others did.

On the night he passed away my mother had some friends around the house, as was happening frequently about that time. The people were gathered in the living room, as was our dog that happened to be sleeping in the corner. On waking he came over and sat at her feet in a way he only did with my father. She informed her guests that Tommy had died. A few hours later the police came to tell her the news she already suspected. When this happened I was in bed unaware of the sequence of events unfolding. At eight years old the concept of death is not something you can visualise. This possibility hadn't been part of my understanding related to his illness, and its likelihood was shielded from becoming known.

In the morning after getting up I discover a number of people in the house, which seemed quite odd. A tense atmosphere was in place coupled with the fact they were acting slightly strange. All of these factors were unusual, but I failed to understand the significance behind them. Leaving the house at the normal time for school I met one of the neighbour's daughters who offered her condolences.

Walking to school I could not accept the facts. Before entering, everything fell into place and standing alone experienced that which became the first major shock in life. It left me unsure of what to do, so I returned home and found out it was a reality.

My father was brought to the house the day before his cremation, and laid to rest in the spare room. It gave me an opportunity to visit him without anyone's knowledge, as I wanted to see for myself this part of life that reached beyond my normal understanding. As an experience it was so strange and unnatural to be in the presence of a dead person, who but a few days ago was my father. The room generated a sensation that could almost be touched. I looked into the coffin and eventually kissed him on the forehead. As a last embrace it was the strangest emotion you could imagine.

During the next few years' life trundled on without anything startling happening, apart from failing to achieve reasonable grades at school. I wasn't very pleased with the end result of my endeavour, because it would not have been welcomed at home. I decided this report wasn't suitable for my mother's approval, and forged her signature. It was in turn given back to my teacher who failed to notice the difference in handwriting. My efforts in the scholastic front during the following year improved sufficiently so that it could be seen this time; unfortunately she happened to notice my handiwork. I got a hiding from her and the belt at school.

At the end of 1969 we as a household moved from Glasgow to Fife in the East cost of Scotland. This proved quite a change because of the different way of life. We had been to Kennoway on holiday staying at relatives various times throughout the years, and my mother thought it would be a better place to live than the city. The move caused mixed emotions from within, but on balance not unhappy ones. On the day for moving a neighbour took me to Kennoway, as my mother went ahead a day earlier to set up the house. Accompanying us was Jimmy who for many years had been a lodger in our household. He was a friend of my fathers, and came along, because throughout the years he associated our family as his own.

Jimmy was a very decent person, although I never looked on him as a surrogate father. The house was located in an ideal position with scenic views from the front. This area was so different to that way of life I had been used to; it allowed me to explore the countryside the day after moving. I experienced a set of emotions in being free of confines associated with a city. It became a time of awareness and discovery. Each of us has fond memories from childhood; this became one of my own.

Attending the local primary for less than two years, moved on to the high school. In that time my personality changed to that becoming more independent of the confines of the home and my circumstances. It came about in a way that at first brought about a conflict of wills with my mother. Looking back I can now appreciate what she was trying to do, but at the time it was not viewed at with the benefit of hindsight. The same can be said for Jimmy as he tried within the confines of his position to make me conform, and I feel sad in a way that these factors were beyond my grasp.

The high school was also a change of life in many ways, but unfortunately not from a work ethic. It held an excitement because of its larger nature. As far as education went there were only two subjects that interested me, these were Art and History. With art it was the only topic I had always been competent at from an early age.

My skills developed to a reasonable standard in comparison to those around me, and in its own way interested me sufficiently to derive a pleasure in creating this kind of work. History was slightly different, as it became a fascination in the facts of bygone ages. There was however one problem with this subject, and that involved my conception related onto paper. This involves writing down the images of the mind into a legible form. In most cases people can manage a competent summery, but not me. My English standard had not improved since beginning full time education, with the writing being no more than a scribble and the spelling at an imbecilic level. My history teacher took into account the differential between my verbal knowledge, and it's counterpart of the written word. These two studies were not enough to allow a meaningful relationship with the aspects of education.

In my new environment there were two people who became good friends; their names were Tom and Willie. Our purpose in life during the first year became that of causing havoc to the teachers and pupils respectively. As a result of our actions we were frequently being belted, which became an unofficial sort of contest. The other part of school life, which interested me, concerned who was the best fighter in my particular year. In the primary, having decided that I was the best of our particular bunch challenged the other boy who was regarded as the best from the other schools. The end result was the other boy did not take up my offer, which kept my ego happy. My new form of identity developed its own set of rules in governing the ideals between right and wrong. One aspect that developed around then involved stealing; it began as many people from my background with shoplifting. This involved basic items that had no real relevance to anything; it was petty theft, which served a point of excitement.

The summer holidays came and went, then on the following year our timetable at school caused my two friends and I to be separated from a number of the lessons. This slightly changed my outlook as to the purpose of being there. In most of my classes there was a boy, who in all reality is the beginning of this story. His name was Steven and although we had different personalities, the one common factor, which linked us, involved a dislike of being in school. He was a mature boy for his age, that is his outlook and tastes were some years ahead of his stature, a quiet person who unlike me did not show off. It proved a strange allegiance, but we got on well. Our strategy on certain mornings involved getting marked in for registration, then leave school to go shoplifting in Leven; it being the nearest main shopping centre. This turned out a good arrangement, as the partnership proved successful. At first these outings were restricted to a few days a week, afterwards going to Steven's house listening to records and the like. On one of these occasions he told me about his use of drugs.

To understand that time drugs were little known about by people of my generation, and it proved a rarity to find someone who actually took them. I did not ponder on this matter;

in fact looking at Steven's appearance now that he said this more of his characteristics fitted into place.

My interest in schoolwork dwindled during the first two terms of the second year. Attending some classes, these were usually the most enjoyable ones. One day we decided not to bother with school. I believe it was during the first term in March 1972. Steven and myself walked into Leven, after telling some friends if inquires were made we had not been in that day. Its lucky most of the teachers seemed unconcerned, almost as if some unwritten rule said if you were not prepared to learn it was no loss to them. This suited both parties concerned.

Taking the shortest route, we arrived in the shopping centre and did the rounds. Whilst in a large department store, Steven asked me to get two tubes of glue. It proved an easy task, as they were located at the back of the shops, and out of view from most people. The tubes were slipped inside my jacket, and then we causally walked out of the store. Thinking he wanted these for some repair job, it was to my surprise when his true intentions were revealed. I had known of the term glue sniffing, but that was the extent of my knowledge. Steven explained it gave you a kind of drunken feeling, with sound effects and the occasional hallucination. He used glue ever so often but preferred pills, or smoking dope. To him it was a cheep alternative, which proved amusing. Felling quite excited by his description; there became no hesitation associated in attempting this, not for one second did I give any consideration to possible side effects, or physical harm within my body. These matters seemed of little importance.

It was decided the beach would be the best spot for its use, with least disturbances. Leven's beach has at its beginning a curved wall, which acts as a breakwater during high tides. This is about five-foot high, with some steps at the bottom. From here we could see anyone coming. Not that it mattered, glue sniffing was in its infancy and the chance of someone realising our actions was very limited. My friend bought two packets of crisps which after being eaten the bags were then used to hold our glue. This was a clear day with few people around, it being too early in the season for tourists. Having settled down on the steps he gave me a brief description on how to use the substance. The cap was removed and a small hole made in the top part of the tube, then it was squeezed into the packet. The aroma at first smelling strong wasn't unpleasant.

After being placed over my nose and mouth the smell increased in strength, but soon hardly became noticeable whilst continuing to breathe in and out. The bag became a centre of my attention, as if it were an extra part of the body. This appeared as a form of synchronisation. It wasn't a major shift, more a different awareness in situation. My attention switched from this, to thinking about what changes the glue had caused, and they appeared to be minor. Thoughts were a little slower that usual. This proved disappointing having expected something more.

Whilst on these steps, in the background I could hear the sound of an ice cream van, or so it first appeared. This wasn't a normal jingle, and when it continued curiosity made me look over the wall to locate its source. Surprisingly nothing could be seen which offered a visual recognition. Feeling slightly bewildered asked Steven if he could hear this tune. "There is no sound; it comes from inside your head". As he said these words, it began to make sense. Thinking in the normal way it should have come from behind. Looking inward its source was soon found. Listening to this jingle internally, it changed to other sounds mainly instrumental based. It appeared strange, as these tunes were abstract in construction, like the ice cream composition not quite recognisable.

I discovered by concentrating on the various effects that it was possible to alter some aspects of this in a limited sort of way. This only lasted a short time, then that tune was remixed into a melody not of my conscience selection. These sounds tended to repeat on themselves, anyway it was hard work thinking about altering it, and it proved easier to let my mind relax and enjoyed the demonstration. Sitting there a strange sensation began to come over me. My body started to feel heavy, and whilst it happened all of my reactions slowed down. This took no more than a few seconds to occur. It was as if someone switched off the power and my functions were shutting down. Being aware of this made no difference. Starting to fall from my seated position I made with supreme effort a lunge towards Steven, and my left hand managed to grab his hair.

I fell as if in slow motion, taking my companion with me. We hit the sand, and then quickly as it had come the sensation disappeared. I was left holding his hair feeling a little silly for my actions, which had been a grab for survival. The shortness in time between the whole events was under a minute. This created a sense of unreality about the incident, and once over it did not seem important, as say a similar act under normal circumstances. I apologised to Steven, and tried to explain what happened. He was content in his own little world until being dragged back to reality. That ended the entertainment for then, and we made our way back to school.

The last few months leading up to the summer holidays were spent much the in same routine, going to school, signing on, and shoplifting. We used glue on average once or twice per week, usually when both in the mood. Its effects on me stayed much the same consisting of various sounds and no visions; also the falling over occurrence did not recur. My control over these interactions was getting better. This happened with time and a little effort. As a comparison it would be like tuning a radio into a better reception. This allowed me to devote more time towards my thought patterns, excluding speech which I could hear as plain as any pitch in the normal wavelength. These effects were mostly musical compositions, or they started of that way, and then deviated with a break of concentration.If I were to relax many different sensations would come and be listened to with interest, trying to understand their nature within my mind. This was in its own way quite amusing, but I did not understand why Steven could see events with relative ease, whilst nothing of this nature happened to me. My first experience of a visualisation took place at the beach during a solitary outing. It came a little way into the session, after playing with the sound effects it took the form of a dog, which suddenly manifested before me.

In distance it would have been no more than three feet away. It looked like a Dachshund in appearance, but not quite real being similar to a three dimensional cartoon of very good quality. Studying this for some time, my first reaction was to stand up and try and touch it. This proved unsuccessful as the dog backed away. Realising it would be a waste of time the next plan involved coaxing the animal towards me.

The dog walked beside my seated position just out of arms reach, then went along the beach and disappeared. There was nothing else to be seen, and my attention returned to playing tunes inside. It must have been a few minutes afterwards when the same dog returned, this time with six pups playing around her. I had not seen them appear out of thin air, for they had arrived from a greater distance. The mother stopped again not far from my reach. She watched me as the others roamed around. I centred my attentions on her offspring, making all the hand movements, which under normal circumstances would have brought them forth. It was also unsuccessful. I gave up and walked back along the beach. A passing observer would have found the situation amusing.

During the remaining few weeks at school I only went to the beach with Steven two or three times. As it was now possible to visualise, as well listen to the effects I felt content with my new situation. The visions only came along at brief intervals, it being the sound show that comprised most of the session. If pictures did appear they tended to be of a simple nature, like the dog scenario. At the time it seemed good enough, for how can one know what to expect under these circumstances. Being as it were in tune with my mind was enjoyable, and not a let down in any way.

On our last day in Leven before the break we obtained solvents by the usual methods, and settled down for an end of term session. Sitting on the steps as normal, poured out the substance. After a minute or so this was having no effect on me. Pouring some more into my bag made no difference. Glue changes one's awareness in a number of ways, and none of these came into play. Thinking there was something wrong with this particular tube, I was about to ask Steven if he was getting anything out his bag, when a clear picture came into my mind's eye. I could see a boy and girl sitting in a grave-yard. The boy was playing with a daisy, half-looking at the flower in a daydreaming kind of manor. The female who was wearing a black dress had blond hair, seemed to be watching me intently.

This vision only lasted a few seconds, and then vanished. It had taken over my normal sight, but its clarity appeared perfect, and put me of my stride. I did not know what to make of that which had just been witnessed, it being something out-side the confines of my understanding. Asking Steven if everything was fine, he reported nothing out of the ordinary. I did not think about it for very long, as then it was not impor-tant. The people were unknown and it wasn't a prominent event. The meanings of these circumstances were yet to come in my life. This being a few years hence, and by then I had for-gotten of this brief sighting, until it was enacted in the same way as shown on that day.

With the school closed I spent most of my time in Kenno-way, playing with other friends of that time. The summer was a particularly good one, and the people here did not know about glue sniffing, for they were different from Steven and his associates. I seldom used the substance in the holiday, as other normal activities took up my time.

Towards the end of the summer I told my friends from Kennoway about glue sniffing; that is what it had done for me up till then. On the day we gathered across from my house on an embankment, which has excellent views of the coastline towards Edinburgh. There were around eight of them, and after a bit of procrastination, we collected enough money to buy a tin. It wasn't possible to steal from the local shop, as their security proved slightly better than my usual haunts. One of the boys collected it, and then returned to our location. Gathering some bags, these were shared out. A few of them were not too keen on the idea, but went along in order to save face. It became the first occasion I had done this with more than one person.

The weather conditions were exceptionally warm and relaxing, the sort of day when you can appreciate just being there. As a group the overall effects were not stunning. It did not bring out any strange reactions, and they wondered what all the fuss was about. Personally I saw another side to looking at nature, in offering an enhancement of perfect conditions. There was a new aspect for me, and it involved echoing. This became apparent, firstly through the crickets which appeared in abundance that year, with their chirps reverberating. The car engine sounds coming from the road behind also had a lingering effect. This created a very relaxing feeling, and rounded off a good day. As the group experience failed to be any sort of success, I did not involve the others from then on. In fact only towards the end of the holidays did my usage become more prevalent.

Whilst at home one afternoon, with nothing to do I fancied a tube in some privacy. My old primary seemed the ideal location. After buying some at the shops I wandered along to the school. Picking a doorway entrance it seemed to be a good spot for noticing anyone approaching. Unfortunately this plan wasn't thought about in great enough detail, because a few minutes after starting the sounds of footsteps could be heard approaching. It appeared too late to make any sort of move, so throwing the bag to one side I tried to act cool. The relaxed attitude took a bit of a knock, after seeing two policemen standing before me. This created a number of problems, of which the first being a side effect of the substance causes a tendency to slur your speech. Being perfectly aware of this, it was important to say as little as possible. They asked me what I was doing. My replies were rather limited, more in the hope they did not want to ask numerous questions.

The police were checking for damage at the school, which apparently had been happening regularly of late. As one of the officers looked around, the other asked me if I had been drinking. This got a shake of the head. It seemed all was in order and they were about to leave, when one of them kicked my bag and the game was up. They're developed an interesting discussion between them as to whether, or not I had broken the law. It being the first time both policemen had come across this situation. Unsure what to do they radioed back to base, and found out no crime had been committed.

They escorted me back to my house, and informed my mother what I had been up to. Until that point she had not known anything about this, and appeared shocked at the revelation. Thanking the police for bringing the matter to her attention, she proceeded to give me the third degree. It was pointless trying to explain why I did this. She became distressed at something outside the range of her normal understanding. A parent's concern is for their children's well-being, and to her this was the worst thing I had ever done. At the end of our talk she asked me to give it up.

The use of solvents by then had been amusing, but no more. I expected better things, which had not materialised, and giving her my promise this would be so, it was half meant at the time. During the rest of the holidays my word was kept.

On returning to school, the class structure was different once again, as Steven on most of the days had other lessons from me. This made it more difficult to bunk of school together. When having time off it was usually alone, and it did not take long before getting back into old habits. In order to understand what this was like I will try and explain in detail the feelings, and sensations during a glue session, as it appeared during my early involvement, this is an individual account, because it varies from person to person.

From the time you take the first inhalation it's roughly thirty seconds to create a change in your actions. It gradually builds up over this short period of time, and can be likened to being slightly drunk. That is one side effect, but is only a simple comparison. Whereas drink makes you forget the physical presence. I found glue brought me into closer harmony with myself. At that early stage this centred on the activities of the brain, which I became very aware of. Instead of just having abstract ideas my conscience was now in the same area as the thought patterns: it being a sort of no mans land. It brought out a different side of my personality, in how I then looked at my surroundings. If the locations were pleasant, I would see this in a truer light. It stimulated an opening to a sense of awareness. This would only happen if studying the landscape, because most of the times were spent on other matters.

Thoughts happened at a slower rate, and were more focuses. I also felt younger than my actual years during those occasions. This is a difficult concept to explain. It was perhaps more one of finding innocence, an escape into a part dream like state. When a vision appeared it proved a bonus; with the passing of time these were getting better in construction and more frequent. The use of glue became an extra part of my life by then. It wasn't an addiction in any way. I would describe its use more like an occasional pastime. After a session it would take you a little while to return to normal. As the beach was our haunt by the time we walked the few miles to school, or wherever all outward indications were gone.

In the centre of Leven there was an old run down public toilet. On one of my visits to the town, after acquiring some glue it started to rain. I did not fancy sitting on the beach getting wet, so went to this building, as it became the nearest dry practical place. Choosing an end cubical it looked dismal inside. The lighting wasn't on and because of the rain, a little darker than normal. This became my first use of the substance in a confined space. It turned out to be a lucky move. My drab interior transformed into a bright new room that changed design during my stay. The one constant feature then became a screen on the front door of the toilet. Through this medium I saw many new aspects that were greatly improved from the beach.

The cubical became secondary, watching the screen that appeared similar to a television. With this I saw cartoon characters enact different scenes, in which my participation was limited to willing the subjects actions in a certain way, or a situation on. It was as a beginning a simple interaction that improved with time.

On that day a most unusual occurrence took place. As well as the cartoons there were scenes in which people were present. This involved seeing naked men standing within the screen on the door, and the number varied from one to four. I knew two of these then as characters from television. The others I had never seen before. What made this so odd concerned the men being pregnant. On seeing them at first it depicted a frontal view. They stayed in that position, then turned sideways and walked off. Trailing behind each of them a newly born baby hung from an umbilical cord. The look on their faces always remained expressionless, as if they did not understand what was happening to them.

This enactment repeated itself many times on returning to the toilet. Depending on when this was, it would sometimes be two or one man. As time progressed the number stayed at a constant one. Accompanying that particular sketch on each occasion were depictions of sexual cymbals, displayed within the screen. Being thirteen, these did not mean anything to me. This is a pity for if I could have remembered their exact position; it could have helped to better understand a strange enigma.

At school certain lessons were being attended more often. This was due to my interest in girls developing. In my group was a particular girl, who on looking back became my first proper crush. We got on well together, but I never asked her to go out with me, due to a lack of courage on my behalf. For some reason or other, I went out with one of the other girls in that class for a few days. It was my first date.

I had been in trouble with the police by then, once for stealing a pair of binoculars with Steven. The other time involved a friend from Glasgow. This proved slightly more daring and we stayed in a shop till after it was closed, hiding in an upstairs store. The plan centred on waiting until every one had gone, then break out with some items. It proved unfortunate the night we chose to do this happened to be the same one the owner did a stock take. For that little escapade it entailed a term of probation. During the same period I was in trouble with the police for some other matters.

My mother received a letter from the school concerning my absenteeism, and she was invited for a discussion with my head teacher a Mr Marshal. On the day we went to his office. At first he talked with her alone, and then called me into find out why I was having so much time off. My mother thought as I went to school each morning, my time was spent there. Between them they also tried to discover the reason for getting in to trouble. It became one of those situations that did not feel too comfortable, for how could you say it was more fun shoplifting and the like, than staying at school. At the end of this Mr Marshal said something, which during the discussion sounded odd. "You will have to grow up more quickly than others because of your circumstances". It sounded like some kind of warning, which appeared out of context. Perhaps I should have listened more closely, for my life was about to change quite dramatically.

During November, this would be a few months after the meeting I attended school on a Friday; it being the same day the first snow fell. Come dinnertime we were playing in the front yard, throwing snowballs at one another. I managed to hit a cyclist who was brave enough to go by the school, which created a great deal of amusement. On the pathway, beyond our confines a woman happened to walking along the pavement, with her umbrella up. By then I was getting carried away, and threw a snowball, which landed on the top struts breaking some of them. Going forward I noticed she was an old lady.

This took the smile of my face. Offering some assistance I felt quit embarrassed for my actions. The woman said, "Why did they do this"? I was not doing any harm. I walked back to the class feeling ashamed of my actions. That night when going home by bus I had a premonition something was going to happen to me. It may just have been a guilt complex from earlier that day, but on arrival my mother told me she was going into hospital in a few days. This was followed by the bombshell, when she said the social work department intended taking me into care. On a previous occasion she was in hospital I had been in trouble with the police, whilst Jimmy had been looking after me. It had been decided in official circles, this should not happen again. I wasn't very happy about this. To move away from home at that age involved a total upheaval from my whole way of life. The timing also proved particularly bad. In school I had been working towards going out with the girl from the art class. This may not seem like a big deal, but she became the first female to take over most of my attentions. Within one weekend all of this ceased to be a possibility.

The next day a social worker arrived in Kennoway to take me the ten or so miles to the children's home. During our journey he explained what kind of set up I was going to. This was a home for people, who through no fault of their own ended up in a long term placement. He said that in my case it should only be a short stay until my mother came out of hospital, not the sort of place, naughty boys went to. At that time I came under the problems at home category.

One of the establishments more famous inhabitants was a former world champion dart player. He went there a little while after me. We arrived in the small village of Ellie passing through the snowy landscape, which thinned out the nearer we became to the seaside. Ellie is one of the picturesque villages spread along the coastline towards St Andrews. The home lay right by the beach, and it looked quite attractive. I saw my new bedroom that was shared with some other boys; basically the building was split up into a boy and girl's section. After settling in I went to see the man in charge, with my main concern being able to carry on attending my own school. After explaining this to him, he said it wasn't possible.

That night was spent getting acquainted with some of the people, in the home. The following day proved a relaxed occasion, being a Sunday. Going out for a walk to discover the location, a shop was found which stocked my brand of glue. I purchased this and took it back via, a scenic route along the shoreline. Although this area was only a few miles from my normal patch, it had a different feel to the surroundings. The place chosen to use it on the sea front created something quite special.

This offered a combination of sensations that were more an appreciation on nature. The timing seemed particularly appropriate, because the sun was about to set. I watched the sequence of events unfold before me, as my eyes had never witnessed previously. It being serenity personified.

During the life span of this tube I did not experience the normal sensations, as my perceptions were encompassed within Mother Nature. When darkness fell, and the glue ran out I returned to the home. The following day it became the turn of the new school to have the pleasure of my company. I found this to be a culture shock in understanding the differences from my own high school, with this one appearing rather formal. In class people took the whole thing seriously. At first I thought it was just a particularly dull group, but it seemed to be the same throughout. After a few days I could not take this starched approach to life, and decided to give it a miss. Telling one of the elder boys in the home of my intentions, he agreed the school was boring. His name was Graham and in a few months he would be leaving both the home, and school to join the merchant navy at the beginning of that summer.

My plan revolved around walking towards the bus stop in the morning, then slip off. Graham said he would come along. On the first day we caught a bus to Leven and went shoplifting. I had told him about glue sniffing and he appeared keen to try it. We got two tubes, and then went to the beach where he used it for the first time. Graham reaction to this took me by surprise he became drunk. It was a total wipe-out, loosing all control over his movements. He attempted to stand up without co-ordination from parts of his body. It looked really funny, saying it was the weirdest occurrence that he had ever experienced hearing no sounds or seeing anything, the effects were purely physical. It wasn't frightening, just strange. I could not comment for it proved a first in my experiences, watching someone act this way. It appeared different to the falling over during my introduction.

From that day onwards if anyone was to use glue as a novice I made a point of watching his reactions, rather than just enjoying my own. We returned at an appropriate time, and planned to go out again the next day. In the home nothing was said about our absenteeism, so it created no problems on the following morning. Instead of going back to Leven we began walking around the surrounding villages. The direction was left to Graham, as I didn't know this area at all. After some hours we passed a pub in a small village. This had a courtyard running adjacent to a field at the bottom. To its right was an adjoining barn.

After walking through it was noticed outside in the yard a number of bottles that could be exchanged for cash. The only problem being, they would have to be taken back to the pub. A little further on was an old brick storeroom with no door attached. Glancing inside I stopped dead in my tracks. There were numerous full crates of beer; it was the gold tops that caught my attention. Going inside we discovered a variety of beers; it became a proverbial Aladdin's cave. Filling our jackets and pockets, walked out as casual as possible checking for people, no one was around, so went to the barn. We could not believe our luck, with it being a rural area must have accounted for the lack of concern for their merchandise. The barn was on two levels, and climbing to the top one of these drank the beers. It did not take long to finish them off.

I said to Graham we should go back and get some more, but he was in no fit state to attempt this, so going alone I got another six bottles. It appeared clear on my return, but I was not in the best positions to judge this objectively. Drinking the rest of these bottles proved to be hard work, but we managed. As these were consumed quickly, it began catch up with me and feeling the full potency, it hit quite suddenly. I thought it important to try a last attempt for the beer depot.

Trying to explain this concept to Graham became somewhat difficult. I was about to go alone, when voices could be heard coming towards us. Keeping silent proved a futile gesture, as down below were the landlord with two policemen. After the initial shock, it wasn't something that bothered me unduly and I found the whole situation quite funny. Graham didn't know what planet he was on. When being questioned it caused me to laugh.

We were taken to Methill Hill Station, then after discovering our names and addresses the police contacted the home, and my social work department. The first person to arrive was the head of the home, shortly followed by my social worker. I cannot remember the name of this woman, but I will never forget something she said shortly afterwards. It was decided that Graham would be taken with them, and I was to be left in the station until something else could be sorted out. The head of the children's home would not have me back because of the trouble caused. That seemed fine by me. It took another hour until she returned, and said I would be going back with Jimmy in Kennoway, until other arrangements could be made. She then went on to say my mother was seriously ill and would not be expected to live much longer. These were the exact words used. I became devastated; it had never crossed my mind her illnesses were of that serious a nature even though she had two heart attacks recently her state of health seemed to have improved. It is not a situation you can envisage happening.

To this day I cannot understand her logic in telling me this information in the condition I was in. It's a difficult enough matter to explain under normal circumstances, especially when dealing with someone in my age group. I have been involved with social workers for a number of years after that; and as a personal observation to be good at the job is something you are born with. There are people in that line of work who act like idiots, this woman comes under that category. Also as an observation, some of them go far within their professions.

One of the social workers took me back to Kennoway in his car. Sitting it silence, deep within my thoughts the car pulled up at the house. I went straight to my room ignoring Jimmy, and those who brought me. Lying on my bed life did not seem important any more. I decided to end it all. This was the most traumatic day in my life, and the decision to kill my self was assisted by the alcohol. It wasn't something I had ever contemplated before.

Hearing Jimmy walk upstairs allowed me to creep into the kitchen and took some of my mother's pills from the cabinet. Returning to my room, I didn't know what these were for, but taking them one at a time, it seemed part of my life slipped away. I cried then for the first time in many years, and it became a very confusing incident.

After lying there for a little while my reasoning seemed wrong. Going into the front room I told Jimmy of my actions. He phoned the doctor who sent an ambulance, and they took me to the hospital where my stomach was pumped out. One of the doctors asked why I done this. It proved a difficult question to answer. The effects of the drink were gone and all that remained was a feeling of stupidity, combined with embarrassment. The simplest reply being to blame it on the drink, then keep quiet.

I stayed in the hospital for a few days, and then a different social worker came to see me. He said I was to be transferred to another place in Fife called Stratheaden. I knew this name, it being the local mental home. Looking back on my actions I did not believe this was a justified response, for it was only a moment of confusion, which caused these circumstances. It wasn't something that would ever be repeated. Being in no position to argue over this matter, it left me unsure as to what I wanted any more. My normal life had been turned upside down. After he left it gave some time to think about my actions. I was not happy being sent to this place. There seemed only one alternative, which involved running away. I wasn't ready for a life on the road just at that point, so leaving the decisions to the will of the state waited to see what happened next.

The following day a social worker arrived to take me to the hospital, he first of all stopped in at his Leven office. This caused us to pass through the top of Kennoway, which happened to be on the same road leading to the hospital. I could see my house in the distance and looked with sadness, at a way of life passing before my very eyes. We entered the grounds of Stratheaden that at first looked draconian in appearance, it being the main building that captured my imagination, and expanded on the pre-conceived ideas people have over these places, however this was not the section that housed adolescents. It being at the bottom and any similarities this had to my beliefs could not have been further removed.

I was taken inside and met a group of people who were quite friendly. My new accommodation being in a small unit that housed about fifteen boys, and girls. These were also nothing like what had been imagined. If you were to meet them on the street, they would seem no different to anyone else. I actually began to like the place and the peacefulness that it came to offer.

There were two people who became central characters in my time in this establishment. The first was a boy called Michael who became a chess companion. Our abilities were evenly matched which channelled my mind in a direction it seldom ventured. This diversion created an understanding of a different kind of person, from my normal associates. He was a complex individual who proved quite intelligent. I found it an appealing trait in his personality, and in its own way this drew me towards him. We talked about many subjects, apart from the central reason for us being there. It was the one thing no one really discussed. I assume they were embarrassed, like me at the fall from grace in normal society.

Michael became an introduction away from the norm, and he is the first person whom empathy could be associated with. My other association was a boy called George, he being a simple individual and his one contribution to my development came through his record collection. I became a David Bowie fan after borrowing some of his albums.

One weekend close to Christmas, George and I were allowed out to spend the money that had been provided by the authorities. This being the first occasion since coming to the hospital I had been permitted to leave. We went to the nearest town, a few miles away. It was called Cupar and after arriving in the centre, wandered around. George wanted to buy an album in one of the record stores, it being a double he did not have enough money. Offering the woman his two pounds, she kept it as a deposit. He then gave his name and address. This caused her to look at us strangely. It proved quite embarrassing and I could not get out of the store quickly enough.When in the town it seemed a good opportunity to get some glue. I had not used any for a few months, and was looking forward to the occasion. It being the season of good will this was purchased, rather than shoplifted. I spent some of the money on glue, and bought something that resembled a Christmas present. We walked back to the hospital, were George and I would use this in some quiet little corner. The storeroom of the gymnasium became as good a place as could be thought of. This was to be George's first use with a substance of this nature. He accepted my description of its effects as a matter of fact, and used the tube as easy as if I had just passed him some sweets.

It wasn't a memorable session for either of us. George only heard buzzing, and I cannot recall anything out of the ordinary. This proved slightly disappointing considering the length of time since my last usage. When glue is not working particularly well, there is no point carrying on. The bag still had a little life in it; so taking the remainder carefully folded it and hid this under my bed for later on. My bed was in a dormitory with five other occupants, and George had his own room. As none of the others knew about glue sniffing, there was no point telling them anything. Besides I wanted the meagre amount to myself.

This became my first use in bed, and more importantly in the dark. Waiting till everyone had settled down, reopened the bag and began. When using glue in the past any awareness perceived had always been beyond my physical body, this is with the exception of sounds which in recognition came from inside. I was about to be introduced to a new concept, that of touch and feeling. Laying on the bed it appeared to change texture to a firmer yet smoother surface, becoming noticeable as soon as the glue took effect. It became an interaction between my body, and another object. I could feel this throughout any part of the physique that came in contact with the sheets. Being used to sound, or vision this proved a pleasant change, but my attentions soon diverted back to the familiar, when a repetitive instrumental tune could be heard coming from the opposite side of the room. Looking over to that direction I could now see a life-sized picture of Alvin Stardust, who was a British pop star of that era. Its colour was black and blue, both of a darker shade, which complemented the room.

There was no movement from the picture that stayed in existence for five minutes or so, until the fumes in the bag became ineffectual. The sound and vision blended in well with one another, it seemed as if they belonged together. This was only a simple depiction, but significant in it's on way. It's a pity I did not recognise that factor at the time. The darkness being a key to upgrading my experiences, but that belonged in another time and place.

Putting the empty bag under the bed went to sleep, not giving a great deal of thought concerning the serious of events for that night. During the week I had an unexpected visitor, it being Mr Marshal my head teacher from Kirkland High School. This proved quite a surprise to think he made an effort to see me. We went to a private room and talked about life in the school, and other local news. It became an informal chat; there was no mention as to why I had ended up in the hospital. Before leaving he gave me a pound of his own money for Christmas. This proved a really kind gesture that will always be remembered.

In late December I decided to run away from the hospital. Nothing had been said concerning my future, and it began to play on my mind. I did not have much of a plan, it being more of a need to get away. This became the first occasion of trying anything of that nature. In the beginning my concept had been shared with two people, both of these appeared keen to come along. By the time we were ready to go the number had risen to seven. It seemed funny how this all came about, as if cabin fever had overtaken the hospital. Personally it made no difference to me if they wanted to come.

Around midnight we all met in one of the rooms, and then slipped out the window, it being an open plan building without security features made our exit trouble free. Getting to the main road, my initial thoughts were to head towards Kennoway then sort something out. After walking a few miles the main group did not want to continue, so persuading them to go on I could see that their hearts were not in it. George and I were the only one's who wanted to continue, and left the others by a phone box, until given a head start before they called up the hospital. We walked some distance and found a road that led towards Kennoway. This being a cold evening with clear skies, it rather surprisingly allowed us to keep warmish whilst staying on the move.

In the early hours whilst plodding on something unusual happened. I began to hear the song 'Star man' by David Bowie, and it came from within me. Walking along the road had developed into a semi-trance like condition, which until then I was unaware off. This combined with tiredness, created an almost glue like state of awareness. The song brought my conscious mind back to the situation, and for the first time it became possible to enjoy a sound show without the use of any stimulants. The lyrics were to be repeated a number of times, and I did not try to interfere with the process, because the song happened to be rather good. It also indicated a potential that could be used when the conditions were right.

We arrived in Kennoway, and by then George wanted to give himself up. Making the same arrangements as before took him to a phone box and said he could call when he liked. It created no problems here, being in my own territory. I went into the woods close by which allowed some time to evaluate my next actions. This brought me to a point that reached the initial objectives. Sitting in the woodland no further ideas came to mind, and the only option left open involved going home. Walking the short distance I got Jimmy up. He phoned the hospital, and they said to leave me there until morning, as someone would come later on to bring me back. Going to my own bedroom, tiredness soon overtook me. This allowed sleep to follow shortly afterwards. I woke up sometime in the morning, whilst still dark and looking around my room it became an unfamiliar place. This felt very disconcerting to not recognise my own home. As realisation came, it failed to offer any comfort.

In the afternoon a social worker arrived for the return trip. On the way he said my mother was slightly better, and should be out of hospital soon. This became the first piece of good news to come my way in some time. Once back nothing was mentioned about my little escapade by the staff. Speaking to the others they were returned by the police, and sent to bed. It appeared this was treated as a childish action not worth a mention When back in class one of the staff, who as well as teaching assessed each of his pupils made a recommendation about my future. He suggested what I needed concerned discipline, and not a placement at the hospital. His evaluation being a List D School, "This was a new name for the old approved school ". I did not understand this term, and would not have been very happy with his opinion had it been familiar.

True to his word, a few days later it became confirmed such a placement had been made. The school was called Balgowen, situated in Dundee. Having been under the impression that once my mother was better, I should have returned home, it now looked as though this was not the case. My first attempt to run away did not have any real motivation behind it, but now circumstances had changed. I intended to get away and stay out for as long as possible. As it turned out the night for my escape was New Years Eve. The last attempt had taught me to wear proper clothing. This time I brought a jumper with me. It was eleven p.m. when I left the building taking a different direction, to avoid using the same route as before. I came into a small village when the bells rang in the New Year of 1974. This first night was bitterly cold and the puddles in the road had frozen over. It proved quite a temperature drop compared with my last outing.There were not many people walking around after midnight in the village. I found this un-usual for Scotland on its favourite night. The cold was getting to me, and looking about there appeared no obvious place, which offered a warmer retreat. Walking around the village I settled for a phone box, this at least kept the chill out. On the ledge where the directories lay, someone had left their change. It turned out to be twenty pence or so, which became rather useful not have any money.

If you have ever been in a phone box, in the cold for any amount of time you will know it is not the most comfortable of places. This became apparent shortly afterwards. Leaving it caused me to find some location that would enable sleep in relative comfort. At least that was the plan. Walking for some time I came across a house in the process of construction, it being the first spot that offered anything like normality. This was an optical illusion. Finding the part that provided the most shelter I covered the windows with some plastic lying around. In another room they had rolls of fibreglass. These were laid out for a makeshift bed. With part on the ground, and some of the sheets over me, attempting to sleep proved near on impossible. Every time I moved due to being uncomfortable the sheets would fall of. If I did manage to sleep it became short lived, only to wake up shivering. This turned out to be the most uncomfortable night of my life so far, and not the best way to start a New Year. At first light I got up and walked around the room, in order to warm myself.

My intentions were to go towards Kennoway and find some friends who could help me out. Leaving the house created a sense of relief, and in reality I was glad to see the back of it. The sun was barely visible that morning, just a red blob in the sky, but a welcome sight never the less. Finding the right road a lift followed shortly afterwards from a man going to Leven.

Travelling all the way he dropped me off on the outskirts. It was still early in the morning and walking to the centre, discovered everything was closed. I then went to the house of Willie a boy mentioned earlier, he being one of my classmates. Telling him about being on the run and my imminent care order, the only matter left unspoken concerned where I had just come from. Staying at his house for most of the day allowed me to eat plenty food, then in the evening we visited one of his friends and played cards. I stayed until ten o'clock and had to move on because it would have aroused his mother's suspicions.

The one place I knew stayed open all night was the public toilet in Leven, where some of my glue sniffing exploits took place. This became my bed for the night. It turned out to be as uncomfortable as the previous sleeping arrangements, in a different sort of way. The temperature had not raised one iota, and the best you could do was nod off. Going to Willie's the next morning I fed, washed and did more or less the same routine until it became time for returning to my bed without breakfast. By the third morning I began feeling very tired due to the lack of sleep. The only conciliation being the shops was now open after the holidays.

I went to the beach and fell asleep until opening time. This morning proved a little better than previous days. There appeared slight warmth in the air that made a pleasant change. I bought some crisps and sweets with the money found in the phone box, and then went to the department store for my first glue of the New Year. Returning to my spot began what developed into the most interesting experience to date. Sitting on the concrete steps it started of in the normal way by hearing different sounds. Looking out towards the sea I became aware of an object coming from very far away. This phenomenon operated outside my line of vision, it being located to the left and could be sensed travelling at great speed. It enabled a first involvement in comprehending a presence beyond my physical boundaries. I had a basic understanding of its shape, which became clearer in recognition the nearer it came. Feeling in a relaxed frame of mind, it did not warrant a great deal of attention just then.

The object now came within the landscape of my vision. This is located to the hills about five miles away. It changed direction to head towards the beach. I felt its every move in detail. My perceptions were still concerned with the sights in my line of vision that is watching the waves lap on the shore. The tide was out during the morning, making each break a gentle movement. As I watched this, one of the waves came in and stood still in time.

I became totally amazed and my first reaction was to stand up and look at this, trying to get up from my seated position proved impossible with my whole body becoming a motionless object. These two actions happened within a few seconds of each other. The only part of my anatomy still able to function was the eyes, which looked on in concern towards a situation outside the realms of my understanding. The presence was now almost at my location and slowed right down just before reaching me. The next unusual occurrence-taking place involved the sand at my feet climbing onto my shoes.

This continued rising upwards over my trousers, whilst the body was incapable of doing anything.

I am not the sort of person who panics in the face of difficult situations, but this proved bewildering. It all happened very quickly and I was unable just then, to judge the situation logically. The presence came and stopped behind me on the pathway beyond the wall. I still could not move and everything took place as before. My situation did not require turning around to see what directed all of these actions, as it became possible to judge its shape and outline in perfect clarity. This was a representation of Jesus Christ on the cross. The sand now almost reached my thighs, when a voice spoke from behind. It asked me to give up using glue. As the last utterance from this statement was heard, my right arm became free from whatever restriction held it. I said yes throwing the bag to the ground.The figure started going backwards on the same course it had come, whilst the sand returned towards the beach. The last event to be noticed involved a resumption of the waves hitting the shoreline. When all of the altercations returned to normal, my body became free. Standing up and looking around me, I thought what a strange experience that was. Without any distractions, it became possible to consider the serious of events taken place. It did not seem right looking at the situation more from a clinical point of view. The stationary wave appeared to be superimposed on the sea line. This presented only a fraction of difference between the vision and reality. At the time it did not allow any clear study, because the serious of events overtook my normal observations. The sand climbing up my legs also looked different to that on the beach.

Going over to the bag of glue picked it up and started again, because I was curious to see what would happen. From my seated position after the fumes took effect the same set of events came into play once again, only quicker this time. Without any distractions it became apparent the stationery wave had nothing to do with tidal movements, this being a clever use of distance, for underneath the normal waves were on their last point of breaking, before returning back to the sea. It seemed strange to behold, for it altered an accepted concept in vision.

My body went back to being motionless; that is apart from the right arm, which remained free. I could sense the J.C. vision coming towards me only at a higher speed. His presence did not have the same feeling as the first time. As he neared, the sand came back as before. It seemed a let down in its own way, a poor imitation of the first. Repeating the same question I replied yes without emotion in my voice then stood up when permitted. I began to feel unhappy with myself. This being nothing to do with the glue sniffing, it was as if all the recent misfortunes became focuses on that point in time. Realising my life had changed, perhaps forever without any clear recognisable future I walked along the beach thinking about what to do, and did not come up with any answers.

Wandering around Leven aimlessly, I eventually went to the social work department and gave myself up. The desk clerk showed me to the office of my probation officer. She asked a number of questions about where I had been since running away. It is unusual for me to have a strong opinion about a person for good or bad, but she became one of the exceptions. Finding no reason to speak to this woman it was quite easy to ignore her. It proved difficult to stay awake with the office being centrally heated. The cumulative effect of this, plus a lack of sleep was catching up.

She left me in a waiting room then went to arrange the transport to Balgowen in Dundee. I fell asleep almost instantly. A young man awoke me some time afterwards. He and his companion were to drive me to the approved school. They explained that my own social worker wasn't available for the journey due to other commitments that at least was one good part to the day, her presence not being one of the more pleasant aspects of life. Once in the car I fell asleep and only briefly woke on passing through Kennoway. This had a touch of irony about it, for at that point the social worker told me my mother had come out of hospital on the same day. I was too tired for thinking about this statement in any detail, and fell back to sleep. When waking up properly we were leaving Fife crossing over the Tay Bridge into Dundee, leaving one county for another, and one way of life to begin something new.

The home turned out to be ten minutes drive away from the bridge. Passing through the outskirts of the city centre, it had turned dark by then. My first impressions gained from looking at the building were one of gloominess, which had an austere feeling about it. Walking into the main entrance, I was handed over to one of the staff members who escorted me to the allotted group. Funnily enough the difference in running away only delayed the inevitable, from that morning when they had been expecting me. Such is life.

The building was sub-divided into different groups. The one I went to was in the main building, and held most of the inhabitants within the premises. This being a large area partitioned into sections, with my bed positioned at the start of one of these. It looked similar to a Victorian boarding school set up. Until then I had not seen many of the boys as they were in the television room, or adjoining corridor. Setting eyes on them for the first time, it looked like a crazy house. They were running around acting like deranged individuals. It caused me to wonder, which of the two establishments was meant to hold mental patents.

The bedtime here was early, around nine o'clock. As things turned out this was close at hand, so going straight to the dormitory it appeared a sensible alternative rather than talking to anyone. The bed seemed the worst excuse for its namesake I had come across. It was lumpy and no more than a mattress on a wooden box, but in comparison to my last three nights accommodation it appeared luxury. I fell asleep shortly after putting my head on the pillow, and did not get up until reveille in the morning.

The boy opposite woke me, then after dressing all the inhabitants of the main building had breakfast in a large communal hall. From here I started to find out how this place operated. It was regimented and strict. We all went into the main courtyard and stood at arm's length, to be accounted for. This being for a roll call of that particular morning, and afterwards you were dispersed to whatever assignments lay ahead. It being my first day I was kept aside and taken to the matron for a standard issue of clothes, each of the boys had to wear. I should have realised what was coming next, a haircut. Standing in the courtyard with the others, it did not sink in at first that everyone had a similar style. After the penny dropped I wasn't happy about this, and put up a feeble argument it had taken over a year to achieve this length. One of the staff said it would only be a trim, and like a sucker I believed him. They had a contract with the local barber who cut the boy's hairs. This trim turned out to be a short back and sides, with the end result looking a right mess. The only conciliation being it was possible to get a comb through my hair, which hadn't taken place for a long time. You live and learn.

In Balgowen there was only one person known to me. By coincidence he was a boy from my former High school, and more unusually had been in the same registration class for the first three years of my secondary education. His name was Eddie Ross, and as a slight digression it is worth recalling a story that happened in one of our lessons. Eddie did not attend school very often that is after the first year made fewer appearances. In our third, I believe he only came twice, and that is what caused him to be sent here. On the second of these occasions it was during a music exam. This being for violin, which had been the main instrument studded during our lessons. In this class no one had mastered these skills very well, it being a basic appraisal of each individual's performance.

Tom, Willie and I were put to the front row for laughing at the attempts, which on the whole were pitiful. The teacher wasn't your average run of the mill schoolmaster. He was more of an extrovert, to say the least. We were informed the next one to laugh would result in the three of us receiving the belt. Luckily two had been already, and we were trying hard to keep straight faces. Then came Eddies turn. I should have known it would be a disaster. He did not have a basic understanding of how to go about this evaluation. The three of us turned around to watch him, because Eddie looked funny at the best of times. On this occasion he picked the instrument up, and then did an impersonation of George Fornby on his ukulele, with a smile on his face. It proved too much. We all burst out laughing to the point of having tears in our eyes. Willie was the worst of all falling to the floor and could not get up.

The teacher went crazy, which added to the hilarity. He belted us as promised, and had to belt my friend by dragging his hand from the ground, which looked ridiculous. I think from all the events during my time at school it was the most comical, and worth a mention. Eddie being my first contact in Balgowen it was through him, I became acquainted with some of the others. I was in the top age group, being just under fifteen. The eldest boy was sixteen and the youngest ten.

Regarding the placement of the youngsters within this establishment, it seemed lunacy. This wasn't only my opinion. It was a view held by certain staff members who could express themselves in confidence; they agreed it wasn't the right environment to bring boys of that age up. It makes you wonder about the people who make these decisions. They are considered capable responsible adults, and have within their powers the welfare of minors; it certainly makes one think.

As mentioned life was fairly strict and everyday events which had been taken for granted such as eating sweets, watching television, and going out had to be earned by good behaviour. In this type of environment I have found you tend to stick closer together, and one's friendships are of a deeper level. This happened to me during my stay in the home. Within a short space of time I meet a boy, who like me came from Fife. We were to become good friends, and had some interesting times. His name was Donald, and like most of the others had a problem with attending normal school. The only difference between us concerned a vice for steeling cars. The first two weeks passed uneventfully whilst settling in. The only matter worth a mention is my taking up smoking. This is something I had been opposed to previously.

In Balgowen because of the different way of life I began reading books. It is perhaps, the only positive outcome of my time there. Prior to arriving the grand total number of books read was one. Through reading I discovered another medium, which diverts one out of a narrow band in life.

The first occasion of being allowed out of the home became on a Saturday afternoon. This was the only time boys were permitted to leave the premises and that depending on one's behaviour. It had taken a few weeks to come about, because they kept you in, until a settling period was over. I met Donald at the gates from where we walked into the town. Donald stayed in a new section outside the main building. This seemed plush in comparison to my accommodation. It did not take long to reach the shops, and as a matter of course went shoplifting. This in the circles I mixed was a routine event, and accepted as part of our culture. It was never a big thing, just something we did. Getting a few items, including glue went to the foot of the Tay Bridge where Donald used the substance for the first time.

We sat on a small embankment to the right of the bridge. From this spot it offered a little cover in case of intrusion. When taking effect I began to see the shape of a man standing within the skyline. He was very large in appearance, and looked something similar to myself. The imagery wasn't clear enough in the facial department to say for definite it was me, but I could feel it was the case. He wore a distinctive jumper of a kind in my possession some years previously. The person in the sky began to run, but did not get anywhere. It proved intriguing looking at the depiction, and found it a little strange witnessing something that had no apparent reason. Donald heard buzzing and echoing, and wasn't bothered about the effects one way or another. We returned to the home before six o'clock, which is the latest you were meant to be out. It had been an average sort of day, and I was happy just to get away for a little while.

On Sunday we had to attend the local church. For this occasion there was a special uniform consisting of a brown jacket, straight black trousers and black shoes. We were marched down the road with the staff at the head of the queue. There became one benefit to this farce, and it involved picking up cigarette buts on the way. I have nothing against the church and believe it to be a good institution, for those who accept the teachings in the bible. My disagreement came through being made to go. If a person believes in a god of whatever religion that is a personal choice. Being an important decision in one's life should not be forced on you, and in essence this is what happened. I can honestly say to my knowledge not one boy enjoyed this form of enlightenment.

I write this opinion as the lead up to before entering the building; that was an experience in itself. It had been some years since my last visit to a church. This proved to be a little different. We were taken to the front and put to one side, under the vicar's nose. He was one of those preachers with zealot type beliefs. When delivering his sermon any part of the speech, which had moralistic overtones, were directed towards us. His eyes would open wide, and began staring as if to say "redeem yourself before the lord and you will be saved". Seeing this for the first time I almost burst out laughing, it was so bizarre. That might have been effective in the middle ages, but he was wasting his breath.

I think the only person to get something out of this was preacher himself. It lost its novelty value after a while, and I along with the others was glad to get back. On the following Saturday both Donald and I had been good boys, and were allowed out for the afternoon. The only place, which held any interest, concerned the shopping centre, and this became our destination. In a department store whilst looking around, I noticed two suited men watching our actions. It was the first shop we had gone into, and being so no plans had been made to steal anything as yet. The men were following us, trying to act discreet and not making a very good job of it

Talking between us about this, it was decided to have some fun. Walking around the store we picked up various items looked around suspiciously then returned them. At first it was done together, then individually. We met up at the exit were Donald had temporally lost his follower. The one on my tail stood back and waited for his companion. During the interval one of the shop girls came up to him and asked a question relating to the store, and used his name. "He replied you must be mistaken madam I do not know you". This seemed very funny at the time. We walked out of the shop slowly, giving them a chance to catch us. The one who watched me asked us to accompany them back to the store. This was performed with some amusement. The end result became a feeble interrogation, by people who did not have a clue how to catch, or deal with shoplifters. I told them to improve on their technique. After a few idle threats we left the store.

That kept us entertained for a little while, and the next few hours were spent looking around the other shops. I suggested we return to the same department store, and get some glue. This was achieved with ease, as the Sherlock Holmes twins were nowhere to be seen.

We went this time to the foot of the bridge, and sat on some steps leading to the water. The tide was out, so going further down it eased the risk of detection. This proved to be an odd session. I had stolen two tubes from the store, as sharing one did not give enough time to appreciate all its effects. I began to feel a sensation within my mouth shortly after beginning. It was at first a tingling that intensified quite dramatically, feeling as if something began pushing my teeth upwards. It was not a pain as such, but quite prominent. I remained seated at first not bothering about the sensations.

As it increased there became a feeling of discomfort, and trying to stand up, found my body was unable to move. At its peak this caused me to let out a squeal, and much to my surprise Donald made equivalent noises during the same instant. It only lasted a few seconds after we yelped, and then everything was back to normal. Looking at each other we laughed aloud and funnily enough was not to discuss the occurrence in any great detail. It proved important in its own way, being the first time of experiencing an interaction with another person, whilst doing the same thing. Even though it was of a simple nature, from what I could gather Donald had a similar feeling in his mouth, but not to the same intensity. He squealed at the same moment because it caused an equivalent reaction. There was however, one difference his movements remained unaltered. This factor wasn't discussed concerning my situation, because it seemed unimportant. I did not look on any of the events concerning the use of glue in a serious light, it being only fun and not something to be taken earnestly. It put an end to that day's entertainment and throwing the bags in water, returned to the home.

The next few months past without incident, my mother was at home and appeared to have recovered from her illnesses. I leaned this through letters received. One day both her and Jimmy paid me a visit. I was pleased to see them, but shocked by the change in her appearance. She had lost weight and most of her hair had fallen out. This being a side effect of the drugs prescribed. Wearing a wig gave some semblance of normality. It however looked odd, for the last time we met I was seeing a normal woman; what stood before now was something quite different. She had also aged in appearance quite considerably. It proved difficult to comprehend the difference a short time could bring about. We went across the road to a cafe and talked.

I was due to return home at Easter for two weeks, shortly after this meeting. The place had a break the same as normal schools during the holiday. Most of the boys were returning to their respective counties that sent its delinquents away. On the morning of departure there was an excitement in the air, generating a feeling, which became unmistakable. At breakfast this transferred into people not eating their food, so I stuffed myself. A mini bus took us in-groups to the nearest large town in Fife. From here we each caught local buses back to our own homes. Before getting on my bus, Donald and I agreed to meet at his place during the holiday.

This was my first proper visit home in five months, and it felt good to be in my own room again surrounded by that which appeared familiar. The item I missed the most being my electric blanket during the winter. The holiday was spent mostly on my own. During the day I would walk to Leven, and the nights were occupied within Kennoway. Although it had only been five months away, life here did not feel the same. This wasn't just one aspect; it covered most of my normal circumstances. It proved an unusual time and caused a feeling of discontentment about it. I did not know if somehow life had moved on, or the change originated within me. Either way it was not the same.

I used glue twice during the break. The first occasion was in the old public toilet in town. The beach wasn't an ideal location at this time of year, and the toilet appeared about as suitable a place that could be thought of. Through the screen in the door I witnessed life in a factory, in which all the staff was female. This wasn't a short sketch of the kind experienced up until then. The factory produced tights and stockings and my introduction into this building began at what appeared its centre. Looking in to the environment became more than watching something occurring, I was actually there. The only part, which separated me from this other situation, was the screen, being equivalent to looking through a window without any glass, into a real event. The woman who worked in this place knew I was watching them, but displayed little interest. They had expressionless faces and movement, which showed a total apathy to their situation. Dressed in white coats and hats they almost seemed automated.

I had a chance to look around through the screen, before touring this location. It all appeared endless. Moving further away from the original spot the machinery and people became as one, as each lost its individual identity. Before changing, the relative normality at the start was gone, and it now appeared cartoon like. This ended and the scenery transformed into a different room, where a beautiful model stood on a podium. She appeared a picture of elegance, changing posture, as her platform moved round slowly to backing music.

The purpose being to display the goods produced in the factory. She was wearing a pair of white stockings that were gradually removed, in the process of turning. To watch this sequence was quite exquisite, and not surprisingly in a sexual context. I could feel this environment within me; it was part of me. On finishing the remaining viewing became more of a normal disposition. This occasion brought me closer in touch with the world on display. That is with one major exception, conversation. For some reason, or other I was not able to communicate with my subjects in any way. Verbal speech had no effect.

My other use during the break wasn't a memorable event, and keeping some of the glue took it back home. This saved around quarter a tube, to be finished within my room. It was used during the morning whilst watching an old black and white television set. It proved to be an interesting experience, in an odd kind of way. I had never tried anything similar to this, and it became a form of experiment to see what difference a change of conditions would bring. The programmes on that morning were not very interesting, and from the outset my eyes were kept on the screen to see if anything would happen. Watching this load of dribble became very comical for some unknown reason, and it caused me to laugh at something that in essence wasn't funny in any way. The odd part concerned my comprehension over these actions. It created conflict of interests and I knew there was no reason for laughing. It seemed strange to think from a rational outlook; such an event could take place. It did not bother me at all; I just wondered how this came about.

The holiday came to its end, and due to circumstances it caused a return to the home earlier than expected. I cannot remember the reason behind this. A friend of the family drove me to the social work department in Leven, and I went in the front door waving as he headed back up the road. My stay only lasted a few seconds giving him time to be out of sight, then left the building and walked to the bus station. I kept my promise to visit Donald by taking the bus to his home. It wasn't a problem being there after he explained to his parents; we had to return at the same time.

The day became spent visiting his friends, and seeing the local sights. They put me up in a spare bedroom, as one of his brothers was elsewhere at the time. On the following day it was decided, for safety reasons I should stay in another location. This would allay any suspicions. I told the family of my intention to go home then, return in the morning. Donald suggested sleeping in an old car close to his house. Early that morning after waking up in the back seat of the car it proved impossible to sleep again. I fidgeted for a little while then went on a walkabout.

At first there had been no plans to do anything other than keep myself occupied. After some time I came to the area in which the shops were located. Wandering around looking through the windows, it appeared an easy task to smash one of these and grab something. The eventual choice was the Co-op, for it seemed well situated in case a quick get away was needed. This whole thing felt slightly unreal because of the conditions, combined with being in an unfamiliar landscape. It took some time to muster the courage, which enabled smashing the bottom section of its glass door. This created such a loud noise when the brick made contact I thought the whole town would wake up, and more especially draw attention in the police station not so far away.

Running from the scene of the crime there was a wall close to hand that allowed a good hiding place, whilst watching the front of the shop. I stayed behind it for at least thirty minutes expecting someone to show, but no one did. It still required a removal of the surrounding glass to enter the store. It was done quietly, and my time in the shop proved to be only a few minutes taking three bottles of spirits, and a large box of chocolates. Leaving by a secure route returned to the car, hiding the items in a safe place. After this little bit of excitement, it proved easier to sleep until first light in the morning. I had breakfast at Donald's and told him of my escapade. He thought I was lucky to get away with it so easily.

That afternoon we picked up the goods and went to an old railway track, which had now become a public footpath.

We started to drink some of the spirits, and it did not take long to get drunk. Walking along this deserted track in a merry mood, there seemed no reason to look behind me. The bottle was swinging in my hand and I did not have a care in the world. Donald told me to throw the bottle away, and not to look back. I did this, but could not help looking around. Following us a little way in the rear was a police range rover. The driver noticing my actions pulled up, and then told me to pick the bottle up. We could not believe our luck, it being a remote possibility them coming along the track at that time

Donald told me afterwards this only happened rarely. It was a case of being caught red handed without any alibi. Still it proved their lucky day and not ours. They questioned us individually in the station, where I was charged with burglary. The home became informed and sent one of the staff to bring us back. On returning all our privileges were cancelled for two weeks. I would imagine this would have been more severe had it taken place within their sphere of influence. At the time I did not look at the situation with any fair-minded appraisal, and started becoming rebellious about my circumstances.

Donald, one other boy and I had planed to run away. It being a slightly romantic ideal in judging our long-term objectives, but at least we had a comprehension of the risks and problems involved. This was gained through experiences each of us incurred until that time. Our plans involved breaking into shops and houses to finance a life on the road.

On the night of departure we met up in a pre- arranged spot and left after dark. Surveying various places as possible targets in the city centre, none of these appeared suitable. It became decided an easier location would be Fife. Walking across the bridge, some houses were found close to hand. Picking one of these proved an easy matter gaining entry, as they were all large buildings, with many access points. It also helped with the house being unoccupied. After returning to the, city and walking through the shopping precinct a single policeman noticed us. He came over to ask what we were doing this late at night. It seemed appropriate to try and bluff him, and false names and addresses were given. He wanted to verify these, and told us we should accompany him to a small office in the precinct.

Inside this place were two other policemen. After checking our cover stories he found them to be false. This resulted in the other boy being hit in the face, as he happened to be nearest to hand. It turned out he knew about three boys being on the run, and on seeing us suspected we were the persons in question. The policemen returned us to the home.

The next morning it became apparent there would be a showdown with the headmaster. This was evident during roll call by the looks received from the staff present. As the others were dispatched to various places, we were kept aside and taken to the first aid room. Nothing being said during this time, the only noticeable difference was an uncomfortable atmosphere surrounding the situation. The headmaster eventually came, and went inside without looking in our direction. We were brought into the room individually. Being the last to be dealt with it became possible to have an idea of how this confrontation would be handled. My two friends were being belted. After coming out circumstances did not allow me to speak with either of them. It was then my turn. I had wondered why it took three staff members to belt one individual.

The reason for this concerned the style of belting that proved different to anything previously experienced. The headmaster said, "Do you think you are going to get the better of me". He then brought out his belt. I smiled and put my hand out. "No not that way". The other two staff took hold, and placed my body face down on the stretcher. The headmaster hit me at least six times on the behind as hard as he could. It hurt, but after being released in seemed appropriate to show a sign of defiance and I smiled at him once again. This response brought an annoyed look to his face, as he sent me out of the room. I decided there and then to leave this place at the first available opportunity.

All privileges were cancelled with no end in sight to being reinstated. The only opportunity we had for making a clean break together came when Donald and I were taken out, with some other boys into a park. A few weeks had passed, and they obviously thought any problems surrounding the situation had been resolved. We made a run for it, but were caught and escorted back under supervision. The next day after being summoned to the headmaster's office, a different approach was tried. He adopted a relaxed attitude and explained our actions were not acceptable to the running of this home. If either of us attempted running away again he would send us to a borstal, emphasising it would be the worst place that could be found. This made no difference, and my plans remained unaltered. The only change in attitude was one of circumstance. It would require better timing. As events turned out my future had other plans in store.

During this period my mother had been taken back into hospital, and Jimmy contacted her other son, who was my stepbrother. The last occasion he came to see us was in the mid sixties. It transpired some argument had taken place on their last meeting, which caused a rift in the relationship. I had almost forgotten of his existence until he came to visit me in home. It was quite a surprised to see him turn out of the blue one day. It proved even more astounding when he asked me to come and live with his family in England. He mentioned this without a reference to our mother. The conditions would also depend on certain legal matters being dealt with, and the transfer of my care order being made to him. He spoke in a confident manor, almost as if the present circumstances seemed irrelevant. I found it difficult to comprehend why events had suddenly changed their emphasis. Until then I had certain idea of how my life was going; now everything appeared different. I agreed with his assumption, not feeling certain anything would come of it. As an option it was defiantly better than my currant situation. We talked of other matters, but my mind became focussed on the last suggestion. It appeared very strange facing the prospect of a new life, speaking in terms as if it were a matter of fact.

This caused me to rethink my position within the home. I decided against anything, which might spoil a chance, if indeed it were a chance. Jim came back to the home later that week, for the specific reason of taking me on a visit, to the hospital where our mother had been sent. She was in a single room, and the moment I laid eyes on her it seemed obvious she was dying. The deterioration in overall appearance was dramatic. It also created quite a shock to be standing there. As the visit came to an end, we were left alone for about five minutes. During that instant it caused me to understand a deeper side to my emotions, than I knew existed this did not cause me to cry it being more a longing for everything to be fine one again coupled by a feeling of closeness developed from within. After leaving I thought my impressions might have been wrong, and perhaps there was a chance she could pull through. The next week proved a difficult period wondering about the many factors in play, and what would be their eventual outcome.

A few days after this I was looking out of the window towards the playing fields, when a staff member said the headmaster wanted to see me. Walking down the stairs an apprehension began to build up; knowing deep down the end for her had come. Looking at his face confirmed my fears. My mother was dead. I heard the words, and in the back of my mind had been expecting them, but there was an unreality about the situation. Before walking out of his office he informed me that I should be leaving the home soon, and hopefully not come back. I wanted to leave, but this wasn't a manor it had been envisaged, going upstairs a new way of life appeared before me. There was no great shock attached to her death, having mentally prepared for it since seeing her. I left the dormitory and went into a smaller bedroom unit for boys who were about to leave, or the eldest in the home.

This little group did not have so many restrictions. The two days passed with relative ease until Jim came for me. Before going we went into the headmaster's office together, so he could explain the procedure. In his opinion there should be no problem in the transfer of the care order, but if there was I may have to return fairly soon. It was good to leave with one exception, and that was loosing a friend in Donald. Before going I went to his unit and talked about the times we had during my stay. As the car pulled away that day I did not look behind me, for it was a promise made in order to forget this particular episode in my life.

We arrived in Kennoway in the early afternoon, it being a Saturday for Scotland was playing football against England in the home internationals, and the match was on the television live. It turned out to be a busy day for arrangements, with a number of people running around doing this, that and the other. I sat quietly watching the game, and let them get on with it. On the day of the funeral three official cars arrived at the house and took us towards the crematorium. The journey seemed to last forever, and we built up a large procession. My mum had many friends, and relatives who came to pay their respects. Some I had not seen for many years. The funeral proved a sombre occasion, being in the front row with our immediate family. As the coffin moved down the aisle I cried for the first time since her death, watching her go forever.

A hall was booked afterwards for a buffet, and many of those at the funeral came for the meal. It surprised me how quickly they forgot what the day was about, the only person, who seemed to be thinking along the same lines, was an elder cousin from Glasgow. His name is Angus and he was very close to my mother. I could tell by the expressions on his face the displeasure at their actions. He had come to Fife with three other people, and left alone shortly afterwards taking the bus home.

The children's panel had been arranged for later in the week. Jim and I attended this hearing chaired by four people who would decide my future. One of these was a boy from my old high school, who must have joined the social work department. As expected the care order was transferred to Jim, and they decided in their infinite wisdom that burglaries etc, were committed due to the upheavals in my life. It seemed funny listing to people explaining the reasons why certain actions came about. If it were not for the seriousness of the event I would like to have said they were talking out of their arses. However this would not have been a wise approach and it seemed appropriate to nod at convenient moments in agreement with the conclusions. Leaving the building caused a wave of relief over me. I was on my way to a new life, in a different country. Once again a sense of freedom prevailed, or so I thought at the time.

The journey down south was in its own way exciting. Our destination was Borden in Hampshire, to a large army base for engineers and drivers. Jim's car was left at a local train station a few miles from his home. We drove the short distance, and were met at the front door by his wife and five children. Everything seemed normal, it being the sort of life I was not used to. I must admit it felt good to be part of something, and settling in proved a lot easier than had been imagined. On the Monday I went to the local high school in Borden. It took its pupils from surrounding towns and villages, with a large number coming from the camp itself. I found this to be a good school in its structure, not too formal or overly soft.

The first problem encountered in this environment being a difficulty of others in understanding my accent. It's not something one consciously thinks about. From here on in it would have to be modified. The biggest help in settling down came from a change of attitude. I wanted to make a go of my new life and create as little problems as possible. Making an effort at school being something never attempted before, and I remember thinking at the time how unlike me it was. The few months spent in school before the summer holidays were trouble free and quite enjoyable on the whole.

During my first three weeks at Borden I had not used glue, altogether it would have been six or seven weeks since the last time in Dundee. On a Friday after walking home from school I bought a tube with the intentions of using it in the woods that evening. , I went in search of an isolated spot. It seemed important not to take any chances, and the place would have to offer reliable views all around. A good location was found, it being an old building, which had a flat roof. These offering a different setting than my usual scenery, it created a new feel to the experiences. In the past I had been used to open spaces. This was a confined area with many trees situated close to one another. I felt more at one with the surroundings than otherwise known. It being nothing to do with anything seen, this became purely an emotional response. In a way it was like discovering another level to something, you only had a partial insight into.

The theme of this show became world war two. At first lying back on the roof I watched a dog fight in the sky that is of the plane variety. One of the aircraft was British, the other German. The battle went on for some time, without a conclusion. I then turned my attentions to the surrounding woods. Coming towards my position were German troops. They wore black uniforms of the SS Division. It was good fun to watch my entertainment because; these soldiers were not quite full sized. It gave the setting an odd sort of feeling. I realised they were stocking my position by the sequence of movements which brought them towards me.

Because the mood had changed as from this day I participated in the game, and hid whist observing their actions. This proved quite funny in a way. The day ended in a pleasing manor, and I walked back to the house, via the long route as to get rid of any tell tail signs. I thought it would be better to keep the knowledge about glue sniffing to my self, for the less anyone knew around here the better. That occasion proved to be an isolated incident before the start of the holidays, and in truth I found myself kept busy until the break, as there were many places to be explored and new friends to see. One other factor kept me occupied during that period. Jim had bought a second hand bike, and it turned out to be very useful for it allowed freedom of movement to visit many places that were different in character from being in Scotland.Life on the home front and at school was both going well. It was now the start of the summer holidays, which had been really looked forward to. The trouble with all this free time was it left me at a bit of a loss. Accompanied by a friend, who lived in the same row of houses, we went cycling to a nearby town. Whilst looking around the shops it struck me how easy it would be to begin shoplifting once again. The security appeared quite lax. There was a lot to consider about resuming, and it involved a number of implications. True to fashion I wrestled with my conscience for a short while then stole something. The boy with me found it quite exciting, and from then on became my partner. At first it was only small items, but after a short while this outstripped anything attempted whilst in Scotland.

The boys name being Michael, and he was a feature in a segment of my past that was to become the present. This event took place with a girl called Lesley, who also lived, in the same block as us. It turned out to be an interesting sort of day. Both of these people had become my friends through different ways, Michael being from the quieter side of life, and I could relate to him on a normal level. Lesley was more an in crowd type girl, who was part of my immediate friends in the school.

It seemed unusual how on a warm sunny day we went to Farnborough together. Although these two people knew each other well enough, it wasn't a pairing, who under normal circumstances went to the same place, at the same time. I think the reason we ended up on this outing was through boredom, at being stuck in the base. The agenda for the day involved having a look around the town, whilst attempting a little shoplifting. By that time both of these people knew about glue sniffing, as I given up on my theory of secrecy. Michael had tried it once without anything startling happening. Lesley had no intentions of even beginning.

We hitched from Borden and got a lift, which took us directly into the town. A few hours were spent in the shops during the morning, and it achieved enough time to visit everything worth seeing. On the way some items were stolen from different places, including glue. I had planed to take this home, for use at a later date. We began making our way back. Michael said there was a short cut through the church that would save walking around the long way. One of the reasons for getting home just after dinner concerned the heat. It must have been the hottest day of the summer so far.

As we entered the church grounds, one of us sat down by some headstones for a rest. This seemed like a good idea at the time. No one appeared keen to set of again, for it was the sort of place you could fall asleep in quite easily. I lay back on the grass with this in mind and felt uncomfortable, not due to the location, but the heat. For some reason or other I had the notion to use the tube of glue in the churchyard. This seemed quite an odd decision for it wasn't a good place, with people wandering through every so often. I went in search of an old crisp bag around the grounds. Returning to the resting-place, Michael was asked if he wanted to join in. This became declined. After pouring out the glue it seemed prudent to find some partial cover. A large tree, close to hand presented the best option. This allowed me to watch anyone approaching from either end of the path. It wasn't an ideal situation, but after beginning it seemed pointless wasting the tube.

My initial concerns were on anyone coming and whilst inhaling I wasn't paying much attention to the effects. It dawned on me after a minute or so; none of the sensations were taking place. Some more glue was poured into the bag, and breathing deeply did not change anything. It became a situation that appeared illogical. I remember mumbling to myself "What is the matter with this stuff". By then any interest in who was coming, had lost its relevance. Returning back with my companions I lay on the ground. Looking towards the grass, all my attentions were focussed on achieving that which should have been expected. It began to annoy me, and no physical changes were detectable in any way. Raising my eyes up from the ground I looked towards the two people who had come with me. Michael began picking a daisy not paying much attention to anything going on; and Lesley was looking at me wondering what the hell I was doing this for.

The realisation struck me instantly; it depicted the scene I had witnessed on the beach at Leven almost two years ago. Dropping the bag to the ground I pointed towards them with my finger. It presented the exact set of events, played out for real now. This being the only two occasions using glue had no effect on me, in all the times it became used. It was so precise in structure and clarity it could not be taken for anything else. If you can imagine the scene shortly afterwards, it was quite something. My first reaction was to explain about seeing this before, and the information became conveyed in an excited manor. Looking back with hindsight it wasn't the best way to go about it. They didn't understand what I was talking about, and who could blame them. In fact I did not understand what was happening. It became a heat of the moment response to an unexplainable event.

As we got a lift back it created time to think about this in more detail. I had heard of similar occurrences before, but they had never happened to me. It seemed strange how on both occasions the substance offered no sensations.

I did not know why this should be, but it concerned an actual physical occurrence that involved two different times. In its own way this proved important because of the significance of the act. From a personal point of view, this should have made me think more deeply as to what I was dealing with. When one sees the future displayed before you in such a way, it is time to wonder as to its causes. As said this is what I should have done. By the time we were dropped of at home the excitement level dropped back to normal.

My philosophy concerning all glue sniffing events were centred on the fun aspect, and taken no further. I did not hold any beliefs, one way or another as to why any of the events witnessed came about. They were just part of a time and place, although it may seem odd to the reader, it wasn't to me. Within the following months the sensations, with the use of glue were to advance in complexity. This caused a re-think to the basic understanding why, and how such matters came about. This different approach proved very important for advancement of my experiences. It being a little way off yet, first I had to face an unsettling period that was to change my life once again.

Jim had decided to take the family on holiday towards the end of the summer. Being in the army he had a two-week break that most service personal take during this period. He chose to visit Kennoway with his leave. As it was a large family we could not all fit in the car. Neville the eldest boy and I went by train unescorted. I looked forward to the trip in two ways. Firstly it was quite exciting travelling such a distance without any supervision. Living in England had been interesting, but in some ways I missed being in Scotland, therefore it would be good to see the place, and my old friends.

On the first night I did not go anywhere, due to feeling tired. This being the same for all the others and we had an early night. During the middle of that week I went in to Leven, on my own, this being for the intention of getting some glue and visiting my old haunting grounds. The beach wasn't a practical place to go at this time, due to the holiday trade. In the same vein the old toilet proved busier than usual during that morning, with all the extra people. It would have been possible to use in that location, but not desirable. This created a little dilemma, where to go. After thinking about the problem for a while, the solution came in the shape of some derelict houses not so far away.

During my times in Leven there had never been any reason for varying my two locations. In a way as with some changes of circumstances, it proved quite interesting. The building was old, but appeared in reasonable condition, because it had not been empty for so long. The entrance was through a small courtyard into a doorway, without a door. I stayed in the front room, which offered a view to the outside. This was through a broken window, and reason dictated it would be better to see anyone coming towards me, rather than being caught in the act. On looking around the premises an old bag was found which seemed appropriate. Before coming I had forgotten to bring one with me. It seemed a bit grubby but looked as if it would do under the circumstances. Sitting in a corner on the opposite end from the window made a start.

After taking effect the first visualisation became that of a woman climbing in through the window. She wore clothing, as an estimate belonged in the 1930 era. She did not seem aware of my presence.

Speaking to her whilst seated brought no response. It became the first time of seeing a full sized three-dimensional person whilst using the substance. Learning from my first experience on the beach I knew it would be a pointless exercise going towards her, so sat back and studded her actions. She was quite young in appearance being smartly dressed, and seemed to be looking for something. Keeping within her half of the building never venture towards me. I wondered what could be of interest, as that section of the room did not have anything worth a second glance.

This went on for a while, and then looking out of the window she called to someone. Leaning outside the frame she picked up two young children, and brought them inside. The children at an estimate would have been aged three or four. They wore clothing belonging to equivalent period as their mother. Both looked at me whilst clinging to her, with faces that were a picture of innocence. I turned my attentions towards them, asking if they would come over and join me. The mother told them to stay with her. She did not look at me once during this period.

I stood up, and in doing so noticed patches of glue on my new denim jacket, which had been stolen during a shoplifting expedition in England. This made me really annoyed, for the stain glue leaves on clothing cannot be removed. Normally I would have been more careful in my choice of bag. This time laziness prevailed; therefore a price was paid. The lining gave way at one side, due to deterioration with age, and it had slowly been dripping on to me.

My attention to the visualisation on offer became more focussed than normal. The reason being for the first time I had seen a full dimensional woman. I remember thinking of a possible sexual connection. As it turned out nothing of the sort emerged. At the point of realisation about the glue on my jacket I became really angry. This became the first occasion of loosing my temper whilst using solvents. It caused a change of emphasis, and giving up the cat and mouse game directed my attentions to those who occupied the other side of the room. Looking directly towards them my reactions caused the children to begin cowering. Walking across the room, a distance of no more than fifteen feet they all departed out of the window with uncanny speed that would have been totally impossible under normal circumstances. Calling a halt to events returned back home.

One point to make about using an old bag, I did not like the feel of putting something to my face in that condition. This sensation intensified after using the glue. It being an awareness that became better defined whilst inhaling and it felt dirty. This was really noticeable, but by then too late. I do not mention it to overstate a point. The reason for an evaluation of this kind is more one of its concerns in the emotion department. I believe it's important to understand one's feelings when explaining cause, and effect. I became more in tune with these as time wore on, and they heightened significantly during such occasions towards a better understanding.

The holiday seemed to pass by quickly, and during the second week I made a brief visit to Leven, for the purpose of acquire some glue. This time it involved lifting a tin, initially for use that evening out in the fields in Kennoway. On returning home I found that Jim and Pam were going out for dinner to a restaurant.

This changed the conditions a little. Knowing Jimmy, he was bound to let the younger children stay up later than normal. I decide to take a chance and use it in the room.

During that holiday I was sleeping in Jimmy's room along with Neville. There were two extra single beds installed, and it made the place a little cramped. After they had gone out for their meal I told Jimmy about fancying an early night. This gave me a good two hours, before anyone should disturb my planned entertainment. Going upstairs the window was opened fully, trusting to luck in not being caught. As things turned out it wasn't much of a problem, and I was not disturbed once. This proved quite fortuitous, as it happened to be by far the best use of glue ever experienced. It wasn't dark as yet, but the light was switched on to save any inconvenience. My bed was furthest from the door, and the furniture had been moved around, blocking part of my total view of the surroundings. The wallpaper directly in front now became as the screen, in the toilets. The one advantage over my normal limitations was an expansion in size covering the whole area of that room. It could be described as a sort of three-dimensional viewing gallery, within the parameters of a given space.

The evening's entertainment came mainly from in front, though very few areas were unused. It started by showing scantily clad women walking about different parts of the room. Laying in my bed it was quite something to behold. I did not attempt to physically interact with the subjects, because experience had taught the futility of such gestures, more the pity. The first serious of figures were scaled down models of the real thing, and they kept out of arms reach, being in bed proved the ideal place to watch this from. If there is one subject guaranteed to get my whole attention, its sex. Thinking back to the sequence of events in more detail the whole evening session became based on sexual manipulation, that in its self-proved unusual and as a method of presentation a potent tool.

After the tone had been set, there appeared in the wallpaper another female who looked at me in a suggestive manor. This one appeared more lifelike than her predecessors did. It was however still a cartoon figure. The wallpaper being of a light colour in this new state of perception it had depth to its two dimensional configuration. At the time I never looked on this with any interest, as sexual thoughts were my main desire. The girl started running towards my direction from a depth within the wall. I looked on with eager anticipation, hoping she would come to me, approaching the dividing line that separated my physical environment from this other. She was prevented in leaving by an octopus like tentacle that grabbed her around the waist. This became a personal disaster. I imagine the expression on my face would have been the same as some child who's just had its favourite toy taken away.

My reaction to this I believe was of the highest importance, never before had I directly interacted with my visions, but then the incentives had not been this high. To put it another way, the carrot was placed in front of the donkey, and it did the trick. With my mind I mentally grabbed hold of the girl and dragged her towards me. This appeared to work, that is until the tentacle pulled back. We became enveloped in a tug of war situation, and it developed into a form of stalemate. My next action was more profound. I mentally directed thoughts towards the tentacle, and cut if off. This proved successful as the limb fell from her waist, and she smiled in a way that offered a thousand fantasies in one alluring expression.

Walking towards me, slowly I believed all my birthdays, and Christmases had come at once.

Life seldom produces such easy conquests, and my alternate existence it did not give up this ethic without a fight, and put another tentacle around her. I cut it off, and repeated the action more times than any beast of its nature should have. I did not know what to do any more, and lost the total commitment which had consumed my being, just a short while ago. In lessening these attentions it caused me to notice other things happening in the room. In the time it took to look at these, the object in front did not have the same importance. I gave up on it as a lost cause.

As mentioned the whole evening was directed towards sex. A funny incident happened shortly after, concerned a French maid caricature. She was relatively small, and dusted around my bed. The counterpane had become slightly ruffled in certain places, and this created a gap between it and the rest of my bedclothes. In a brief instant she appeared to enter one of these spaces. It was so quick, that at first took me by surprise. Pulling the blanket to one side and looking around in the hope of finding her proved, rather elusive.

The wallpaper continued being an interesting feature all night, as it constantly offered something new. This took place in other areas of the surroundings, as my attentions where focussed on that directly in my line of vision. A good example was a particular incident which distracted one train of thought. In the right hand corner of the room, I began to hear singing that was unmistakably female. My view of this side happened to be blocked by a wardrobe, placed in such a way to facilitate the extra beds. As it continued curiosity forced me out of bed, to see whom it was coming from. The effort proved certainly worthwhile.

That which appeared in the line of vision was by far, the most attractive proposition of the night. It being a woman dressed in a showgirl's outfit that stood in a pose that took my breath away. She told me her name was Za Za Gabour. The size was scaled down, but it made no difference to her captivating abilities. My attraction to this effigy was the strongest of the night, and there did not appear any way to attract her towards me as she walked around the wallpaper. By then at least two hours had passed, and its duration would have exceeded any previous sessions. Glue like alcohol has a tolerance level, although circumstances could have allowed me to carry on; it involved pushing my luck. The most important factor of these increased the risk of detection. By creating a little time in removing any trace of the fumes, it would have rounded of a perfect night. By then darkness had fallen, and before switching off the light my tin was closed, then along with the bag it was hidden under the bed.

I walked over to the light and turned it off. What happened next took me completely by surprise. Instead of seeing darkness in the room, it became a myriad of coloured shapes. For a few seconds my bearings were lost, and only through feeling around were it possible to gain a perspective of my location. The first object that gave a semblance of normality was Jimmy's bed. It took a few seconds for my eyes to accustom themselves with the normal darkness of the room. Intermingled within this these colours were still in place, an irregular block similar to crazy paving. I edged myself along the line of beds and lay down frontward, with my face covered by the pillow. In the darkness of the mind's eye I expected normality to return. This concept proved far from being the case. The shapes and colours that offered partiality visibility now appeared in their fullest extent. I was in some sort of tunnel, which consisted of many colours, and they appeared similar to neon, only purer.

These conditions under normal circumstances would have effected my vision, but it became apparent shortly afterwards normal sight had nothing to with it. My initial recognition only lasted a few seconds, because whatever function in my body witnessed this began to move. The simplest description would be to say, an area of my consciousness occupied a space hither to unknown, and travelled within it. At first the take of speed was slow, but within a short space of time it built up, and reached a constant. There were no sensations of travelling at high speed, such as wind resistance, or any physical reaction, but I certainly was there. At its peak the colours became blurred, then faded away as the potency of the glue left my mind, and normal darkness returned.

The whole event could not have lasted very long, because the residual experiences of the fumes will only continue for around a minute at maximum, after inhalation ceases. This occasion had been of the highest importance, although its relevance wasn't grasped, as perhaps it should have been. Through mentally altering this environment, my capabilities had increased. On the night it became simply a matter of wanting the girl, with sex as an incentive. The tunnel of coloured lights were in fact the beginning of another journey to be to make at a later stage, for its end had not been reached. Unwittingly I had attained another level, in terms of experience. This was to be made clear, in the not too distant future.

The holiday came to an end, and we were on our way back to England. It left a few weeks before the schools restarted, and during this period I found myself steeling from the shops a great deal. What caused the upsurge in these activities has never been fully understood. As well as shoplifting, the use of glue was becoming more frequent.

At home I was beginning to run into problems. It had been noticed the amount of clothing, in my wardrobe had increased since arrival. This became difficult to explain away. Stupidly I gave the denim jacket, with the glue stains to Pam for washing. She went off her head. To manage this problem I made a point of keeping out of the house as much as possible. With a tense atmosphere now in place it caused an unhappiness from within that became a standard feature. To take my mind of the oppressive situation I would quite often get hold of some glue, and go into the woods. On one of these days something happened, a little out of the ordinary. I was now taking more caution than ever, to reduce any chance of being caught. My walks into the forest were deeper that before, to keep unwelcome eyes away

It became very hot towards the end of that summer, and this day proved no exception finding it quite humid, deep within the woods. Sitting down on a clump of earth, slightly higher than the ground I made a start. This part of the forest was thickly planted, with nothing else in sight. It seemed very much the same all around that area. I soon became aware of something happening to me whilst looking around the terrain, as it changed. With my eyes open I was visualising another type of woodland. This appeared very different to the place my physical body occupied, just but a few seconds ago. The trees were thinner and more openly spaced; also the ground was of a different structure. Accompanying this became an overbearing desire not to move from my seated position. This created a strong emotional response that obliged me to re-main in that spot. I complied knowing the choice was a free one. It became so strange that to describe the situation with mere words is an inadequacy.

At this point my body had not moved. Turning my head slowly, I began witnessing an alternate landscape, to any-thing, which should have been there. My eyes were looking around the area in which the physical body inhabited, but saw nothing they should have. Even the feel to land was dif-ferent. To one side on a downhill stretch it became possible see a fast flowing river. This had a concrete wall along either of the banks within my line of vision that must have been in-stalled to prevent erosion.

My initial sighting of this had began to its right, and fol-lowing the path downward to the left just over half way I could see a boy looking into the water. He appeared to be in some distress. The clothing on his body was not from this time, it being a tweed suit with Knickerbockers trousers. As an estimate I would say it came from the 1920 period. The cause of his anxiety concerned another boy who had fallen in the water. He was battling against impossible odds, and the efforts proved futile. The currant was very strong and carried him down the river, with his friend chasing in the hope he may be of some assistance. They departed from the field of vision, and I was left watching an empty landscape once again. Shortly afterwards my normal sight returned, and all that remained concerned an atmosphere which could almost be touched. It left me in awe. I put the bag on the ground, and walked away.

I knew this sequence of events witnessed through other eyes, but, did not understand why this should be so. The setting, its river and the boys were familiar. From the point of conception it offered more than being a spectator, it became interlocked with my identity, or part of some unknown aspect within my personality. It left me feeling disturbed on the return journey home. This being the first occasion since using glue it had caused any emotion of that nature to surface. I tried making sense of these events, and couldn't. It was by no stretch of the imagination a normal experience of the kind associated within the standard format. The purpose seemed different, almost a revelation. In describing it, I must stress the importance of feeling, with the emotional upsurge becoming significant. It took me to a new level in terms of involvement, which befitted the occasion.

At home things were going from bad to worse. We had started back at school, and during the first week on the Friday after returning home a major argument developed between Pam and me. The ends result being she said I was not wanted in the house. Until then my course of actions had seemed uncertain. It now offered only one alternative, and that involved leaving the house there and then. In a way it proved quite sad, for all the recent upheavals were back in place and the new way of life had been short lived. Funnily enough I had wanted to make a go of this and in my own way tried within certain limitations, still that was past and something would have to be sorted out fairly soon. Going upstairs an extra pair of trousers was put on, and a tube of glue recovered from its hiding place. Before leaving I explained my predicament to Neville the eldest son about going away. He seemed to understand, and then all that remained was to walk out of the house. London seemed an obvious place to go, so I went to the nearest town with a train station. After telling the guard I was expecting someone, he let me wait for this non -existent person. The circumstances were fairly good as no one else was around, and it allowed me to use part of my tube without too much trouble. Considering the situation thus, it turned out to be a good session.

The platform had an older feel to it, which became reflected during the twenty minutes, or so waiting time until the train would come. At first the song Lucy in the sky with diamonds could be heard. This seemed a funny choice because I now like the Beetles, at that time they held no interest for me.

The station transformed its outlay, depicting an earlier part of this century. I could see a porter dressed in attire becoming that era. He was a cartoon caricature with cobwebs hanging off him. It looked very funny just then considering the importance of my situation. All of his business was tackled in a slow, drawn out manor with the pipe he was smoking a prominent feature. His whole persona gave off comical overtones, and on seeing this I laughed out loudly. Following him were some policemen dressed in costumes from that period, and they asked the guard if he had seen a runaway. I was sitting on a bench, no more than twenty yards from their position. They had bloodhounds in tow to search for this person. It proved a very comical set up. There became alertness in purpose, and searching for this runaway had an element of pomposity about it, looking in every place apart from my location.

It seemed light-hearted, and the mood of the sketch was appreciated. At that time it helped ease my burden, although I do not wish to state glue sniffing became a substitute to the difficulties of normal life. This proved an unusual situation, and helped deal with a problem in a relaxed sort of way.

The train came in and putting my bag away it was boarded. This area happened to be a commuter belt, and most of the people who travelled would come back at a later time. The outward journey was almost passenger free, and whilst the effects of the glue wore of it caused some concerned about the lack of people on the train, because if a guard came into my carriage I would be in trouble. As events turned out there was no such difficulty, with the journey to London being problem free. The train pulled into the city, and it did not necessitate the bother of giving some phoney explanation.

My good fortune continued whilst getting off the train as I managed to walk through the barrier in which you hand over the tickets unchallenged. The collector came to his place after me and a few other people went through. Looking around the crowd a man was picked out to ask where the motorway began. After mentioning it to him, he replied I seemed a bit young to be hitching such a long distance. He must have deduced my predicament, because he went on to say that circumstances caused him to run away from home some years ago. This was from Ireland, and during these travels it brought him to London, where he ended up working on the building sights. That was his job at the time. I felt he could be trusted, and told him that he assumed correctly. He asked was I in need of a job, and if so could arrange one on the sight where he worked. Considering a few minutes ago my position seemed vague, this appeared something out of the blue.

The thought of working here became appealing, and certainly an answer to my problems. Improvising on the situation, I asked if it would be practical to bring one other boy with me. He considered my statement and said it should be possible to get both of us a job. Explaining to him about Donald in Scotland, and how I imagined he would jump at the opportunity, we arranged to meet at this place on the following week during a certain time. Telling me the directions, he then gave me a pound of his own money.

In life one needs a purpose to achieve your aims, and this created the circumstances, plus motivation to make it worth the effort. Taking his advice involved a short trip on the underground, which led to an area for the commencement of my journey. I had been used to hitch hiking, although these were mainly lesser distances. Speaking from experience it's difficult getting a lift out of a town, or city unless you are in the right spot. The distance travelled in the early stages, was no more than twenty miles. By then it was still light and a good frame of mind had developed. Before restarting I walked up a grass bank, to the side of the motorway and used the remaining glue that had been saved from earlier.

The bank was quite high in relation to the road, and it gave a good overall view of the landscape. My location offered a reasonable setting, with calm conditions that changed the whole emphasis surrounding the environment. One other little bonus concerned watching the sun about to set. To my left after it had taken effect, an Arab man appeared as the first visualisation. He was dressed in white robes going through some kind of ritual, of which the actions were mystifyingly, being to my limited knowledge a sort of religious preparation. These sequences of body movements seemed very precise, and were followed by a powerful display of singing. He used a language outside the bounds of my experience, and all these actions were directed towards a certain area. I did not know what point on the compass this could be, not knowing my own position.

Watching this proved fascinating, and the feel it created blended in with the pleasant evening. Turning from his position on the grass bank, he then faced the road. Starting to sing again, this time in English asked the drivers to stop and give this boy a lift. He offered alms to the person who would do this. Needless to say, his proposal was not taken up. It proved quit amusing to watch, and a good end to that particular tube. I went back to the hard shoulder and started the long journey. The lifts were at first patchy until the early hours of the morning, which by then had taken me within a hundred miles from the border with Scotland. Having been dropped off outside a transport cafe, the best lift off all was achieved. From here a lorry driver picked me up, going to the south of Edinburgh. This was quite lucky as by then tiredness began taking its toil, and once in his cab I fell asleep until we crossed into Scotland.

The driver of the vehicle asked me home for breakfast, as he was finished work. It became apparent to most of the people who had given me lifts I was quite young, and some of them offered to help me without making the fact too obvious. His suggestion of food proved a welcome gesture, which under the circumstances could not be passed up. Before leaving he offered me some money, which because of his kindness already had to be turned down. I thanked him for everything, and went back to the main road. It was quite early in the morning, and as luck would have it my next lift took me straight to Dundee. This created a two-hour gap until the boys were allowed out for the afternoon. Waiting at the gate of the home, at first there was no sign of my friend. I did not want go very close, because the fewer people who knew about the circumstances, the better. When showing up he was with the boy who had joined us, on our first attempted escape. After noticing me he let out a gasp of surprise.

We walked to shops where I explained the events leading up to me being there. In town it created an opportunity for a little shoplifting mainly for food, and it was then I mentioned about the offer of work in London. This gave him a lot to consider, whilst going about our business. After our visit in the precinct, he went off by himself to think over the options. Staying for a little while he came back with a smile on his face. It wasn't a wasted journey after all.

We said goodbye to the other boy, asking him to mention nothing of this, and set off. To start the return journey it involved walking across the bridge to join the road that led south. Our first lift was from a man going towards Glasgow. The only difference it made concerned a change of route, going to London by the west rather than the east. We ended up with a few odd lifts that where quite disconcerting, and I hoped the rest of the journey would not be like the last two. It was now after six o'clock, past the point of redemption for Donald. Looking at each other we laughed.

This stretch of road appeared really quiet, and apart from the last driver I wondered if anyone else knew of its existence. I was on the point of giving up for the evening, when a mini bus came by. It looked fully loaded and sticking out my thumb, there seemed little hope of it stopping. Much to my surprise it did, and we were on the move again. Dropping us close to the town in Carlisle, we did not want to wander too far from the motorway and found a motel that had a number of fibre glass boats, with cabins in its front yard. It seemed a strange combination, all of these boats were small, not the living in variety. Picking the best on offer did our utmost to get comfortable for the night. The timing proved particularly appropriate as it started to rain. This at first was quite light, and then became much heavier. We did not manage to sleep very well due to the cramped conditions, nor did the rain show any sign of letting up.

In the morning nothing had changed, it was still raining and we hung about hoping it would go away. This only wasted valuable time, and left no option other than getting wet. Walking back to the start of the main road wasn't a pleasant experience. The traffic proved quite sparse that Sunday morning, and we were having no luck. This concept multiplied after seeing a police motorcyclist coming along the other side of the road. He changed direction and headed towards us. It left little time to work out a cover story, whilst the bike was parked and his helmet removed. This did not allow any time to discuss the matter further, as he came within hearing distance. Looking at this policeman he seemed quite young which offered a little confidence. Giving him the information I believed my address would we be safe, but Donald's was another matter.

As it turned out both of these came back clear. I think an older policeman would have understood the situation better, but you have to be grateful for small mercies. After explaining our destination he suggested walking further on, as it offered a better spot. When he left I gave a large sigh of relief, and taking his advice walked to the new location. As it turned out this proved ideal and got under way shortly afterwards. From here on in there was not much waiting time, with the first lift coming from a lorry that allowed us get dry. The last ride came from a group of workmen going to Luton in a works van, and finished off the need to travel by road.

It proved quite satisfying to have achieved my aims, and shows what can be done with a little determination. If we could get by that night without any problems, the next day should be plain sailing. Finding a place to sleep became a little more difficult than at first thought. We eventually settled for the luggage compartment of a Single Decker coach, in some yard they were parked for the night. Early in the morning we visited various shops in the West End, stealing some food and glue that supplied two basic needs. I found that being in a busy city did not offer many suitable places to use one of these tubes.

Somewhere near Leicester Square there is an underground toilet and at first going in for a call of nature, I thought it would be as good a place as could be found, under the circumstances. Telling Donald of my intentions returned to the toilet. This was the busiest lavatory I had ever been in. Waiting until a cubical became free, went inside and began. Unlike other buildings of this nature come across whilst pursuing my hobby, it appeared very plush. The walls were tiled, and its lighting evenly spread. This became reflected in my session giving the cubical a feeling more akin to an office, than it was originally intended for.

There followed different scenes connected with offices. These were not important, and because of the immediate situation not enjoyed. The screen appeared on the door before leaving, depicting a sketch concerning the naked men with babies. This was still a complete mystery. Putting the unfinished bag in my pocket went back out to join my companion. It was now around lunchtime, and luck began to run out. We had drifted into the vicinity of Bow Street. Walking down the pavement minding our own business a policeman spotted us from the other side of the road. He came over to ask what we were doing. Because this was a large city I thought at first he must have assumed we were skipping school, or something of that nature.

As an automatic response we tried bluffing our way out of the situation. Once he heard the Scottish accents, his attitude changed. Deep down from within I knew at this point, we'd had it. Giving him false addresses waited for the inevitable reply. During the interval an older woman came over, and started asking a serious of trivial questions. This at least created the opportunity to throw away the bag of glue, whilst his attention was distracted. The next problem to be tackled involved getting the unopened tube from the box, into my trousers. The policeman was getting annoyed with the woman, by the expressions coming from his eyes, although he handled both situations well. At that point I managed to slip the tube down my trousers, whilst the station called him back. It proved good timing, with the difficulty factor in getting this inside two pairs of trousers. They informed him no such address existed. He told us not to make a run for it because one of us would be caught. Telling the woman he had business to deal with escorted us to his base. It seemed funny to fall at this stage in our travels

I will say one thing for the police at Bow Street; they were very decent towards us. This is more than can be said for a number of others, from past experiences. At first we refused to give our proper names, or addresses, as neither of us wanted to go back to our respective lives. These however changed nothing and were told if they could not find out, it would result in us being placed in a remand home until they did. We realised it was a futile gesture, gave them the information they wanted.

One of the officers then searched us and took away the few possessed acquired on the way, but not the tube of glue. It was noticed I had two pairs of trousers on, but only the pockets of the second were searched. I asked the one who arrested us what had drawn his attention. It turned out to be my scruffy appearance, another lessons to be learned. They contacted Balgowen, and Jim in Borden. We were put in a cell and awaited the inevitable outcome.

I asked Donald why he had not made a run for it. His reasoning turned out to be similar to my own. I knew that one of us would have been caught, and in a strange sort of way it's like leaving a friend in the lurch. We started of together, and if a problem involved one, it concerned both. At the time when the policeman began questioning us, it crossed my mind to dash off. This idea had soon been rejected. All of this fine camaraderie did not change our circumstances; we were both in trouble. Donald believed he would be sent away from Balgowen, to where he did not know, and I wasn't looking forward to meeting Jim, expecting a beating of the kind never received before.

The tube of glue was still down my trousers, although it had avoided detection there appeared no way it could be used. In the cell there was a radiator, enclosed by a form of grill of which your hands could not be put through. The various people staying in this cell had pushed different sorts of rubbish inside the small gaps. On closer inspection at the bottom someone had eaten a packet of crisps, neatly folded the bag and pushed it inside. This was really annoying being out of my reach and try as I might it seemed impossible to retrieve. This became one occasion in which the use glue would have been most welcome in order to take my mind of the immediate situation. It proved highly frustrating.

The answer to my dilemma came in the form of a policewoman who brought us some food. This was the first proper meal eaten since coming from the lorry driver's home in Scotland. When the meal was finished it occurred to me the plastic fork might be able to reach the bag, but it wasn't quite long enough. Donald suggested gluing two pieces of the cutlery together. This worked and the impossible, had been achieved. Separating the cutlery it was cleaned then put back on the tray. Shortly afterwards the policewoman came to cell, for our empty food containers. She had an easygoing personality, and happened to be very attractive. Giving us both a cigarette continued with her duties. We both had the same thoughts concerning this woman. Fifteen is a good age for fanaticising.

There seemed no reason I could think of why the police should return to the cells, in the immediate future. Jim would be the first to arrive and that would take a few hours, at least. Taking out the bag and solvents did something I imagine very few people have achieved a glue sniffing session in a cell. As it turned out this wasn't very enjoyable. The format of the visions revolved around situations with the police. Under the circumstances, this became the last thing you would wish experience. It transpired Donald found little pleasure in his attempts either, being his third time and not the best of locations. Throwing the bag behind the grill, the fumes dispersed before anyone came back. The only message coming from beyond the cell was that Jim would be here shortly, and someone was flying down from Scotland to collect Donald. I would be the first to go; not such a pleasing aspect; it even crossed my mind to refuse leaving. We knew the chances of seeing each other again were remote. In some respects I would not have liked to be in the cell alone, waiting my retribution.

Not so long afterwards footsteps could be heard walking along the corridor. The cell door opened, and I was informed someone was here to pick me up. Saying goodbye to Donald going into the main interview room Jim was sitting in the far corner. All he said to me was "You have really done it this time, haven't you". I did not reply. Signing the papers for my release went out to the courtyard. A friend had driven Jim here, as his own car had mechanical problems. He did not speak very often during the return journey, apart from informing me my time in Borden was over. That seemed inevitable, and only confirmed a factor that already had been known.

It was around six o'clock when we came into Borden. The car came up to the junction that led towards Jim's house, and then carried on up the road. This took me by surprise. Our new destination was the local police station. After going into the main enquiry section, I could see Michael the boy who had accompanied me on a number of shoplifting trips. He was sitting in the waiting room, and we did not have a chance to speak. I was ushered in a room that had a number of my belongings lain out on the floor, some of these pieces had been stolen. A police sergeant started asking me where each of the items came from. This proved a difficult situation with Jim sitting behind. I had to admit some of them had been shoplifted, or taken from outside people house whilst delivering papers during the summer. Of all the times I had been questioned by the police, this proved the most difficult. The sergeant then went on, to accuse me of other unrelated crimes.

I do not remember the end result of this, as it wasn't very important at the time. The questioning developed in to the realms of fantasy, this being a small village attitude. After being released we returned to the house on foot. Once inside

I thought here we go, but nothing happened. Jim told me a social worker was coming to take me away in the morning.

I went upstairs to the bedroom, and told Neville about all the events during the last four days, then went to sleep. It was good to be in a proper bed again. In the morning everything seemed as normal. The children went to school, and life in the home continued as if nothing happened. Today became different for me; it was the start of a new beginning. Jim took the day off work, and Pam continued doing the housework, she did not speak to me. I packed a few clothes and some other items the police had not taken away, and then awaited the social worker. He was late in arriving, and once in the house only stayed a few minutes". With that I left Borden for good. Getting into the car, it created a feeling of relief at vacating the premises. I did not know what type of establishment was awaiting me; it could have been anything.

The social workers name was a Mr Hedges, and it turned out we were heading towards Winchester. The home was called Ashbourne Lodge, it being an assessment centre. This became a new term, of which the reference proved unfamiliar. During the journey he asked a little about me, including an understanding into glue sniffing. He was the first adult person who had shown an interest in the subject. It seemed quite surprising considering the line of work he was in; it had not cropped up before. In the short time the journey took to complete I tried my best to explain about what this did to me, its effects on others, and reason why I used it. My understanding of the subject just then was of a limited nature. That was to change very soon

We arrived at the home, it being situated close to the centre of Winchester, about ten minutes walking distance in all. It was a large building set in extensive grounds. On either side of the home were two other establishments of a similar nature. One for naughty girls, the other was for younger boys who were placed in care on a long-term basis. A staff member called Frank showed me around, it was a routine I was getting used to by now.

My social worker did not stay long, having other appointments to deal with. Frank issued me with some clothes, of a type worn by all the boys in the home. This conformed to the same system operated in Balgowen, but that is where the two establishment's similarities ended. I soon came to like Ashbourne Lodge, as did most of the boys who were there. This wasn't an oppressive place in any way. Their purposes being to evaluate an individual's character, then recommend what type of placement should be made. The whole set up was so good in a contrast from Dundee; it made me realise the difference of being put in a home in Scotland, and here. In the mornings we attended a school that was held in a large portable building, situated in the grounds. It being split into two sections, and run by very able teachers, who taught basic subjects, put over in a constructive manor. I actually found myself enjoying these lessons. The building was used in the evening for handicrafts, on a voluntary basis, and usually run by the residential staff, whereas during the day the teachers were proper teachers. I made a chess set, with board in my spell there. It was based on a very old design copied from a book, and required a lot of effort getting the detail just right.

The boys, who stayed in the home during my time, were affected by the whole ambience, in a similar manor to which it had on me. You had a number of options to keep yourself amused, with one being an assault course that took care of any surplus energy. The game room became the centre point of most of our free time, and wasn't used in a negative way. The staffs were also good, which completed a well-balanced set up. Considering the circumstances I was very glad to have come here, and could not think of a better outcome to my present situation.

This really became a beginning to a change in my life. In the Lodge we quite often went into the countryside with the staff doing various activities. Through this I saw more of the place than if left to my own devices, it's quite easy to understand why Winchester is reputability the richest town in England. On the Saturday it became possible to visit the cinema in town, if you paid a small percentage of the cost. Ever since I was child in Glasgow the pictures have always been a special occasion. The one cinema in Winchester was split into three studios. As we were all under eighteen, it proved difficult to watch the X rated films, and no one really tried. This was only a temporary setback to my way of thinking. Once the film had started it became possible to slip out of one studio, into the other. I did this on the first week and found it a simple matter. It became standard practice after then, and a number of us would make the switch on each visit.

On the following Saturday none of the films were particularly good. After flirting around the studios, I wondered if the usherettes would let me out of the building for a short while, on some pretext. I explained to them about having to see someone, and would it be possible to return before the end of the film. There seemed no problem with this suggestion, as far as they were concerned.

The reason I had to get back was a staff member accompanied us, and it may have looked a little odd with myself being outside, when everyone had meet up in the building at the end. This gave me ample time to explore in the town centre. As luck would have it, this wasn't very far away. After a quick look in some shops, a homing beacon guided me towards my favourite department store. Most of their buildings are laid out in the same fashion, and this proved no exception. The glue was in a retrievable area that is from a shoplifter's point of view. Taking a single tube returned to the cinema before the end of the film, to watch something that wasn't very interesting. As a group we walked to the Lodge, then after tea I used the glue outside in the grounds for the first time. My most recent experiences with the substance had shown an increased depth in quality, and in reality I should have been happy with this, but it left an afterthought there was something missing, though what it could be was unknown. This began to concern me, for reasons beyond my comprehension. I tried to ignore it, putting it down to stupidity on my behalf. Because I had come to the home with very little in the way of clothing, the social work department issued an order to make up a basic requirement. This was good on two fronts. It would replace some items the police had taken off me, and more important-ly create an extra opportunity in acquire some glue. Although the regime seemed fairly easy going at the home, to disappear for the time it would take getting to the shops, and back with-out detection would have been difficult.

During the middle of the week one of the staff took me shopping. The clothing order was for specific items, but the choice became my own. After picking all that I was getting, the last shop by manipulation happened to be near the glue depot. Asking the staff member if I could go to the toilet, he waited by the shop for my return. It did not take long to get the tube, and come back without drawing suspicion. We walked up the road towards the home. This left a feeling of content-ment on both fronts. The tube was kept until that evening, as I was hoping to use it inside the building. The difference between an outdoor session, and an indoor one became quite substantial in construction. The choice of location usually de-pended on my preference, and how safe it would be to use in the presence of others. On this occasion a chance was taken indoors.

I chose my timings with considered thought knowing the routines that evening of the staff and boys. There is a lull in activities before bedtime, with the boys in the television room, or games area. The staffs are usually in a relaxed frame of mind, unless there had been trouble. On this evening every-thing was fine. Picking the toilets as my location opted for the middle cubical. The area of the toilets and showers were quite large, therefore my assumption being if anyone appeared it would give me time to sort out any problems. This session proved slightly different in format, than I had been used to. It was very detailed, and stayed with a subject for longer than normal. As mentioned the events seen recently were getting better, but this one contained a higher level of complexity than previous incidents.

Within the door of the cubical a cartoon format came onto the surface. It involved an arm wrestling competition. There appeared a queue of people waiting to take on the champion, who was seated at a large table in a forest setting.

The man at the table looked like Bluto from the Popeye cartoons, only he was larger. The champion took on the various challenges one after another, and beat them all. These men were also represented as being bulky, but none had the stature of the champion. As the competitors moved down the line, I could see a representation of Bruce Lee taking his turn with the others. He waited behind the largest challenger of all. Shortly before it was his turn he looked towards me with an expression on his face, which said, "Well I will give it a go". It was now the turn of the man in front. Bruce patted him on the back, and they shook hands. This showed the difference in their physical sizes. The challenger appeared almost as big as his opponent did, and as he locked in battle put up the best performance yet. Bruce was shouting in his support, and the contest lasted longer than any previous challenge. It proved a valiant effort, but he too lost. It was now Bruce's turn.

After he sat at the table it became possible to judge the difference in these two characters physical statures. It appeared a miss match of such immense proportions, that it caused me to wonder why it should be taking place. If I were to watch a cartoon on television and viewed such a sketch, the reality factor would not have entered my head. This however wasn't the case. Under these conditions, instead of just watching I was part of the setting, and that changed my whole perspective to the contest? The two figures locked arms and began to take the strain.

In the early seventies Bruce Lee had developed cult status, and I admired his capabilities as a fighter. This however did not change reality. The competitors started making their attempts to defeat each other. At first there seemed little movement one way or the other, and the signs of strain could be seen on their faces. I watched this with interest, and at first mentally began supporting Bruce's efforts. Against the concepts of belief, he started doing well. Both characters pushed each other's arm towards the table. Seeing this I could not accept the outcome, and gave up my support for Bruce. The set changed, and returned to a recurrent theme of my visions. That of the naked men with babies attached, being dragged along the floor.At that very point footsteps could be heard entering the toilet. As an automatic reaction the bag was folded over, and I remained silent. Whoever it was stopped, then came up to the toilet door and knocked. The voice belonged to one of the older staff members called Mac. He called my name, and then asked me to come out. It appeared obvious he knew what was going on, as the smell would have been quite strong around that area. The only way I could think of saving the bag was to put it down the inside of my pants, and hope for the best. I flushed the toilet whilst doing this to cover up the sound, and then opened the door.

The staff at the home knew about my glue sniffing, and this became the first time any one of them had come onto contact with it. He asked were the glue was. I told him it had been flushed down the toilet, after hearing him come. He gave me a quick search; not looking in the place it was located. Accepting this was the case told me the headmaster would be informed in the morning. It happened to be close to bedtime, and under the circumstances suggested going up early. I walked along the corridor and up the stairs with the greatest of care. The glue started to burn my skin through the bag.

I did not know how this could be, but once out of sight quickly pulled the bag out and transferred it to my pocket. Once in the dormitory the remaining substance was put under the bed for use when everyone was asleep. I waited until the night watchman checked our room, as he did most evenings at a certain time then began. Unfolding the bag, it appeared my entertainment would be short lived.

Most of the glue had been used up in the toilets; still it should have been at least ten minutes worth. By that stage I could roughly guess the life span of the substance in a bag. There had been three previous occasions in which it had been used in bed. One of these concerned the hours of daylight. The second had been in similar circumstances to these, with a little glue left. The last involved a time in Scotland, which proved to be an eventful night, as before the texture of the bed changed shortly after beginning. This time it became more profound than the last, and I underwent a set of emotional experiences.

On the whole it was unlike me to enjoy sensations through the sense of touch, or to derive pleasure from my innermost self. Being British it is not the done thing to search, or express emotion. I like many other people have been brought up this way. It took me by surprise when this happened, but I did not resist and enjoyed feeling the sheets, bed and my body. It being an awakening to something I previously only had a partial awareness of. My perception was contained within this small area surrounding me, and under the circumstances wasn't interested in anything else, until something caught my attention.

When in bed at night if the sheets cover you, there is certain darkness that surrounds your environment. Whilst wallowing in my newfound sense of being, I looked into the obscurity and noticed it appeared different. Until that point I had not heard, or seen anything associated with my normal experiences. This caused a diversion in attentions away from the self, to my surroundings. At the time it caused a slight annoyance, as I would have been quite happy to use up the remainder of the glue, on nothing more than this experience.

My surrounding darkness seemed to have depth to it. At first no features were visible to judge what I was looking at, but it was definitely different. It appeared as if I was in a large cave, which only had minimal light within. This being so did not allow any perspective to be aware of the boundaries.

I had by then given up on the self-indulgence and focussed my full attention on the new situation. The first change to this environment came in the manor of an instrumental tune, which was of a repetitive nature. It seemed to be coming from within the space. Shortly afterwards whilst this music was still playing, a silhouette shape of a man appeared before me. He had no features to his body, only yellow outline. The shape facing me turned around and began to run. My alter ego, which viewed this, began to follow at a set distance. This action took me away from the point of origin, and in doing so gave an awareness of the surroundings.

The silhouette started running towards some pillars of light in the distance. He passed the first of these, and I followed shortly afterwards. It appeared similar to an obelisk of pure neon. The pillars put my environment into a more manageable perspective, although no end could be seen to this space, it did not matter. The mere fact of witnessing this from an internal position contained the important ingredient.

These pillars were large in comparison to my being, and in passing each one gave ample time to study them. They contained the primary colours, and were three-dimensional. The pureness appeared quite spectacular, almost unnatural. I must have passed six of these, and then everything began to fade. The glue in my bag had lost its potency, and shortly afterwards the normal darkness returned. This became really frustrating being poised on the threshold of something new.

If it were at all possible I would have left the building there and then to get some more glue. At that time of night no place came to mind in which it could be acquired with ease.

Through being caught earlier on it had caused a change in my patterns of usage. This was a complete stroke of luck, that had it not happened I could have carried on using the substance by conventional methods for a long time, experiencing inadequate results.

To try and explain how important this was I could use a simple analogy. Until now if I had been seeing anything whilst using glue, it was presented in such a way that it occupied my physical environment. By this I mean the visions superimposed on actual physical objects. At certain times I had glanced into their source, but had never been able to view a situation from inside this environment. What effectively happened tonight created a bridge over the threshold, and more importantly I recognised this was so. It put everything generated from the past into a secondary league, and I knew there was something waiting to be discovered better than anything experienced so far. Even my wildest imaginations did not compare to that awaiting my next visit. This evening had solved one little problem on a personal basis. That being the niggling feeling something had been missing. Tonight it had been found and awaited discovery.

The following morning I was called into Mr. Gibbons office, he being the headmaster to discuss my glue sniffing in the toilets. It had been the first time of causing any trouble in the home, and because of my previous dealings with people in authority I expected you shouldn't do this and that routine. Much to my surprise he approached the subject from a different objective. This was more like an informal chat, with the emphasis on why I used it. My answer if asked yesterday would have been different from today. Saying little about the experience side, we just talked in generalisations. He did not pressure me in any way and the matter became left at that. I was impressed at his attitude, and found it on the whole a better response than normal. Even as we were speaking my thoughts revolved around the quickest possible way to get out and acquire some.

During the next three or four days it proved impossible to get into the town, without causing a major problem. My chance came when one of the staff wanted a hand carrying something from the shops. As he uttered these words I jumped up to offer my assistance before anyone could say anything. The particular shop was not so close to the large department store. I had to run quite a distance to get there and back within reasonable time.

Once in the shop it did not allow time to worry about the normal precautions. The best that could be managed involved a quick look around. Taking a tin put it inside my jacket, trusting to luck. As it turned out everything was fine, and returned without arousing any suspicion. Before meeting up I transferred the tin under my armpit, and walked back to the home slightly uncomfortably.

It was hidden in my dormitory, with the metal undercover removed to avoid causing any problems at night. Returning to normal life waited the evening to come. It became a long day going through the rituals, and my mind was not on any of these. In the classrooms I tried to comprehend what a three dimensional environment would be like. If by judging what happened on the previous occasion as a guide, it should be very interesting.

We finished classes and had our evening meal. The rest of the night was spent in the television room trying to take my mind off the situation. Our normal bedtime being ten o'clock I went to the dormitory before this, checking everything was in order. The tin could be felt inside the pillowcase resting on my head. I watched the others come into the room, and go to bed. All that now remained involved a waiting period, for everything to settle down.

The nearest I can recall to being this excited was during Christmas, as the presents were given out. That of course was as a child. The time before commencement became savoured, waiting for just the right moment. It had now come. The life span of a tin was in excess of six hours if used continuously. I had never gone much beyond two hours before, but tonight it seemed quite conceivable to exceed that record. After pouring out the glue I went under the sheets and started.

My attention from the outset became focussed on the darkness surrounding me. As it took effect a difference became perceived, in depth and shade, the only change being minuet specks of colour seen within this space, with nothing else outstanding. Coming from beyond my bed, in the area of the dormitory a song could be heard drifting through the sheets towards me. The first line developed after the musical introduction 'This is your golden day'. Because this happened it caused me to pull back the bedclothes, to find the source of the music. Looking around the dormitory I was completely taken aback. The whole room had been transformed into something more resembling a palace, than a ten-bedded area for naughty boys.

The bland setting now had furniture, from different time periods appearing in front of my very eyes. These were superimposed within the existing structures of the room. Where a bed stood, more elaborate four-poster versions moulded around these. Its design looked authentic to my limited knowledge of antiques. The change affected all aspects of my environment. The carpet became multi-patterned, having a depth and quality that would never fall within the budget of a local authority. The ceiling altered to a much-decorated area, with additional plaster patterns all around. That, which had once been lights, was now a chandelier. To see this was to look at a real chandelier. Curtains adorned the new design windows, and the whole imagery became quite stunning.

After my first good look, the room was filled with golden speckles falling down from the ceiling. This tied in with the song. It indeed was a golden day. The whole set began changing before my eyes, that is every aspect that had been previously witnessed, the beds, chandeliers, windows, curtains and carpets, all assumed different designs. None of these were of a lesser quality, just alternative pieces. The total transformation would take around twenty seconds, and begin over again. It was all very stunning. The complexities on display proved extremely impressive. Other events happened in the room as the changes were going on. One of these concerned an elongated style of cinema screen that appeared in front above my head, showing a film similar to One Hundred and One Dalmatians. It was in cartoon format, concerning spotted dogs. This wasn't an extract copy from the original film, more a likeness. It did have one aspect of difference and that was in quality, it appeared much better. It would be impossible to remember all of the events that happened, during the first sequence of my education that evening. It was like taking a deprived little boy, dropping him in Disneyland with a free pass to go were he pleased. It proved so spectacular that I would not have believed it could get more diverse, I was wrong.

This show had taken my mind of the original intention. Going back under the bedclothes, a whole New World awaited me. That which had been a black cavern was now filled with light, combined with imagery. I began seeing well beyond my physical space, it was totally awe-inspiring. Ahead in the distance appeared a large set of gates that opened shortly before coming to them. Going inside there were many buildings surrounding me? One of these was consciously chosen and some part of me went towards it. As well as seeing a different environment to that which my body occupied, I had to come to terms with moving independently. This combined with looking at objects, not with my eyes, but some other function that I had been only partially aware of up till now.

That is quite a simple explanation of my immediate recognition, in conjunction with this place that my alter ego inhabited. The building in front had a door to one side, and moving towards this it opened to let my presence in. It appeared to be a backroom that housed stage props, because everything in the room seemed authentic. I noticed two men working, moving various items about. Both of them were aware of me, or whatever version was on display. The men were dressed in clothing that belonged to the nineteen twenties, or thirties. From the limited visions seen until then, it gave an appearance of America during this period. I moved closer towards them, and in doing so they stepped aside to let my mass enter the space they had occupied. I knew instinctively not to try and touch them, for whatever part of me occupied another perception did not have hands as such. It did however accompany a presence that felt human. Being in a new environment did not warrant any sudden actions, and I was feeling my way around, carefully.

The two men continued working, and at one point wanted to come back to the place they had been previously. By simply thinking about moving backwards, it happened. They did not seem at ease with me being there. Nothing extraordinary happened during that time, unless you count just being there. I wondered what was happening back in the dormitory. Lifting the bedclothes it appeared as before, constantly changing. The range of furniture going through the room was quite astounding. Each of the ten beds was of a different design, not all four posters. It became possible to look at the nearest ones in more detail. It illustrated stunning craftsmanship. In the top left hand corner of the room; there appeared a small version of the bed I had been studding. This was identical, apart from having sizes, and numbers around it. Looking back and forward at both of these it appeared the smaller one was nothing more than some form of catalogue description, for its full sized counterpart. It may sound strange, but that became the first time I began to consider my mind could not be conjuring this up. It was too complicated in structure and detail, for an individual imagination.

Because I was in the middle of something, the fundamental ideas behind this theory would have to wait until a more appropriate. I had returned to the stage area that was now minus the people. There appeared something odd about them, thinking back to the previous encounter. They looked real enough, that is all there features, sizes and mannerisms were identical to a normal body and compared in visualisation to anything I had seen whilst using glue. It is hard to put this into words. Because I now inhabited another environment it gave me a much clearer feel to my surroundings. Although appearing authentic, they were not. The imagery lacked something that is unmistakably human, and did not possess that quality.

There seemed little point in staying in a deserted building, and moving across to another door went outside. This created an unusual sensation in leaving the room, as it went straight out into a pavement. They're being no space that one would normally find in doing such an action. It is a small point of comparison, which struck me at the time. The scene now visible was different than my first encounter. I saw a road that could have come from a major city in America during the early part of the century. The buildings and surrounding fittings were exact, as one could have imagined them from this period; however it was not real in the true sense of the word. On this street there were people and vehicles corresponding with the setting. I moved up the pavement and encountered people walking along to the side of me, as you would find in any street setting. The differences were striking in a number of fundamental ways. The first noticeable one being it seemed very quiet for such a large area.

As I came upon these individuals going about their business, each looked at me without saying anything. Continuing onwards watching the people gave a chance to study them closely. They wore clothing from that era, and were all very smartly dressed. It was evening, but did not have the ambience of such an occasion. It proved really strange. My initial impressions being this appeared a very good copy of a scene from that period. The first car I came upon was a black limousine. Crossing on to the road, it was a real car in every sense of the word. There were however detectable differences; the first of these being it was in pristine condition. No indications were visible that informed me as to its make, or model. Without any badges or labels it could not be distinguished from any other black limousine. One other little pointer being the lack of exhaust fumes from a running engine.

These changes to one's concepts were very apparent, but not so important as to make you think different about the events on display. It appeared more like creating an imbalance to one's perception. Why this should have been, was unknown. It offered another part of the evening's entertainment that would have to be thought about at a latter date.

My total attention had been focussed on the many occurrences going on around me at the time. All of my presence was encapsulated within this environment, which proved to be fascinating. Until that point there had been no concern about anything seen, or the fact that some part of me inhabited another space. For some reason that was totally unknown I began to feel uneasy. This happened suddenly, and nothing could be detected which should cause this to be so. Carrying on up the road it grew to such a point that I could not concentrate on anything going around me just then. To put this into context at that time, it was such a strong feeling that I can't ever recall experiencing a comparable emotion at any event in my life.

That included real circumstances, or through the use of solvents. It became such a strong sense that I eventually found it impossible continuing through this setting. Pulling back the sheets my concern switched from the bed, to the dormitory wondering if there was anything that could account for this uncanny sensation. I did not have to look very far to find the answer to my problems. All the changes stopped, and it had returned back to a normal bedroom. I only noticed this however for a few seconds, as there was something else in the room looking at me. Standing by the doorway was a being not from this earth.

With my many experiences through the use of glue, from the beginning until this time I had witnessed numerous events, settings, and people. In all of these cases I had never accepted the subject matters being alive, in the same context as life that is known to me. They had been visions, copies or representations. Even the more extreme times, such as the boy drowning in the fast flowing river became a depiction of an event. This however was in no way, the same as any of these. I was looking at a life form that could not be mistaken as a fabrication. To describe this individual for the want of better word is all that can be attempt. It was formed in a similar way to the human shape, being at an estimate five feet six tall. My judgements of its size came from seeing it standing within the doorway. Its colour was green, with a larger than normal head in comparison to the body. I could not see ears as one over-whelming part of the face caught my total attention that was the eyes. Everything else became unimportant after staring into those. They held within their gaze an intelligence, which seemed so overpowering, I could not come to terms with the differences in our statures. I panicked, and acted like an os-trich facing a problem beyond its comprehension. Pulling the bedclothes over my entire body stopped doing anything. Staying there for two, or three minutes remained motionless. From the first sighting until my demise could not have lasted more than ten seconds? So much for being mister cool, in the face of adversity.

It is funny looking back on the event to those things I did not remember, such as was the being wearing any clothes. To this day that cannot be visualised, it is something that should have stuck out a mile. One other quandary-concerned lapses of memory associated with the time spent under the bedclothes. This I imagine was to do with being in shock; it had caught me off guard in a big way. It is important to stress how real this was to me at the time. I did not know what I was dealing with, but it was certainly way and above any-thing experienced, getting to know this other existence. By the time my faculties had been regained, I was clenching the bag tightly. The effects of the glue had worn off, and my next decision to be made involved venturing out, or not. Pulling the bedclothes from my face, there was only one area in the room that interested me.

That, which had been the most astounding spectacle in my life, was no longer there. It had never really occurred to me that source of my visions could have been influenced by an external force. This is because the use of solvents, for a personal point of view had only been regarded as entertainment. I felt up until then incidents seen from the past, were somehow part of me. I had not understood the manor and method of their presentation and in truth not thought about this a great deal. It is not necessary to understand the mechanisms of something, to enjoy it.

Between the ages of thirteen and fifteen I did not consider fundamental issue very deeply life is about fun. This was my philosophy until challenged by more pressing realities. Tonight had brought about one of these challenges. That, which had been seen standing by the door, did not just appear as another vision. It created a build up, which affected me in a strong way, before even laying eyes on it. This being no coincidence, it was designed to show that which I was dealing with, and certainly achieved the purpose.

My next decision involved a more serious matter, and that was should I carry on. Being now in a position to rationalise the last set of actions, it had not been delivered as a threat. A better way to describe this would be to say it was portrayed as a dynamic realisation. Once you have opened Pandora's Box, there is no turning back. I felt it imperative to continue.

Reopening the bag still held tightly within my hands, I sat upright in the bed. My gaze was directed towards the door whilst inhaling the fumes. After regaining an awareness level, the room remained unchanged. That which revealed its form did not returned. There had been very few instances whilst using glue that nothing appeared different. I could not understand that why after a flurry of activity, everything had gone flat. Keeping my attentions within the room for some time did not alter anything. I stayed longer than normal in an uninteresting position, just in case something unusual happened. It did not appear anything of the sort would come about. The only other option involved returning under the sheets.

Having done this I was now seeing a different landscape than had previously been shown. The setting now viewable consisted of two prominent objects. I was back in a large cavern with a stationary escalator, which had no visible end. After seeing this I found myself placed upon the escalator, which began to move upwards very slowly. Looking around this landscape on either side, the only structure that could be seen was the dull blue walls. I stayed in this position for quite some time, expecting some form of change. It just trundled onwards, without the slightest difference. After what appeared in excess of ten minutes, I became very bored of these conditions. Because it was a totally strange environment, any action I could take may have brought about unknown consequence; even so travelling on this road to nowhere seemed pointless. Coming out from under the bedclothes it was hoped something would be occurring in the dormitory. The room only had one change to its otherwise normal furnishings, and that was a full-scale escalator going from the centre of the room to the ceiling.

On seeing this it began to move upwards, at an even slower rate than its counterpart. From the comfort of my bed I watched this boring spectacle, with a disbelief, which could not have been foreseen that long ago. Going back underneath, nothing had changed. To compare the heightened pleasure first achieved during the beginning of the evening, to the frustration now felt covered both extremes in one's emotions. Whist back on the escalator, I started to think of other times associated whilst using glue in the past. One of these occasions involved a particularly good session in Scotland in which I wanted to physically touch a girl that was coming out of the wallpaper. Because the desire existed to attain, the un-attainable I mentally interacted with my environment, causing physical changes to that set. I wondered if by trying this again, it could have the same effect.

My plan centred on stopping the escalator, and the first idea that came into my head involved placing a metal bar across its path in front of me. No sooner had this concept been formulated, it became a reality. The escalator stopped moving shortly before my presence came upon the bar .It proved very pleasing to have achieved it, although the relevance of the action did not strike me at the time. My smugness was soon overtaken by surprise, when a voice said, "Well done William". The sound of this voice appeared as if close by, but I could not detect its source. This did not allow any time for further searching, as my whole environment changed. Instead of an escalator I now found myself in an elevator with its doors wide open. Looking out of these was a bottomless tract, downwards this time. It started to move on what could only describe as an endless journey. After a few seconds I thought about placing the bar in my path to stop its progress. Once again after completion the voice congratulated me.

I listened closely to the structure of the sound trying to detect some form of accent, or tone that would give an indication as to the orientation. It was spoken in perfect English who gave no hint to any of my ideas. Once again the set changed, this time to some form of obstacle course. There became one major difference between it and a normal circuit. My participation involved thinking a way through the various obstacles. At first this seemed relatively easy, as the initial objectives proved to be of a simple nature. After the third it became gradually more difficult to mentally react with my environment. The speed in which the problems had to be dealt with, plus the complication factor became too intricate for me to handle. When this point had been reached, giving up in my attempt the remainder of the course passed me by.

At certain times in my sequence of writings there will come situations that are difficult to transfer on to paper. This is one such instance. In describing an event such as the course passing me, I cannot draw a similar comparison in real terms to the reader. One has to judge this in a viewpoint of special effects from high-tech films, only it is three-dimensional and you are there. I found myself back in the stage prop room. The transfer from one scene to another happened instantaneously, without any form of fading from one to the other. The two men had returned and were working as before. One of them spoke directly to me asking the location of the box was he looking for. I replied no. This answer had come from me, though not spoken verbally. I thought the word that came across clear as any speech pattern from my own mouth. This was turning out to be an extraordinary night. From the first day of using solvents I could create sound effects, and tunes, but at no time in the past had I ever been able to master the art of speaking with my thoughts. It felt quite strange to do this, almost like uttering a foreign language for the first time, where you say the words but are unsure of their soundings.

I had been using glue in the region of three hours by then. At some point during the experience I must have fallen asleep. It was now morning, and the boys were getting up. Unbeknown to me the bag of glue had spilled out over the bedclothes, my pyjamas and hair. It was particularly bad timing when I found this out, as a staff member came into room to wake up the stragglers, trying to get out bed proved difficult with various items stuck to my person. One of the boys became the first to notice my predicament, and let out a loud laugh. It must have been quite funny because I was trying to be inconspicuous, which proved impossible. When the staff member saw me he had a look of amazement on his face.

After separating the unwanted items, I was taken straight down to see the headmaster in his office. It turned out to be an informal telling off, with more emphasis put of why I did this.

The headmaster's wife happened to be with him at the time, and she cut the chunks of glue out of my hair. The only comeback in the way of a punishment involved having to pay for the sheets to be cleaned. They were under the impression glue stains could be removed. I knew otherwise.

During breakfast my exploits were the main topic of discussion that morning. What surprised me was how careless I had been last night, this being caused by the astounding set of circumstances surrounding the whole event. It was certainly something that should never be repeated. Well, what to make of the whole episode. It certainly involved a quantum jump in terms of experience. I think the best way to describe my understanding is to deal with the issues of that time.

It would be inappropriate of me to say I understood what appeared to be going on, for I did not. If there became an outcome to last night it was certainly to disregard the idea of an over active imagination boosted by a stimulus. The events were patterned, and purposeful. They were presented in a complex manor not only beyond my imagination, but anyone's. It caused a major rethink of the many events that happened during all of my glue sniffing exploits. My brain was working overtime through the rest of that day trying to comprehend something way beyond understanding. It certainly made sense of circumstances, which had been until then a complete mystery.

Two boys who were in the lodge expressed an interest in using glue. Since my capture it had become public knowledge, and a curiosity arose as to what it involved. After telling one of these whose name was Michael he managed to get hold of a tin whilst in the town. This proved rather satisfying, it being an unexpected source of supply and lessened the need to get some by my own devices. It was during the afternoon when I knew this.

My interest level in using glue, through the hours of daylight had all but disappeared by then. As the tin was his, it would have seemed unfair introducing him to something at night while I was totally engrossed in my own circumstances. We went outside into the grounds and climbed up the fire escape. This part of the building gave cover from most angles, and lessened the chance of detection. The only real drawback was a window that looked out from the top part of the main home, to our position. Going to the corner of that flat roof, we began using the tin.

Because my last session had taken the word 'experience' to a new level, I wasn't that interested in seeing the normal outdoor display, and looked on this more from a study perspective, watching Michael's responses. It's funny how blasé one could become within a period of days, to something that would have taken my full attention prior to the last occasion. My eyes stayed on Michael whilst inhaling the fumes. He is one of those individuals glue has a strong visual impact on, and his facial expressions changed to a comical, dopey response. It proved similar to watching a baby amusing itself within a pram. He began laughing in a quiet contented manor, and could be left without further supervision.

My attentions were switched to the wooded landscape, being on a higher position it became possible to see my surroundings from a different point of view. Looking at a number of events going on around me did not register high on the interest level, and it seemed a waste of a good opportunity to be doing it this way. I wondered if by simply closing my eyes, could the circumstances of darkness be mimicked, and produce the conditions relevant to achieve the same results. Checking the area beforehand seemed like a good idea, because it would have been somewhat annoying getting caught attempting a simple experiment. If you shut your eyes there is a normal blackness surrounding, one's visual perceptions. It no longer existed within my alternate level of consciousness. This proved quite astounding, and something that had not happened before. By the simple blink of an eyelid it became possible to see two different environments, operating within one state of awareness.

My first recollection did not show any visible objects to make it blatantly obvious, and like the other occasions it appeared as a large empty space. This required my attentions focussed on a different wavelength. As you would imagine my eyes remained closed through most of the session. Within these surroundings a voice spoke to me, it being the same one that said well done on completing the basic tests. I concentrated on talking with my mind, and found it to be much easier than the first attempt. My initial conversation involved asking the voice, which had a masculine tone, his name. The reply was 'Gong' and this became accompanied by a visual description in imagery. I witnessed a man striking a large gong, of a kind similar to the Rank film introductions that were popular during the sixties. At seeing this it caused me to laugh, because it appeared such an unusual title.

My next serious of questions were more of an informative nature. I wanted to know where I was, what I was seeing, and why all of this was happening. There were other enquires of a similar nature. After running out of questions to ask, my reply came, who, what, why, where and when appeared on a large screen that occupied this other level of consciousness. The voice said none of these questions could be answered. Well that certainly dealt with my inquisitiveness .There was no point in asking why this should be, as it became covered in the initial reply. Although this was disappointing, it did not lessen the interest surrounding my circumstances. The changes that occurred during the last week to my awareness were quite astounding. This covered many aspects, which at one time I would have let pass by without a second thought. A good example to this happened after opining my eyes to check everything was fine.

It all seemed reasonably quite in the grounds, apart from the induced differences. The one window running adjacent to the stairs revealed no people walking towards the top half of the building. I looked around to see Michael, who was still sitting contented, and did not have a care in the world. Above his head appeared an object that resembled a pillar-box. It was roughly the same dimensions, and seemed to be located within the wall no more than a few feet above him. This was an object associated with the other side of my consciousness.

What makes this so interesting is there was also one of these close by my position. If attempting this by myself, the object would not have appeared visible as it would always have been out of my line of vision. Because the new state of awareness presented capabilities to see two people's environments, it offered a deeper level of understanding, and I think this was not per chance.

In talking about unusual concepts such as this one, I will try and make the relevance as clear as possible. These boxes were not part of a surplice decoration scheme. They had something to do with the external visions, which could be seen around me. I felt they were, to use a simple comparison akin to a projection outlet. That may sound like I am doing a lot of assuming based on little or no evidence. It did not occur to me the possibility of trying to make Michael aware of this, for I imagined my superior state of focus could not be attain by a novice.

A friend of mine experienced similar conditions in the not too distant future, only this involved six or more people, without any pre- discussions to that on display. At the time these intricacies did not overly concern me, as I was getting to know my new circumstances. The pillar-boxes were to become a regular feature, whilst using the substance in a day-time situation. They always held a certain fascination, that if it were possible to see beyond my limitations into their function, a better understanding of that on display would be more complete.

One of the problems associated with using glue outdoors, concerned time devoted to matters not related to the subject. If there was a noise, or your concentration became diverted it spoiled the occasion to a certain extent. It really required a totally peaceful environment, such as the bedroom at night. After using the bag with its little amount of glue, I spoke to Michael asking how it had been. This proved a formality, as it became plain to see the way it affected him. He revealed what I expected, with only one minor deviation. That was a strong ringing in the ears. He seemed pleased at the outcome, and rather sensibly gave me the remainder of the tin for safekeeping. This created an opportunity to continue where I had left off. The next time would be just right, and now that my inauguration was over, perhaps it could return to a stable format.

The tin was hidden within the grounds, because I had no intentions of wasting any of it on trivialities. If there is regret associated with this time, it concerns not collating some form of written record. To have recorded the events, and put them in their correct order would have greatly increased the substance of this story. At the time it wasn't a viable option, with my English standard being appalling, If someone had told me then, I would be writing a story of this length and detail in the future, it would have caused me to laugh in their faces. It's quite amazing what the passages of time can bring to an individual. This also reflected in my attitude to life during that period. Although it's now possible to view the circumstances with informed hindsight, at that juncture my opinions were still based in the amusement aspects.

I believe this partly resulted in the way issues were dealt with. Most information of this other society was delivered throughout the medium of vision. It became a sort of three way split. You had the subject me, the source, a highly advanced group of individuals, the method of presentation the visions directed to a middle ground. My only actual dealing with the source involved the other night when one of them stood by the door, and changed my awareness to the situation. The format of my dealings really began during that night. The other occasion served as an introduction, laying out the ground rules. It was a more business like approach that faced me now, incorporated within the guise of amusement. I can only assume this proved the most competent way to communicate with, a lesser life form and get results wanted, causing the least concern. That evening made me understand the purpose to the many different scenarios, appearing before me. They were quite simply tests, designed to gauge my responses in a given situation. After retrieving the tin brought it to my dormitory and began approaching the fundamentals with care, hoping to avoid the conditions of last time. When the correct level of awareness had been achieved, I found the initial stage of the proceedings belonged to me. From the outset of the dealings I had a guide who accompanied me through this other environment, and explained what became required in the different settings. A blank stage became my introduction, as to the capabilities on display. He explained thought would become reality, by simply concentrating on any object that came into my mind it would appear to create the setting of my desire.

The stage at the beginning was empty area laid out for my convenience; it set parameters to attempt something, which at first seemed a little daunting. My initial conception was to build an animated set, which expanded with each projection. As the foundation objects appeared it did not amount too much, until more items came into place, then began to resemble an actual creation. With the final piece completed the whole set came to life, and the efforts of my thoughts had a semblance of meaning. My choices during this early stage were of a simple nature, but then only being fifteen I didn't think to use this facility to its full capabilities. As a rough estimation that segment of the program lasted ten minutes, or so, then afterwards my presence left the area and went on to something else.

The ranges of subjects encountered afterwards were quite varied, and to remember these in sequences is impossible, only the more prominent events can be recalled from individual occasions. In the early days my memory of these is quite good, and in describing it will try giving my opinions of that time, rather than a reflection from the benefit of hindsight. That night gave me a better understanding of how events would be directed. This happened shortly after my playtime in creating an animated set, and it took the form of a race that could be likened to a steeplechase.

To my left appeared an opponent who seemed very keen to get under way. This wasn't a conventional contest; it had one major difference. Instead of just running its length, I had to think my way over each obstacle. These barriers were different in construction, and would incorporate the need for speed and accurate responses. By nature I'm a competitive person, and it does not take much prompting to achieve the desired results. It was possible to see most of the course, although the end section failed to be so clearly defined. We set of and at first there being little space between our respective positions. As the race progressed I managed pulling ahead slightly, enough to ensure victory with only two obstacles to complete.

On the penultimate barrier I noticed a little man working on part of my apparatus. By being there he created a problem in negating this object, and the only way to overcome this difficulty was to ignore him, believing it would be possible to jump over his position, then deal with the obstacle itself. On the point of attempting it the lower section, which he was working on, fell down, completely blocking any way around the problem. My opponent passed by on the other side, and won the race. This proved frustrating to have almost achieved the objective, only to be hindered by incompetence.

Looking at this man I could feel my emotions transferring from thought into action. By directing this anger towards him, it generated an electrical charge, which stunned his body.

These set of actions were very sudden, and only afterwards did I understand the significance of my response. The purpose of the race had nothing to do with winning, it being an evaluation in real terms to disappointment, with no restrictions attached. I became aware to the capabilities of my mind in this environment, and realised they would have to be kept under control in similar situations. The difference between my two levels of experience had quite a profound effect on me.

In the past these offered only partial insight into the emotional awareness surrounding the alternate existence, by this I mean the feelings and responses were not fully developed. Having committed the whole of my consciousness it allowed me to comprehend certain feelings from a much deeper level. This was to manifest itself in a number of different ways that previously had only involved a limited realisation. The part of me, which embodied these beliefs, was of a purer state of existence. I felt younger in this environment than my actual years; a better phrase would be more innocent. It seemed as if two separate pieces of the consciousness had come together. They were both intrinsically linked, and having developed to this plain became as one. To feel this was a unique experience, an understanding of the depths to one's being. I cannot fully explain its substance; perhaps it is lost innocence. Whatever terms one could chose it is a very enlightening part of my inner self.

This emotion tied in with a closer harmony to my senses. On experiencing something it would be understood from an emotional perspective. I do not mean it helped me comprehend situations more fully, or increased my intelligence quota. It allowed an expanded awareness to the whole of an event, rather that a limited view the senses normally observe. The voice that had spoken to me 'Gong' would ask my opinions on a number of different matters. These questions were usually directed during an interval that is going from one set to another. They did not appear to have real importance in depth and were more informal in tone, almost small talk. I found this to be out of context with the environment that was highly structured. The choice of discussion did not on the whole give any insight to that which I was dealing with.

One of these talks stuck out from the rest during my early involvement in Ashbourne Lodge. It concerned the subject of music, and more specifically a certain band who were popular through the seventies. These were the Osmands. Gong asked my opinion of this group, and did I like them. My response was to laugh at the question, replying no. This answer wasn't based on the fact they were bad, it more concerned the image they presented of being a girls band. I became surprised when this was not dropped shortly afterwards. He seemed it important to let me know they were very popular in his world. The words 'here' and with all of us were used. This pertained to more that one opinion.

I could not understand why a higher level of intelligence could be interested in such a form of entertainment. This burst of enthusiasm became accompanied by a visual description. Looking back on this from the present, it wasn't quite as silly as it first appeared. The Osmands were an unusual phenomenon in the pop world by their music and presentation, which represented a set of ideals that seemed to mirror Gong and his compatriot's approaches to life. These conceptions were not the only one's depicted in my time there. I had yet to be made aware of his counterparts.

The tin Michael had given me lasted a few more times. Through the week I had a chance to conduct myself in the manor decided after the obstacle race, during one of these occasions. This part of the session involved playing table tennis against an opponent, who was depicted as a fully-grown man of large build. The style of game was somewhat unusual. Instead of hitting the ball with a bat I had to use my thoughts. This proved to be more difficult than had first been imagined, and it was lucky he wasn't a very good player, which balanced the game up. The match was about half way completed when my opponent became agitated through missing the ball. His anger at first became directed at himself, and then transferred to me. It proved a totally unexpected turn of events.

My reactions were the same as if happening in real life. When danger threatens one personally there is a chemical reaction in the brain, which heightens the state of awareness. I could feel this with a force outside the range of normal perception, and it took the concept of understanding my emotions into a different reality. I felt every reaction in total clarity, as if watching the changes from within. It did have one benefit in a round about sort of way; at least it seemed possible to comprehend my reactions with the same intensity as my hosts.

The lesson had been well learnt during the previous encounter. I knew it would be possible harm this man if so desired and with that knowledge responded with silence, waiting for his next actions. He continued being aggressive until it became obvious that I would not bite. The set changed. These references are contained within the lifespan of that particular tin. There were many other incidents, but with the passing of time have slipped in obscurity. The memories of that period are fondly recalled, if somewhat diminished.

The home arranged an appointment in the local hospital for a brain scan. I assume it was taken in official circles to see if glue sniffing had caused any damage, and this interested me in a way the authorities could not have guessed. Because of the changes to my perceptions I wondered if these had altered any principles governing the thought process. As those actions originated in the brain, I hoped some form of difference could have registered on the EEG machine. On the day I was taken by one of the staff in his car, the few miles to the hospital. By that time my interest level had built up considerably, and I viewed this in the same way as a test conducted during my glue sniffing exploits. After being wired up I tried concentrating in order to cause some form of deviation. The markers whirled away on the paper throughout my efforts, for ten or fifteen minutes. On completion the doctor removed the electrodes and looked at the results. I asked him in a half expectant manor if everything seemed fine. It turned out normal, as the readings showed nothing out of the ordinary. This proved disappointing from an achievement perspective. Leaving the building and returning to the home, felt slightly disgruntled.

Ashbourne Lodge was only a link in the chain for placing of boys into more permanent situations, and being so it caused a continuing turnover. An aspect of this movement concerned the availability in sleeping arrangements. The dormitory in which I stayed housed most people and there were two of these, with one small room that slept four. A bed became free in the smaller room due to one of the boys moving on.

Having been there a few months, and being one of the old hands the option of changing accommodation came about. As this presented fewer distractions in perusing my hobby I moved in the same day. Life in the home proved very good in terms of activities. We were taken out in the minibus to various localities, at different times. On one of these occasions the trip involved going to a fair in Basingstoke. There were around ten of us in the bus, and one of the boys lived within walking distance to where this was situated. His father ran a public house and seemed quite enlightened as to the develop-ment of his son. After spending an hour or so amusing our-selves, four of us slipped of to have a drink. His father gave us beers and cigarettes whilst we mingled with the punters. It felt good to be accepted into the adult community; being my first occasion in this situation it left a strong impression.

I think my companions were in the same frame of mind being roughly the same age. We sat at one of the tables and talked as men of events in the future. In this environment life at the lodge did not seem quite as good as it had been. We collectively decided to run away in the not too distant future. The theory involved making the transition from childhood, to grown up overnight. It seemed a plausible idea sitting round the table, and we were all of one mind. It would not have been advisable leaving there and then, as it could have drawn attention to the landlord. Returning to the fair, our plans would be left to a more opportune time.

Our chance came on the following Monday and it seemed quite odd how the occasion developed. There was no pre-planning, just an opportunity. Three of us ran out the building along the main road. This proved really idiotic, as it had no chance of achieving anything. As expected the police picked us up a few miles away and returned our carcasses back to the home. Nothing significant happened over the incident, as far as two of us were concerned. The one boy who seemed to receive the brunt of any attention was Michael. This brought to a head a dispute he, and the headmaster were having. It was one of those situations where mutual dislike developed and he was always going to the focus for any retribution. I knew how Michael felt having experienced a similar condition in Balgowen.

It wasn't until the following Saturday that the right circumstances came about to run away. I had gone to the pictures as normal, which allowed access to my own clothes. Towards the end of the film it dawned on me that a better opportunity would not present itself. Leaving the cinema my intentions involved breaking in somewhere to finance this plan. My morals at that stage of development had diverted from their basic premise in a downward direction.

It took quite some time before a suitable target was found which presented an easy option, and led me past the boundaries of Winchester into a surrounding village. After breaking in I rummaged through the rooms and took some items, which could be sold easily. There were also a few pounds in money lying around that ended up in my pocket. Returning to Winchester, the train was used to reach London. It being around midnight on arrival in the capital, experience had taught me not to wander about. Going straight in to the downstairs toilets, it became a makeshift accommodation for the night. In the morning after a wash and tidy up I went in search of a pawnshop.

My directions led me towards St Paul's Cathedral where a man of dubious morals bought the items for fifteen pounds. This being a lot of money in those days, it allowed me to have a good dinner in the West End of the city, and then afterwards take in the sights.

To someone of my age a place of this nature is about as exciting as it comes, and the first port of call was to the cinema. In this area there are a number strip clubs, ranging from the tacky, to well choreograph shows. I had never been to such a venue in my life, apart from one's sexual imaginations. I wondered if it were possible to bluff my way in. On reflection my appearance would seem slightly older than fifteen, so going to the cash desk I tried appearing as casual as possible. The cashier gave me the ticket, which proved expensive in relation to the money in my pocket.

Walking up the stairs became quite an experience; with my heart beating faster the nearer one came to the main door, shortly before coming upon this some showgirls came out of a side entrance, and I almost walked into them. Right up to the point of sitting down I could not believe my luck would hold out, expecting someone to say you're not old enough. The show turned out to be very good, from a professional aspect.

Money was whittling away at a faster rate than I had believed possible. With three or four pounds left my last fling involved going into a small bar in some side street. It said topless waitress service and I imagined one could get away with spending relatively little money. The inside of the building did not match my thoughts as to what it would be like. In one corner a single man had four girls standing around him, they were all fully clothed. Sitting down in the opposite side of the room, I waited to see if anything would happen. After ordering a drink discovered its price was the same as the large club I had just come from. One of the girls who had been by the bar came over to me and said hello. She sat down in an opposite seat and asked if I would buy her a drink.

The most striking feature of this person being her eyes, they were lovely. I became really taken aback when she started speaking to me, but the illusion was soon to end as she was a prostitute. The bottom lines involved giving the hostess seven pounds, and take the girl back to my place. If it had been possible on both counts I would have done this. Due to the lack of money, and accommodation it spoiled what should had been a perfect end to a good day. Explaining the circumstances offered my apologies and left the club.

The realisation this kind of life could not be sustained, unless you had a lot of money was dawning on me. Thoughts turned too more pressing aspects, that of the longer-term objectives. The only option that offered a semblance of normality was making my way to Scotland. As it turned out the train was leaving sooner than I thought. Making my way to the station it was quite easy to get on board, but there weren't many people about. Going to the far end, a carriage was found to be unoccupied. The situation offered a less than a perfect scenario for avoiding detection. Shortly after the train pulled away a man came into the carriage and lay across the three seats opposite, face down to sleep for the night. This seemed like a good idea; from a pretext of fooling the guard into thinking I was a heavy sleeper. That became my intentions for an hour or so, until falling asleep for real. The first sound to wake me came in the early hours of the morning. The man was getting off at his station, it being Newcastle in the North of England.

There had been no interruptions through the night, or I would have woken. It seemed unlikely anyone would come at this late stage in the journey to check the tickets. All that was needed to make a good ending being a little luck when the train pulled in at Edinburgh. I envisaged dealing with a number of different situations. As the train came alongside the platform my luck continued, it being the end track. Instead of bluffing my way past the guards it became a simple matter of jumping over a small barrier.

I made my way to Kennoway, and walking up the road saw Jimmy working in the front garden. He seemed surprised, but I managed to persuade him about being on holiday for the week. It proved fortunate he did not know the in. and outs of the social work department. Accepted my word everything appeared fine. Events had turned out better than expected. There however became one potential problem that could not be dealt with. At the start of our road were two police houses. My friend lived directly opposite these, and the chance of seeing him without being detected by one of their wives was nil. I hoped the police in the village had not been informed to my absconding. Once again this was trusting to luck, a little too much this time. After visiting my friend I returned home.

The last couple of days had caught up with me in the sleep department, and my plan involved having an early night after dinner. Whilst walking up the stairs I happened to glance out the side window and saw a police car stop at the next-door neighbours. For a few seconds nothing happened and caused me to believe it was any more than a coincidence. This wasn't to be. It crossed my mind to make a run for it, but I couldn't be bothered. Opening the front door apologised to Jimmy for deceiving him, and they took me away. I was brought to the local station and kept there until officials made alternate arrangements. This took quite some time and it was quite late when I was transferred to a remand centre in Edinburgh.

The overall experience of this event brought some perspective back into my life, and in its own way became a good thing. It made me appreciate Ashbourne Lodge a great deal more than before coming here. Sometimes it's better to have a good kick up the arse to lessen the complacency generated by an easy life. I spent a number of days there, and ended up flying back to London, after being taken to the airport by some social workers.

It felt good to be going back. After an hours drive we arrived at the lodge where I told the other boys in our room of my exploits. Security has its own rewards, and sleeping became an easy matter for the first time in a number of nights. In the morning before breakfast I was summoned into the headmaster's office. He informed me the police wished to make inquires over a burglary that happened during my first night away. A policeman came to the home in the afternoon. To save any time messing about he said my fingerprints were found in and around the house. This became another charge added to the list for my court appearance, who's dated had not been set.

I settled back into routines at the Lodge, almost to the point of never having been away. During my absence no form of solvents had been used. Consciously it was decided to steer clear of any trouble during the foreseeable future. This included going down the town and stealing some glue.

About ten days later a serious of strange events began happening. This started on a Saturday with finding out that Michael had run away from the home that morning. He left with the boy, who by coincidence was the other person to have shown an interest in glue sniffing. The fact Michael had gone wasn't in its self-unusual. His problems in the home centred on a clash of personalities with the headmaster, which became compounded by a mutual dislike situation.

Michael had run away before, and when coming to my attention it generated little surprise. On that particular Saturday as events turned out I was the only person sleeping in our dormitory. This was the first occasion during my time in the lodge, circumstances caused me to sleep alone. Two of the occupants had gone home for the weekend, and the other person left the previous day due to a longer-term placement.

The day had been spent in a quiet sort of way. Towards the end of the evening I began to develop a headache, it being unlike anything experienced previously. To describe it as a headache is not a very accurate description. This proved similar to having my strength drained slowly. As the night progressed it began getting worse, developing to a point where concentrating on the normal events became impossible. At nine o'clock after telling one of the staff about feeling unwell, I went up to bed early. Switching off the light, then resting did not ease my situation any. I could not get settled, and sleep when it did come offered little comfort. These effects were really wearing me down, causing restlessness, which resulted in tossing and turning throughout the night, half aware of my predicament. Whatever this was it must have lasted a good four hours at least, and during that time it had been relentless.

In the early hours of the morning all the symptoms stopped, which caused me to waken. There were no after-effects and on getting up it felt similar to coming out of a strange dream. My faculties were not fully restored, in the sense of thinking about in detail that which been occurring. The first recollection of the circumstance came in realising my vest was soaking wet. This appeared quite strange, and discovering this noticed at the same time the sheet was also damp. My attentions had been till then focussed wholly on me. Switching from the self, I now looked about the room.

In the far top hand corner a small Arabian tent could be seen flapping in mid air. This appeared no more than a meter tall. Seeing this for the first time it did not register how out of place it was. The movements it produced were really gentle, and in a way very relaxing. However, circumstances did not allow me the time to watch this for very long. In the centre of the room I could see Michael, the boy who had ran away earlier standing looking at me. He was wearing a black tuxedo with white shirt and top hat. My initial reaction was to say "Michael what are you doing get to bed". There became one problem with this statement, and it involved the method of delivery. Instead of speaking these words verbally, they were relayed by the mind as thoughts, to be heard as clear as any speech.

Michael, then rose from the floor and levitated towards the ceiling. As he did this a feeling of extreme evilness generated from his eyes towards me. The time elapsed from getting up, until this point could not have exceeded one minute. Whatever uncertainty had remained during that period because of waking disappeared in an instant. My mouth opened wide whilst watching this in a state of amazement.

The effigy hung in the air for a few more seconds, and then vanished in a dramatic manor. As he went the tent which stood in the corner accompanied him. During this period when the body levitated it generated intensity in the atmosphere, which also returned to normal everything was now, as it should be.

My next set of actions still amazes me, even to this day. The whole event was briefly contemplated as if it had been a matter of no importance. These reflections only lasted a short while, and I decided it seemed pointless thinking about the reasons behind it all, at that time of night. Removing my vest lay back on the bed and promptly went to sleep. This wasn't a bad dream or anything of that nature and I failed to understand how my reactions had been so casual, in responding with such an indifferent manor. It must be regarded as my strangest response ever, to a major situation.

In the morning everything appeared fine and I felt no adverse reaction to the events of last night. It certainly required a great deal of reflection, and not something to be discussed about over breakfast with the other boys. The person whom it involved could have been anywhere, and it was only him it bore a relevance to. Shortly after finishing the meal, whilst leaving the dining room I saw Michael and the other boy coming in through the front door. They were taken straight into the headmaster's office, which did not allow any chance for a discussion. As soon as they had been dealt with we were able to speak freely. Because of the extraordinary developments I was keen to explain the sequence of events. My statement did not get further than a basic introduction, when Michael began relating their circumstances, which had, became interwoven with my own.

After leaving the home they wandered around Winchester looking for a place to sleep through the night. The most suitable location turned out to be a house in the process of being built. Inside this building were different materials that would have been needed to continue this work. It included some industrial sized tins of glue that were used on jobs of its nature. They took one these each and inhaled fumes directly from the tins.

Both of them had used glue before, but it was only the second occasion for the boy accompanying Michael. Soon after taking effect, in a simultaneous experience both of them saw me tossing and turning in the bedroom at Ashbourne Lodge. This happened at the exact same time, without any pre-discussions. Their sighting failed to last very long, and once over returned to mundane matters. This offered the first vision either of them had experienced, and its significance cannot be underestimated. Michael asked me if anything unusual happened concerning me. Explaining the events surrounding my side of the story we tried to make some sense of it all.

These events were important in a number of different ways; the most prominent being it involved three people. This set of actions takes the issue into a different level of understanding. If you are of the opinion my interpretations are no more than elaborate delusions, it is a valid argument. I can comprehend this line of thinking implicitly, and understand the reasoning behind it. I obviously do not agree with that theory for my reasons put forward to date. If this one issue can be broken down into specific instances, and looked at separately there are circumstances, which are beyond the capabilities of my imagination.

To deal in hard facts Michael and his friend were located some distance from my location. Because these individuals had access to solvents, and used it they were able to see an actual event-taking place. Not only was it a reality they witnessed, it was by no stretch of the imagination a normal incident. The simple fact that both of these people were able see this at the same time, indicates a level of understanding far beyond normal perception. What makes this even more unusual was it being the first time either of them had witnessed anything by the use of solvents. In trying to understand the circumstances that surrounded me, I should cover a number of different possibilities. The first important one of these involves not using any glue for around three weeks by then. If one considered the possibility of flashbacks, this is not a property solvents have the capabilities of doing.

My introduction to this three way split, came in the form of seeing Michael who saw me. Taking the possibilities of coincidence what would be the odds of such an incident occurring, given the many thoughts encompassed within the mind. From developing the headache that proved unlike anything previously experienced, to seeing the different events became a totally unique occurrence on my behalf. These combined with the visions had some connection with the other side of conciseness, though its purpose seemed a complete enigma. If you are still of the opinion it was a delusion, then it has to be the same for three people. The circumstances could be compared to one of my glue sniffing episodes in some respects, although it differed in essence.

The priority during that day concerned some way of acquiring glue, in the attempt to understand the reason behind its meanings. It being a Sunday did not present any easy solutions how this could be achieved. The chance came on the following day through one of the procedures, which happened in the lodge. Part of the system in the home involved working in the kitchens to help the cook out, it being something that only occurred on the odd occasion. On that Monday it happened to be my turn, and it made a change from the normal routine. Working here did not initial the same form of supervision applicable in the classrooms. After my work had been completed I asked the cook would be possible to take a break. She allowed me the time necessary to run down the town and back, which did not entail a difficult explanation as to my whereabouts. Getting out of the building was fairly easy, and it proved a simple matter of lifting a tube in the shops, then returning to the home. The whole venture took under an hour, and did not create any problems. I continued working for the rest of the day, and awaited my opportunity that would come through the night.

Because of circumstances surrounding the last ordeal I was impatient to get started. Avoiding the normal waiting, time got under way shortly after the lights were out. My introduction did not follow its usual pattern of creating a set, or something of this nature. Gong spoke to me saying I had failed the test. This statement wasn't elaborated on and the first visual encounter involved being met by a cartoon delegation comprised of six human representations, and one alien. The caricature was of Gong who headed this group. The purpose of the delegation was to offer me their condolences for failing the test. I asked the real Gong when he first spoke to me, why this should be so. That line of questioning proved ineffectual. Trying the same approach with his facsimile worded the question in a number of different ways. This offered no better results. It proved quite frustrating to have something take place, and not be able to find out its reasons. This delegation began annoying me, and by the fact of them being there it offered a chance for retribution, if only in a limited sense.

The line of responses put forward seemed very patronising. As this continued I realised its purpose was to evaluate my reactions, and how it would be responded to. After understanding the meaning, I let them continue without offering any response and the set changed. I wondered afterwards what would have taken place, if this particular test had been passed.

Help in answering the question came in an unusual manor shortly after giving up glue sniffing. That was some way in the future, and it's timing, as with other revelations came about, after the moment had gone.

During that night the format of my visions changed to a more structured, and purposeful presentation. In the past it seemed to be directed towards finding single responses to a given situation. The events were constructed in such a way that insured it would be a natural outcome. I did not always realise this at the time, and only afterwards did some of its meanings become apparent. If I were to use glue for two hours, this would be broken up into different sections that proved quite diverse. A good example, which began during this night, involved life on an ice station, and remained a constant theme from here on in. I spent around twenty minutes in this place and became introduced to the aspects of survival involved with existing in such an environment.

I will attempt to give an explanation of how my understanding had developed until this point. Firstly it would be incorrect to say my comprehension of the reasons behind this, were now somehow better informed. I became no more enlightened due to the manor of presentation, which gave away little information in its delivery.

It would be inappropriate to say I knew, or understood why all of this was happening; my analysis is more of a personal theory. The visions witnessed came from a specific place, though its origin is unknown. By the use of solvents I had been able to reach a certain level in which my participation became acceptable, to be dealt with on a personal basis. In order for this to happen I had to react correctly to a variety of situations put before me. These spanned a period of two years in my case, and individually they would have given the parties interested an evaluation of my mannerisms well in advance of revelation.

The purpose of these tests insured I would conduct myself properly within the framework of their environment. The reasoning behind this suggested my responses were appropriate in their actions, not to be overwhelmed by the situation. By this approach it allowed a manor that remained consistent, and not one altering my dealings with them. This being important to the individuals who controlled the way our interactions were set out. I do not believe these events were laid out on for my benefit, no more than a white mouse could expect enlightenment in a laboratory.

The voice that guided me through this place belonged to the being, which revealed his physical shape by the door. The purpose of this encounter developed in line with my thoughts, and was a focal point in realisation. Gong was my mediator in this land, and during most of the dealings he became my main source of contact. There seemed to be a number of different reasons associated with my being in this place. They were mainly involved with testing to find out reactions, and responses. Gong's factions did not conduct all of this work. There were other parties involved who had different objectives as to my purposes.

As well being involved with alternate sets, there was another awareness that accompanied some of these. I recognised this immediately when confronted by these feelings. It made me understand a separate conception that existed in this environment. My first encounter with it came in the form of visiting a building in which a number count began. Something within me did not like this, as if another sense became alerted to danger. Being in this room did not threaten me in any way, and nothing could be seen that offered an explanation to these feelings. Because this was a new experience I waited until it finished, then moved on to pleasanter surroundings.

During these early sessions I had become aware of similar feelings, though not as strong. It seemed this room, became a focal point in matters related to its conception. Being more in tune with my senses caused a different perception to this problem, which initiated a level of distress. I remember quite clearly trying to avoid taking part in this section of the pro-gramme. My objections were directed towards Gong who was speaking to me shortly before entering one of these places. No one had said that my next involvement was such an area they didn't have to. It generated a feeling that became unmistak-able.

Talking to my guide asked him "Do I have to go in there". He replied yes, and then proceeded to show me a cartoon sketch, which helped explain the reasoning behind it. This de-picted a scene in which two aliens were at opposite ends of a workspace. The one nearest was a representation of Gong. His counterpart formed in the same way, and appeared to have similar capabilities. They were both taking materials from a conveyer beside them, and assembling nuclear weapons. In this place I had come to learn, any form of material could be created with the greatest of ease. This told me without any words being spoken the aliens were involved in some form of war. They were not fighting over a theory, or some ideological dispute. The battle was over me.

Even though I was only fifteen this proved a disturbing revelation. It expanded an understanding to the situation and heightened my concern to the involvement being dealing with. During the recent ventures at this level it became appar-ent the society, which governed my involvements, was based on two sets of ideals. They both had different mannerisms, and feelings surrounding their presentation. This does not require a lengthy explanation in explaining these concepts. They are good, and evil. In talking about the fundamentals these are relatively simple matters to understand. If one were to expand on this reasoning, developing the concept to ex-plain the motives of higher forms of life, you would have to comprehend their purpose of existence. In describing my level of understanding that did not come from the spoken word, I am talking about ability not in normal use.

This is more than supposition at forming one's opinions. It belongs to a higher awareness that I would assume is part of our makeup, which under normal circumstances is not brought into use. This ability-helped deal with actual problems associated in this environment; namely I could not ask why certain occurrences happened.

The guidelines of asking who, what, where, when and why where kept too strictly throughout my time with them. Therefore if the powers that be wanted me to understand something without infringing on there own rules, this may have been a way around the problem.

It would also help to explain my being able to understand certain events, without the use of an explanation. In suggesting these various ideas, I have to stress they are only opinions deduced from evaluating my circumstances. In describing the conception of higher thought processes, it would help if I could draw a comparison, which the reader would have experienced. Unfortunately it is not a common occurrence, so you will have to suffice with my evaluations. These writings are associated with a two-month period in the Lodge. There were other events that became important to my future, on a more fundamental level. The court date had been fixed for November, which drew ever nearer. It had been suggested my care order would be transferred back to the social work department, and I would be put in a longer-term placement. It was the last part of this statement, which caused more concern.

The day of judgement arrived and my social worker took me to court in Alton. This is where I was being prosecuted for the crimes committed, in and around Borden. Since leaving the charge sheet had a few extensions from my little jaunt to Scotland. Jim came to the courts to relinquish his responsibilities over me. We met in a small room and talked before the actual hearing. There was no animosity between us, which seemed pleasing under the circumstances. In court it went better than expected, with all the changes being wavered. They judge decided being put back into care until my eighteenth birthday was enough punishment. This could have been much worse, with other conditions being envisaged. That became the last time Jim and I was to meet up. Going back to the home, it made life a little clearer.

I felt happy at Ashbourne Lodge, and the homes in that area were certainly better than their equivalents in Scotland. It was around that time when the evaluations about my personality had been made. The next development concerning my future involved finding a permanent home. One such possibility mentioned was a place called St Edwards in Wiltshire. As events turned out there was a mini-bus going to this home a few days after my court appearance. The boys in the lodge were asked if they would like to come along for the ride. It became an ideal opportunity to see what I may be letting myself in for. Around six of us went along for a variety of reasons. We set off early in the morning for this journey in distance, about twenty miles away. One of the boys left the lodge recently, and the reason for going to this place involved taking some of his belongings on to the new home.

St Edwards at one time had been a palace, which had been taken over by a Catholic Brotherhood. They used the building for taking care of Catholic boys who had strayed from the path of righteousness. With the passing of time it became discovered that other religions could be naughty as well, and more importantly the state would pay for their upkeep. In this way all denominations could live happily together, and as it had become a private business make those who held the purse strings life a little more agreeable.

The grandeur of this place had remained throughout the years, whilst retaining its identity with the change of use. We stayed there until the afternoon, which allowed some understanding of the system that operated the running of this home. It was an authoritarian regime, with the staff in the top pecking order. This worked its way down from the eldest boys, to the youngest. On reflection it would not have been too pleasant for the junior members of this society.

During this visit I met the boy who moved here from Winchester. He used to be quite a boisterous character, but in the short time since changing homes these traits, which had been prominent, seemed to have left him. I could understand the differences in the two set-ups, and recognised why the change came about. On the return journey after some consideration, it was hoped St Edwards would not be chosen for me.

As events turned out my destiny had other plans in store. A few days afterwards the headmaster called me into his office to explain a placement had been found on the Isle of Wight, and if everything went according to plan he envisaged it going through soon. This settled any debates concerning the future, and in a way it seemed pleasing to know what lay ahead. There was a down side, and that involved leaving the lodge. Through the many changes that occurred during the last few years, my time in Winchester had been the happiest. Still life moves on, and we cannot live in the past.

During early December my social worker came to the lodge, in order that I could visit this proposed establishment. He explained how the home was run, and from his description it seemed quite different from St Edwards. The place we were going being called Eastmore House, and it appeared to be a liberal regime. From the time in Kennoway after being put in care there was usually a feeling of apprehension about changing my circumstances. With this move these emotions did not surface at any time, since it had been made known.

Driving from the lodge involved travelling to Lymington where the ferry departed for this short crossing. My first view of the harbour in Yarmouth was that of a picturesque setting. After disembarking we were met by one of the homes staff who drove us the mile, or so to the building. My first impressions of this area were very positive, it being pleasing to the eye. Entering the grounds through a side entrance gave a first sighting of Eastmore. This seemed really strange because it looked familiar. As a visual impact it was like being reunited with something known to me in an obscure way. It appeared most odd considering I had never been on the Isle of Wight before. My curiosity over this situation required some explanations, so asking our driver the history of the home received a brief summery.

He said it once belonged to Lord Canarven who financed the Tutanankamun expedition as a summerhouse. After his death it had been taken over by Catholic priests who ran the premises on a similar basis to St Edwards, for degenerates like me This in turn became run down through the early seventies. His story proved interesting, but it failed to offer any hints that would help my understanding of this little puzzle. He carried on saying the County Council took over where the priests left off. The thinking behind the new approach to its management was experimental in concept, and the theory incorporating these ideas were to bring boys up in such a way they would make decisions for themselves. By these actions it was hoped the individual would mature, and eventually fit into society, then in time become a responsible adult.

Walking around the back of the building we entered through a side doorway. He brought us to the section called D group. At the time there were only three groups, a b and d as the home wasn't at full operational capacity. Taking us into the office we met the person in charge of this section, called Mr Campsy. He gave us a guided tour of the building and grounds, firstly showing me the room that would become my own, should circumstances bring me here.

It seemed small in comparison to some of the others, but well furnished with a little sink by the wall, which made it appear comfortable and a pleasant lay out. In comparison to some other establishments, it became the equivalent of moving into the Ritz. The home was very spacious and the more one looked at it, you could not fail to be impressed. There was a large gym, which offered facilities unmatched on the Island during that time. When a boy came to Eastmore he was given the option of attending one of four different departments. This being alternative to normal lessons and their purpose were to prepare you for the job markets in the real world. This actually proved a very good idea, rather than learning something that served no benefit to most of the home's inhabitants. After being shown round the first three options, the last call was to the nautical department on the sea front. It offered the largest facility from an educational aspect, with the classrooms split in two sections. This was an elongated building, which took more boys than any other department.

I met both teachers whose rooms were divided by a partition. This separation signified different teaching methods, for both men were opposite in their outlooks, and ways they presented themselves. On speaking to a Mr Thompson he explained the objectives of his department. Taking me around the boathouse, then after seeing most of its workings I indicated an interest in this operation over the others. At the end of his tour he explained on completing the course your name would be forwarded to the merchant navy offices, to join the organisation. That settled it; this was the place for me

We returned to the main building where I met the headmaster, Mr Crosbie where he asked my opinions of the home. In answering this question the reply was a totally honest one, saying it appeared better than could have possibly been expected. The conversation switched to the subject of glue sniffing, which had been mentioned to him by the other headmaster. It became obvious from the tone of speech; his knowledge about these matters seemed limited. This proved quite beneficial, and it could be turned to my advantaged. My involvement was toned down indicating a phase, or something of that nature.

After playing the bluff my thoughts turned to the prospect of using the substance here, and if I were to get caught my arse would need kicking. We left shortly afterwards. On the return trip my social worker asked if I wanted to come to Eastmore. It seemed ironical thinking one had to do wrong in life to come to a place like this. Back in the lodge the other boys were told about Eastmore, and how good it appeared. Considering the alternatives, this seemed the best offer imaginable, even if the choice had free one. The phone call that settled the matter came sooner than expected. Because of the closeness to Christmas Mr Gibbons gave me the option of staying there, or leaving to start a new way of life. I chose the latter, as it seemed an exciting prospect.

The departure was arranged within a few days. My time remaining in the lodge became pretty much my own. It did not require attending classes to the same extent as the rest of the boys. Looking around the building and grounds caused a sense of nostalgia, remembering events and occasions, which had become special memories. Because of these circumstances it allowed a visit to the shops, with sightseeing as the pretext. My intentions were two folds during the outing. Going into the department store did not create a pressure to acquire glue in such a hurry.

Whilst looking around the shop something caught my eye that rekindled a memory from Scotland. It involved a conversation Steven had with me concerning the subject of solvents.

He explained there were a number of products that could be used which created the same effect. In this shop by one of the counters was a certain shoe cleaner that came under this category. It being a small bottle of clear liquid and its name was well known to me. Taking this proved no more difficult than lifting a tube of glue.

The reasoning for trying something different was to see if it would create a noticeable change. As this was effectively the last visit to Winchester for the foreseeable future, the remaining time became spent sightseeing. The pretext and the reason were not so far removed from one another. It turned out to be a pleasant day visiting the Cathedral and looking at the beautiful buildings, I wandered back to the lodge a few hours later.

In the evening our classrooms were in use for creative hobbies. The shoe cleaner had been kept on my person through the day, with the intention of using this whilst in bed. Having it on me did not entail the same problems associated with a tube of glue, because its purpose could have easily been explained away. Both classes were in use that evening, with one staff member supervising the two different rooms. The main activities were in the other section, from a few other boys and me. Michael also happened to be with me. We spent the time taking about certain matters, when I mentioned about having the shoe cleaner on me. After informing him, he wanted to use it in the room.

This is something that under normal circumstances would not have been considered. He seemed keen to attempt it, ignoring the possibility of getting caught. The aroma of this substance did not have the same potency of glue, whilst it could be easily concealed within the palm of the hand. Pouring a little away down the sink he held the bottle to his nose and started inhaling. It had the desired effect, which by that stage in his involvement allowed a better conduct of action, so they were less noticeable to the untrained eye.

It seemed unwise to let him use this for too long, and taking the bottle of him tried it. My

Attentions were more focussed on the door, rather than the substance. It became apparent shortly afterwards the feelings surrounding this fluid, and glue were quite different. This happened before any visions became prevalent; when coming they too had a different quality in visual perceptions. To draw a parallel in proved similar to watching the same picture through two different televisions, and with the shoe cleaner it created clearer graphics.

The subject of this brief endeavour concerned an alien being. It wasn't a representation of Gong, because his facial structure appeared different. This depiction involved a cartoon presentation, and created a different feeling surrounding my awareness of the subject. After seeing this, which initially mixed with the classroom due to my eyes being opened, closed them to have better viewing. The alien could only be seen from the top half of his body upwards. He began transferring thoughts from the mind, which appeared in bubble form, and these were similar to drawings you would find in a comic. The thoughts rose upwards beyond his environment.

Each idea encapsulated a different vision, and the subjects came along at intervals. This allowed time to study them before leaving the range of his perception. The first one concerned a landscape setting, and appeared basic in its construction. The pattern followed a similar premise with alternate ideas, of which no two were alike.

This proved quite interesting, but due to the circumstances I could not devote the attention required. After watching this setting for a few minutes, my concerns returned to the prospect of being caught in the act. Opining my eyes the room was checked in case the teacher could be on his way in. Everything appeared fine, but not ideal. From then on in the visions were viewed in sporadic bursts.

The setting changed to seeing the thoughts from a higher angle, with the alien no longer in the picture. I watched this at intervals for a few minutes, and decided to carry on would be pushing my luck. Giving the bottle to Michael the remaining time in the classroom concerned returning to normal. This had been an unusual setting in every sense of the word, and it continued to be so with the after-effects. When using glue these sometimes left me feeling a little groggy, which usually passed fairly quickly. The shoe cleaner proved quite different, being of a higher concentrate than glue fumes. I did not like this and when leaving the classroom about an hour later the substance was poured down a drain, by the outside of the building.

My reasoning behind these actions went like this. It seemed obvious this form of attainment would offer a deeper level of awareness, but the price paid would have been higher, in terms of damage to me. Solvents allowed an adequate connection with this other existence that proved sufficient. If this substance could upgrade the visions, it caused me to think what something like LSD would do. In times that were yet to come I did try one variation on a theme, but that was a little way off.

The day had arrived for my move, and the social worker came during the afternoon. There weren't many belongings to be transported as most of my possessions had been dispersed through different living arrangements? He decided to take his car on the ferry and drive into the home, which seemed a little lavish considering the distance involved. We arrived in the building around teatime, and after helping me with these few belongings he left soon afterwards. It did not take long to arrange the room, which looked tidier than the first visit.

There followed a period of reflection of my circumstances shortly after this. It could be summed up in the word 'contentment' as an accurate description to my feelings. Spending a little time alone, I then went to the common room and spoke to some of the boys. There were no others from Ashbourne Lodge who were known to me. The staff members in this home were very easy going, and whilst eating the communal meal I asked if it were possible to go out. They did not have the same restrictions associated with state run establishments' come across in my experience. The only requirement being to tell someone you were going out. As this had been mentioned in the question, there became no further need to ask. Freedom is a special quality and unless it has been taken away you don't realise its value.

It was now dark, and the only place that seemed worth a visit was the centre of Yarmouth. Walking along the sea front held more significance than any action for a long time, and going into one of the pubs ordered half a lager and lime to celebrate the occasion. The next morning after breakfast I went to the nautical department and spoke to Mr Thompson, who said it wasn't worth starting the classes till after the holidays. It turned out the following afternoon was the last day until the beginning of January. Walking back to the main building created ample time to have a good look around.

Eastmore being on the sea front presented opportunities for exploration that were appealing to someone of my age. One of the priorities, which had to be established, involved finding a supply of solvents, in easy reach. As it was daylight, and I had plenty of free time my next actions combined looking at the surroundings, and checking the local shops for this purpose. Going back to Yarmouth it was discovered two shops sold this product. One of them had it placed more conveniently from a shoplifter's point of view. A tube was taken and on returning to the home, it caused me to think the owner of these premises would believe sales in this commodity had taken an upturn.

The tube was hidden in the room, in a fairly casual manor due to the system that operated here. After the departments finished for that day, most of the boys were getting themselves ready to go home on the Friday. It turned out six of us were staying in the establishment over the holidays, and we all were moving into one group. The fact that I had been to Scotland recently did not cause a sense of resentment at missing a time of family union. Being here was like a holiday itself. That night after settling in the tube was brought out from its hiding place for my inaugural use in Eastmore. The proceedings began with a conversation. Gong asked if I liked my new situation. The discussion about the home continued for a little while, and covered different aspects of life here. The theme of our discussion was broadened to the subject of imprisonment.

There followed a sketch in which Donald "My friend who was in Balgowen" and myself locked up in a jail. We were planning a way to break out of such an establishment. On seeing this it caused me to laugh, because if we had remained together for any length of time, this would have been our destiny.As this sketch finished Gong asked my opinions of the penal system. Answering this question I replied, what else you could do with people who broke the law. He seemed to have strong views on this subject, and stated 'It was wrong to imprison the individual, and he should be made to reimburse the people he stole from'. This is a reasonable viewpoint as far as stealing went, and not something I would argue with. The subject wasn't developed to cover more serious crimes. I did not take this to be a reflection on my own actions; it appeared more of a generalisation, which left me a little, dumbfounded. It seemed a pity he did not offer a deeper insight to his views pertaining to other issues. This being the first occasion a discussion concerning moral ethics had taken place.

There were other events during that night, but the imprisonment debate and sketches were the most memorable. The tube lasted a few hours. Getting out of bed to open the window so the fumes could disperse, I noticed my reflection in the mirror above the sink. This wasn't very clear due to the darkness, and would not have warranted a second glance if something else had not caught my eye. There appeared to be other images placed behind my own reflection. Studying this more closely, three people could be seen whose facial features were indistinct.

The person who occupied the first space wore a similar vest to that of my own. His hair was quite short, and different to the fashions of the time. As an estimate he would have been around nineteen, or twenty. If I moved my body, the extra reflections would match this action so it wasn't possible to look at the images from a different angle. The next vision also wore the same vest appeared older than the first. He was much wider than his predecessor, and had quite short hair.

It became possible to estimate the age of this person, being about thirty. The final individual was a man in his early forties. The vest was still there, and his physical appearance consisted of a well-built stature. He was bald on the crown of the head, which can be associated with someone of his years. Each of these people held a different perspective within my line of vision, and it became possible to study them individually without interference from the other. The only feature that remained unclear involved the face, as my own reflection seemed to get in the way. At the time this was no more than a curiosity, but it remained a constant theme from that point onwards.

When using glue in darkness and passing a mirror the same vision would appear. On the first occasion whilst wearing a vest it caused the reflections to don similar attire. The actions that followed copied my dress for each occasion, whilst keeping the same theme. It may sound naive but any connection this could have been to me did not occur at the time.

An understanding of this occurrence came after giving up glue sniffing whilst on location with the merchant navy. I was on a ship that travelled between Central America, and The United States. We had docked in Albany New York on our first trip. It was Sunday and I visited the city that morning. Walking to the centre of town I went into to a paper shop, which also sold a variety of books. After looking through the selection, one particular title caught my interest. The subject of this story had a similarity to my own experiences. Considering the titles on offer it proved quite lucky this could be found amongst all of the books. The author was called Franklin Merrell Wolff, and the title being pathways through to space. Reading the introduction it became obvious there was a common connection in our experiences. Apart from visiting a museum that morning it seemed the only event worth a mention.

The book was purchased and I read part of it during the voyage. In comparison to my own experiences the author became involved with the similar circumstances, but on a higher level due to his intellectual abilities. He is a man of considerable brightness who wrote the events of his own observations. It became apparent after reading a few pages; this man thought most people had the intelligence quota of Albert Einstein. His writings were very difficult to understand, with an abstract use of English that employed over-complicated words to explain his situation. In essence this book was read in snippets, searching for relevant information. There were a number of points, which proved to be enlightening, if not fully understood.

The author, without the aid of a mirror, experienced the part relating to my reflections. He was shown images of himself throughout the remaining years of his life. By that time I suspected the reflections in Eastmore were a progression of my own body during its lifespan. This became a form of second opinion, if such a thing could be possible under the circumstances.

Speaking from a present day position the first two images were spot on, regarding physical size and hairstyles. The last one has not come about yet, and my hair is still intact. When this time does come to pass, it shall be an interesting prospect facing my ending with prior knowledge. It's not something that bothers me unduly, and perhaps more importantly is the timing of this occurrence.

I will have to update the final description of the last image, as time moves on towards the end of the last century the final phase of my development has not arrived. It could also reflect my judgement in estimating the age of a man without a face. In the last chapters of my story I will try and make some sense of different incidents, such as this one and unite their importance within an overall framework. That will require a great deal of work, and a certain amount of restraint. This is not one of my better qualities, but time and experience have taught the need for such characteristics.

The following morning after my inaugural session in the bedroom, there was a certain buzz of excitement generated throughout the building. Some of the boys were leaving to go home without attending the departments, because they lived further away. The rest had to wait until dinnertime. For myself there was no change in tempo, and watching the pace take an upturn proved quite amusing. When the last of them had gone, the home acquired a certain calm that by its peace created a different atmosphere. Moving rooms involved going from one end of the building, to the other. The remainders of us were staying in A group. My new bedroom was similar in size to the old, but its furniture appeared shabbier. This became my accommodation for about three weeks.

The Christmas holidays turned out well, with most of the time spent overeating and watching television, and it wasn't so different from the family occasion. Those of us who remained were given some money to buy our own presents. Following tradition that began the previous year, the money was spent on an album with the remainder going towards a tin of glue. In keeping with the festive sprit I believed this should not be stolen.

The tin would last me over the holiday period, providing it was used economically. The first of these occasions concerned my alternate room during the night. This proved quite special in a way. My initial usage involved sitting up in the bed, and looking around the surroundings. After reaching a level of awareness my environment changed its perception. At first this became apparent in a feeling of total peacefulness engulfing the whole room. In terms of experience, it was unique.

The level of calmness was almost a religious sensation. A vision appeared by the door, which added to its enhancement. This was a shepherd who complemented the seasonal aspect. He began singing, and it became the most beautiful sounds I have ever heard. The language was unknown, and in truth it made no difference because all relevance to time and space became lost in the song, which overwhelmed me.

When he finished Gong spoke to me asking if anything appeared out of context with the vision. It took a few seconds in bringing my attentions back to normal. The feelings remained after he finished this ballad, thought at a reduced level. Looking closely at this man he was wearing glasses, which seemed out of context with the attire, which belonged to a different century. After mentioning the one obvious anomaly the set changed.

This tin was used on three occasions, which because of the different aspects were longer than normal. The second time in the game's room under a stage during the hours of daylight, because it had the necessary darkness to create the conditions of night. My experiences were varied, but not so memorable to give a detailed description of them. The last use was back in the bedroom towards the end of the holiday. After creating my animated set, the location changed to a domed amphitheatre of considerable size.

This was a gloomy building with a damp atmosphere. I seemed to be lying on the floor looking upwards into the galleries that surrounded the top half of this structure. Amongst the isles could be seen many eyes watching my predicament. There was some form of restraint holding my presence in this particular spot. It appeared quite dark in the new setting, which prevented seeing the faces behind the reflection of their eyes. Coming towards me was a man who became the inquisitor, on behalf of his audience.

He seemed full of self-importance, which became apparent shortly afterwards, by his line of questioning. I treated this situation rather light heatedly, without being rude. My reactions were indented to be helpful, because the reasoning behind this could have alternate meanings. In answering the questions, they had no real substance to them, which made the situation rather silly. The longer it went on, the more stupid this became. My initial line of assistance began to wane. The inquisitor said that if his advances were refused a great pain would be inflicted on me.

This caused a renewed interest, as to how such an action could be enforced. Keeping silent, the man started ranting and raving. There followed a mild electrical charge, detected in the area of the brain. This did not hurt at all, and it proved quite amusing to see his reactions. He told the audience the pain had caused me great discomfort. By then my attentions were more focussed on those watching, rather than this pompous character. He informed me the level of suffering would be increased, unless total compliance was given. There followed another charge of slightly higher voltage than the first.

The most interesting part of this occasion became the building itself; it had a certain authenticity to the fabric of the construction. I could not accept it was a genuine structure, because the level of assimilation proved a very high standard. The set changed shortly afterwards, with no apparent outcome to its purpose. However this continued on a similar theme within a period in time. Leaving that building to see the outside world it seemed not unlike Venice in its heyday, during the seventeenth century. The architecture proved stunning, and visiting this for the first time caused quite an impression. It depicted a bustling city with many canals, and structures that had no equals to my knowledge.

The tour was short lived, and the next method of visualisation became very special. I found myself free of constraints and had the ability to fly. It was like releasing a bird from captivity that found its purpose in life. Rising into the air was as natural as any motion my physical body could have made in an enlightened state. The choice of direction became a conscious decision, with nothing holding me back. There was no fear of flying, travelling above the tallest towers. The overall view of the city looked spectacular, and my only regret concerned it didn't last longer.

There are two points worth a mention regarding this event. The freedom of flight wasn't an induced sensation, it seeming inherent within my being. I am not qualified to expand on this statement, for it involves the essence of our makeup. An understanding goes way beyond the level of knowledge mankind has to the purpose of creation. This is not a question of physical dynamics, it relates to the soul. It's not possible to further expand on my experience, for the subject is no more that a theory to the understanding of our time.

To write about it and try relating my feelings as a fifteen-year-old is not appropriate. I will cover this in a little more detail from the present date, towards the end of my story. This statement does not propose that somehow my knowledge has increased to understand the essence of life. All that can be offered is a more in-depth analysis. The second issue concerns the setting. It wasn't totally unfamiliar. There are many arguments that exist as to why a person seems to know a place they have never visited before. I do not want to debate this premise, for it covers a range of subjects my intellectual abilities can't compare with the experts. There is no reason, which can be offered to substantiate my feelings, but they existed. As far as this issue goes, no more can be said on my part because I am unable to explain it further.

The remainder of the session dealt with other subjects, but the former became the most significant. The holiday came to its end, and during early part of the New Year I moved back to my room in D group. On the first Monday after all the boys had returned, it became time to join the department that would one day take me into the Merchant Navy. The teacher was my preferred choice of the two, being Mr Thompson. He handled the boys very well considering the mixed bunch at his disposal, and it is quite rare when a person can gain the respect of most of the people he is teaching. Throughout my time in this department I cannot recall a bad word being said against him.

The course on offer proved enjoyable from a number of different aspects. The practical subject of sailing and learning to use the elements to your advantage, were a new form of challenge, and it wasn't something I would have been involved with in my normal ways of life. These types of diversions broaden your horizons, and make you see things from a different angle. My feelings were not restricted to the department, Eastmore during that stage proved completely ideal. Talking to former boys from the home in the years that followed, it was discovered these observations were matched by their own memories of that period. It became standard practice to keep a tube of glue hidden in the bedroom, when and if it was required. My main time of use was during the weekend, because that period proved to be the most suitable. On one such occasion it was used before everyone settled down for the night. It wasn't so much of a problem, because the supervision became more relaxed during the weekend and being so, it allowed more freedom than normal.

One of the boys in a room opposite was playing the record Mr Postman by the Carpenters. As the glue had taken effect at relatively the same time as this was playing, it caused a link-up with the first vision. There followed a symbiotic relationship between both circumstances. In modern terms this would be called a musical video. It appeared unusual seeing the relationship between both cultures being portrayed this way and a first in my experiences. There seemed no end to the little surprises that could be conjured up, and this trend never ceased to amaze me.

On that night I began feeling tired and did not finish the bag off. They're being only a small amount left; it was placed under the bed for use latter on. In the morning some field activity had been planed which caused certain of the boys to get up early.

After being woken by the others noise I decided to finish of the bag, rather than leave it to latter. Shortly afterwards there was a knock at the door. This caused a little panic because the boys wouldn't bother with such formalities. My concern involved the level of fumes in the room, and would they be detected. The bag was put under the bed, and I said for whomever this was to come in. It turned out to be one of the female staff members who asked me if I wanted to join the outing.

This involved speaking to her which also caused a risk of detection. My replies were fairly limited, more in the hope she would go away as soon as possible. This happened to be the first time we had spoken at any length. It appeared she wasn't aware as to what I was doing, this being due to luck more than anything else. Her name was Ann, and she looked rather attractive. After failing to persuade me to come along, continue with her business. The bag was soon in its proper place, to resume where it had been left off. When this took effect I began to cry. There was no reason known why this should be happening and it seemed quite incredible, because as an emotion it very rarely surfaces within my personality.

In the previous writings there have been two mentions concerning crying. This proved so infrequent that I can count on one hand the number of times, such an event has occurred since being a small boy. It became a profound experience, and in coming to terms with the feelings, not an unpleasant one. Whilst this sensation overtook I had been speaking to Gong. It seemed to take him by surprise, because he asked what the problem was. This question could not be easily answered as it involved a complex level of emotion, which in depth took me beyond any sense of feeling that normally could be understood. This failed to amuse him as the remainder of our time together involved sarcastic comment and imagery. I witnessed a representation of myself dressed in nappies, plus a little hat of the kind babies wear. The alternate likeness began rolling around on the floor. It seemed my hosts had difficulty understanding such feelings. Speaking from a personal opinion it proved enlightening to delve into the depths of one's being. Although this can be seen as a frailty, depending on your point of view, it is still part of my construction. In life we do not comprehend these emotions, and cover them with a facade of other expressions. It showed me for a brief period my inner self.

The use of glue was only a small part of my time in Eastmore, as there were other circumstances, which required more attention. In a new environment there is a need to make friends. My first acquaintance on this level being a boy called Derek who came from the Island, arriving in the home shortly before me. We became shoplifting partners, as circumstances dictated. These outings usually took place in the main town of Newport, which happened to be his hometown. The stealing involved mainly small objects that were easy targets. This offered little risk of detection and proved successful in terms of not being caught. On one of these excursions in early February, our various attempts failed to bring forth little gain. As closing time came for the shops, it became viewed as an unsuccessful outing.

These occasions happen every so often, and the only thing left involved making the trip back to the home. It was during this journey, when Derek told me about the time; he broke into a certain department store in the high street. After explaining the intricacies of there operation, it occurred to me that we could repeat the objective in similar circumstances.

This discussion began whilst walking by the shop in question and the amount of time it took to decide we could attempt this covered the length of the building. It seemed prudent waiting an hour, until everyone should have left the premises.

Our starting point was a toilet wall, to the side of the shop. This involved the same route taken previously by Derek. After reaching the top of the building, it became apparent the company had taken precautions against such an eventuality. The place Derek entered previously now had bars blocking our path. This seemed an impassable problem, and my initial reaction was to call it a lost cause, when Derek noticed one of these appeared slightly loose. He suggested removing our socks as makeshift gloves, to avoid incriminating evidence.

The bar was pulled back and forward in alternate turns, until it became free enough to come away from its fixing. The window was then smashed when a bus came by the front of the building. Derek managed to get through this space easily. I had more difficulty being slightly larger than he did. It took a while to find our way into the main store, from the darkened room. Once this had been achieved Derek ran through the store, and dived on the floor to avoid detection by the pedestrians walking outside, along the pavement. My entrance was no less dramatic, involving running then sliding in a similar fashion.

We knew the layout of the counters fairly well, and proceeded systematic plunder of the goods required. Derek concentrated on accessories; I dealt with the record department. This proved very exciting, and we collected as much items as could be carried. Once back on the roof it became apparent another way would have to be found to reach ground level. It seemed infeasible to take the excess baggage, by the same route. The other option involved travelling a longer and more complicated path. It took quite some time to achieve this, and in the process an old wall, which I had been climbing over, collapsed on me. It felt a strange sensation that luckily did not hurt too much. We came out in a side road without any major problems.

The bulk of the loot was hidden in a derelict house, and we walked to the main road. Hitching back to Yarmouth our lift was from one of the smallest cars imaginable. The timing seemed particularly good in arriving at the home, being just before bedtime. It was lucky the back stairs were closely situated to our bedrooms. This meant we could avoid meeting any people and it became a simple matter getting in without detection. Going to our separate rooms I felt quite pleased with myself. The goods were laid out on the bed to see them before settling down for the night. To my utter horror one of the staff members walked in the room, without knocking and told me to turn off the light. It involved the worst situation imaginable being caught totally off guard. My mouth dropped open, and it was fortunate he only stayed a few seconds to repeat his action in the remaining rooms. This proved a lucky escape, but it was short lived due to unforeseen circumstances.

About four months afterwards two boys ran away from home, and caused major problems for the inhabitants and staff alike. They stole a motorboat from the local harbour, and then went to the mainland. As this craft was found adrift it caused the coastguard to be called out. After that little jaunt a number of cars were taken, either to be wrecked or abandoned. When being caught they were in deep shit. It involved an unlikely partnership, with arguably the most intelligent boy in the home, and the stupidest.

In order to save his own skin, the latter of the two told the police all criminal activities he knew which occurred in Eastmore. This included Derek and me. On the weekend following his revelations, the local police station was very busy.

As a result of this eight boys appeared in court on the same day, and we were dealt with as a job lot. Because of the scale of events our expectations were fairly bleak. It turned out better than most of us expected. Derek and I were fined fifty-nine pounds each. This option presented quite a relief, and similar fines were imposed on six of us present on the day. There were two exceptions that had been saved until last. The legal system has to set examples, which became evident during the proceedings. Two of the boys were sent to detention centres. This seemed an odd decision concerning one of them, because he committed the least crimes by far. After sentencing him, the boy who was not the brightest of characters asked his fellow detainee, what did he get? It was said loudly enough for all of us to hear. This seemed so funny under the circumstances that we all burst out laughing. It relieved the tension, which did not go down well by the bench. By that time it did not matter so much, as the decisions had been taken.

The fines were taken out of our pocket money, which defeated the object of the exercise. After that showdown it caused a certain period of reduced activities in the criminal department. From a personal aspect my stealing only involved shoplifting, which entailed little risk.

The next major event in the home involved opining a new group. This was to be called C group and it consisted of two large dormitories. After the painters and decorators finished their work, it looked quite a pleasant set up. The home was expanding, and the staffs that were to control this section came from the various departments within the buildings. On the whole this new group took the best people, from a staffing point of view. It proved slightly disconcerting to break up a family unit that spoiled a certain harmony, which existed in my life. After the section had been decorated I went to look at the empty rooms, to see if they were worth moving into.

The boys already in the home were given first option to change groups, if they so desired. There became a pleasant feel to the one of these places, and it offered a homely quality that seemed quite appealing. The main issue, which helped sway the move from being self-contained, to a dormitory set-up, involved messing about on a larger scale. It was possible to imagine what a selected group of people could get up to in a room of this size. Being in a single room has its restrictions, making you a little too responsible in the conformity front. One had to balance this loss of privacy, verses excess amusement. I thought both arguments through standing in the brightly lit dormitory. Being here would not affect my use of glue, as the outside disturbances should be minimal

Going from the room to see the head of my section, I inquired if there would be any problems in changing groups. It turned out my request was first from within the home. He agreed, which left me free to persuade some others to join me in this venture.

The group became officially opened on the following weekend, and it had attracted five or six boys. Being the initial volunteer gave me a choice of beds. It seemed sensible picking one close to a window, and far away from the door. This would allow the fumes to disperse, and the size of the area made detection less likely. As events turned out I was the only person in our dormitory on its first weekend. To celebrate the occasion it involved going into Yarmouth and stealing a tin of glue.

The circumstances created by having such a large space to myself were quite unusual. In the home no one bothered you, unless excessive noise could be detected coming from the room. On past occasions this created the problem of expressing oneself in such a way that could be picked up by those closest by. The quietness surrounding my environment was almost perfect. After making contact I began speaking to Gong verbally, and continued doing so because there were no restrictions. During the conversation he asked me why I chose to communicate this way. Explaining to him there was no chance of being overheard, due to the circumstances it allowed me to speak naturally. He did not reply to this reasoning, instead there appeared a large musical stave in front of my alternate environment. Gong asked me to sing a few notes. I could not understand the meaning behind the statement, and it caused an unexpected embarrassment for my singing standards were not operatic quality. Trying to get out of this, without mentioning the reasons did not lessen his insistence.

After singing the first note, its equivalent lit up within the stave. This action was to be repeated a number of times, and it became possible to see my results in a notation pattern. The tone of my voice was appalling, and it proved difficult to advance in higher pitches, being condemned to the lower end of the scale. When my, and anyone else listening ordeal was over it seemed quite a relief. Gong then asked me to play the musical notation within my mind. Starting at the bottom the first of these lit up by the act of thought. This proved to be very easy, and after repeating the exercise a few times found I could cover the whole range. It was simple as running your finger along a piano. If one needed a graphic description as to how the abilities of the mind were better than the physical act of speaking, this was it.

Looking at the argument from a logical perspective, it cuts out the need for the thought process to use one of chains of command. Normal speech is hindered by different needs such as breathing, and hesitation. Pure thought at this level is uncluttered by distractions from within your own brain. My choice of verbal speech over its mental counterpart had been governed by conformity. From now on higher of the two abilities would be used.

This evening's session had one other event worth a mention. It involved going into the room in which a number count was about to take place. I recognised the feeling of this building before entering. Since my previous visit to this place, a conceptual understanding as to its purpose had formed within my mind. I must stress no one had given me any indications to the reasoning, behind its intentions. Being there made me feel uncomfortable and initially it took a few seconds to control these emotions.

The count had started by this time, and on reaching the number three or four, called for it to be stopped. This may sound stupid but I believed the count represented people's lives being taken, here on this world. There is no rational reason that can be given to justify my statement. It could have been an exercise akin to the Pavlov dog experiment, with me as the dog. However this is not my belief, because it wasn't a trait of either side's presentation. By this action it alerted something within my psyche that deals with matters of understanding beyond comprehension. People call this sixth sense or premonition; whatever terminology one uses it became under the circumstances very prevalent.

Derek my friend from the other group had changed accommodation, after some persuasion. He believed in the same philosophy of mucking about within a larger set-up, and was enjoying living in the new section. During our acquaintance his knowledge of glue sniffing was rather limited, because I did not want any of the other boys involved in my venture. The reasoning behind this was self-motivated. If it were to become known to one, then by the law of averages it would spread and bring the attentions of the staff upon me. I tried to explain this to him, and became reluctant to share in the method and experiences. It was during one afternoon, after being pestered by Derek that I gave way and passed my tin of glue to be used by him for the first time. My attitude changed after accepting the fact Derek was to be brought into my circle of one.

I explained the best results would be achieved by closing his eyes. Derek's response to the substance seemed deep routed, and he appeared to be in some form of trance. After inhaling the fumes for a few minutes he stopped communicating with me, and rested his arms with the bag on to the legs. There followed a period of around five minutes when he remained motionless. This being something I had never witnessed, or experienced personally. When consciousness returned and his eyes opened, he made a most unusual statement. "Are you one of them"? This caused a certain amount of confusion to me, and the nature of the question appeared thought provoking.

It was obvious he attained a level of awareness, far surpassing the norm. I asked him what he meant by this statement, which proved as much a mystery to Derek as it had been for me. He did not recall any time after our conversation, and wasn't even aware of the missing period in his life. This offered neither of us a satisfactory explanation and it had to be left unanswered. There was nothing more to be said considering the issue, and I did not devote any more time on it. Sometimes events happen which are beyond understanding, and to make sense of them will get you nowhere. This occurs at certain times in conjunction with your experiences, and is part of the overall picture. They are however not arbitrary statements to be disregarded at will, and have a context within some period of your life. It wasn't a matter, which held any relevance just then, but the issue presented itself in other forms at different times.

My initial assumptions that glue sniffing would spread after showing Derek proved to be the case. In total during my time in Eastmore there would have been twenty, or more boys who used it at some point in the following year. They mainly comprised from the two groups in which I had stayed. The reason behind this involved a unity that existed between certain sections. In the home we tended to stick within territorial areas, and the activities from the groups consisted with those we knew well. This is no different to any other section of society, and being the case kept solvent use localised.

In my time four of the boys continued using it on a longer-term basis. The others would have tried it as a novelty, perhaps two or three times. As its use became more widespread I did not view this as a social activity to be joined in as a group practice. That involves a different conceptual pattern, which, in my opinion fails to achieve the best results. There are however alternate experiences that can occur under these circumstances.

One such incident happened to Derek and some friends whilst sharing a tin outdoors. They each witnessed the same hallucination, on a simultaneous basis without pre-discussing the object in question. That is quite amazing considering there were six or seven boys present during that occasion. I am writing this down as Derek described, and not stressing my opinions. There is great deal of understanding, which should be undertaken concerning the whole subject matter. To disregard the incident as a mass hallucination is not good enough. People who make statements of this nature have very little comprehension of what they are talking about. I can look at the group's experience, as a lesser event in comparison to my own. Even the word 'Hallucination' is ambiguous, and not the correct description.

It appeared obvious to me even during that period, of the gap, which existed between professional knowledge over these matters, and the realities. It is a pity that my own level of understanding was limited to the amusement side of the issue. I feel from a present perspective that more relevant knowledge should have been gained from my time with them. The opportunities at my disposal were not used to a fuller extent. This being partially caused by my age, comprehension, combined with limited abilities. On the day that Derek began using the glue for the first time, I continued where he left off. This was a short session because it involved unnecessary risks. At the time if memory serves well the subject of our conversation wasn't discussed with the other side.

There became however one piece of information that was forthcoming, and this being a partial answer concerning my failure of the test in Ashbourne Lodge. There appeared a model of my body, with red markings covering various parts of the anatomy. These were to signify defective functions to limit its operational capacity. The areas concerned were the left shoulder, right eye and part of the stomach. I contested this description saying there was nothing wrong with aforementioned areas. No reply was given, but then my argument could only be based on present day knowledge. Those who I was dealing with knew my condition from the time of conception, to its termination date. This became apparent to me shortly after the futile argument.

There were two other incidents that can be recalled from that session. The first of these concerned a woman who began preaching Communism. She was a typical feminist, and proclaimed her cause with a great deal of vigour. This wasn't directed towards me, as my view was from a side angle. After she finished a new voice spoke to me. Once again this was masculine. He asked my opinions on the subject. This required a little thought as my political doctrines were only based on limited understanding. I implied some of their ideas seemed better than the Capitalist set up. This statement being followed by explaining my knowledge was fairly basic. The speaker decided it seemed important for me to comprehend the system practised in Russia was based on evil. He did not elaborate on this message, and it became relayed in such a way that my attentions were fully focussed on his opinion.

The reasoning behind this wasn't particularly understood, and I could not respond with any practical arguments to advance the discussion. This seemed a bit heavy for me to analyse, and I conveniently left the matter unresolved.

The next subject proved a lot simpler. It involved a boxing match between two cartoon characters. The graphics of this match were very basic, and it consisted of a black fighter verses his white counterpart. My choice was to pick the winner of the contest. Studying both protagonists my decision became to pick the white fighter. This wasn't based on colour prejudiced, because that goes against any beliefs inherent within my personality. The match commenced after the choice had been made. Considering this was a basic cartoon my involvement became entwined to the same level as watching a good professional fight on television. The battle was evenly fought, swinging one way then the other. It appeared during the climax that my man was going to win, as he had his opponent on the ropes, and seemed about to put him away. The black fighter pulled a punch of exceptional quality from the reserves of his strength, and knocked out my fighter.

When you are so involved with something, as it consumes your whole being this caused a deep level of disappointment. My emotions had been worked up to a heightened state, and only afterwards did I realise the purpose of this contest. It gauged the responses, in real terms to my emotional involvement on a given subject. The most outstanding factor of this was how it had been achieved, by the simplest method possible at this level. In the past I kept my feelings separate from most given situations. It showed me two different issues, the first being that my counterparts could create any condition to get the response they wanted. On a lesser level my awareness had been fooled as to the purpose of the test, by the simplicity of its nature.

These were the more important incidents of this session, and the rest of the tin was kept for more appropriate times. The next significant event, which happened within the home, involved taking on new staff members due to its expansion. One such person who came along was a man called Alan Taylor. He proved slightly different in his approach to the way he dealt with the boys. Alan had a certain drive, which seemed lacking in his other operatives.

To understand better the home was a very easy going establishment, and this being the case most staff members followed its pattern. This is not a criticism as to their method of dealing with us; it was appropriate under the circumstances. Alan affected a number of different boys, whose aims in life were indistinct. I came within this group, and became caught up with his enthusiasm in an unexpected source. He proved a multi- faceted character, which adopted many hobbies that were shared with the boys. He caught me, and quite a few others by deciding badminton could be an interesting sport he would like to try out. The man could not play the game; neither could any of the boys within the home. His enthusiasm caught on, and a number of us took it up from the basics and progressed onwards.

Speaking from a personal point of view, this became the first time I made any real effort to achieve something that wasn't negative, and it produced results, which affected the whole of my life. From hitting the first shuttle we advanced into the Island leagues, then after a few years produced some good players.

This sport created the opportunity to mix with decent people, of the kind I would have not met under normal circumstances. It developed different relationships, which altered my actions for a considerable period.

This period covered the spring of my first year in the home. Most circumstances had gone well during that time, with the court case being the only hiccup. In writing of the glue sniffing episodes they can be related in sections of roughly one month at a time. My conditions were becoming more familiar, in the respect of understanding how my alternate environment operated. It had a major difference in comparison to one's normal existence. This concerned the terms of movement.

Since reaching this level, with one possible exception it seemed geared up to advance in a forward direction. All sets or situations had at their base route this principal. The only occasion, in which this guideline appeared to be flexible, being on my first visit in Ashbourne Lodge whilst moving backwards to let the store men continue working. That had been an instinctive reaction, and in terms of distance relative to the environment only a few yards. It was during an interval whilst travelling along a corridor when this subject was brought up with my guide. I informed him of a desire to retrace the passage. He told me this wasn't possible. At the time it did not seem a logical statement, and was ignored in an attempt to go backwards.

A stronger force than the entity, which encompassed my thoughts, met my actions. It was a battle of two energy sources, with my total mental capacities transferred into pushing against an unknown counterpart. My efforts lasted a minute at most, which proved to be quite tiring. It reached the point where it became obvious no ground would be taken. The reluctance of my hosts to allow what appeared; on face value a simple request seemed unusual. From today's perspective there could be two possible explanations, which may explain this.

My other environment became geared up to gain my responses to given situations. If one looked at the mechanics of how this was presented, and more importantly which type of machinery would be required to generate the images, the word computer springs to mind. This would be a super computer by today's standards, but still only a machine. The term virtual reality perhaps is more apt, making a return journey the way you have just come is a waste of time. This commodity is precious, as you are limited to the involvement spent in this stage of the experiences. This being something I did not realise then, but it was to be made known very forcefully during a later date.

The one other possibility involves going back on a set programme, which the machine wasn't designed to deal with. This is not a criticism of its makers, more a reflection of its uses. Either way this observation covers two possibilities, from my understanding of the situation. It is not a definitive answer, only an opinion. The programmes move on to its next encounter, which involved meeting a vampire type creature. He had risen out of a coffin to my side and stood before me, in his entirety. There appeared no obvious reason why this should have taken place. After questioning the purpose of such an exercise, it proved quite surprising to receive an answer. My guide said 'To gage your response to fear'. I challenged this reasoning quite strongly, for no adverse reactions had come over me during its appearance.

My arguments were responded to by creating a repeat showing of the same event. This time my attentions were focussed inwardly. It became possible to more understand the chemical reactions that the brain generated during these circumstances. By refocusing the point of consciousness it became apparent there was a change in my response. This appeared slight, and would not have been noticed unless a repeat demonstration had been laid on. Taking this one simple test as an example, how many other responses were being evaluated without my awareness as to the reasoning behind them. It made me realise that visual perceptions were only one part of an overall scheme. This argument could be expanded as to what I achieved during my time in this state of awareness, and that which my hosts benefited through the same period.

This night produced a return visit to a setting from my early experiences in Scotland. It was the factory, which manufactured tights, and stockings. On the previous occasion my viewing consisted of watching the events from within the toilet door. For its time this had been quite advanced. What now transpired involved an internal tour, rather that seeing the environment from behind a gateway.

My last visitation had presented an extensive journey. In that setting the main components, of people and machinery had moulded into one functional entity. This trip proved similar in construction, and no less pleasant. It is quite depressing to see representations of people who experience no emotion. They had become part of the scenery, and as one advanced into the location their personality became further removed from the individual. The end result was the machine, which enveloped all traces of their being. The previous visit had not taken me quite this far.

As a visual impact it seemed difficult to imagine circumstances of this nature could ever take place. Having worked in a factory life can become mundane, but this touched on a different subject. One could speculate as to the purpose of this showing, but its meanings were unclear. The most basic analogy could depict man's relationship to the machine, taken to an ultimate degree. If it was intended to teach me something, the purpose failed. I was glad when the showing ended, and moved on to more comfortable matters. The next subject involved the ice station, which became prevalent during most of times that were yet to come. This being my second visit to this station, and it was to a quartermaster's store that became the first stop of this trip. The room being quite large, it housed every conceivable item needed in this harsh environment. I met the man in charge who issued me with clothing relative to the conditions. He did not ask any measurements relating to my sizes.

This seemed unusual, and enquiring how he knew what they could be, wasn't given any answer to my inquiry. His lack of response was par for the course. When he finished his duties, these items were put to one side and leaving the room I went for an extended tour. This complex seemed massive and my movements involved travelling through part of the grounds to see the sleeping arrangements. The other sections of the buildings did not concern my attentions, though it became possible to notice many of the different structures. It was an incredible piece of engineering far surpassing any man made habitation, on either of the ice caps. The rooms, which housed the sleeping quarters, were partitioned into cubicles; housing thirty or so single beds.

These beds had a covering on them of a kind similar to the protective wrapping, which keeps goods on a lorry. It consisted of criss-cross strips that appeared to take the place of blankets. In all of the beds this became a standard feature, and looked out of place. The reason behind its meaning was not enquired in to. That was demonstrated on a later visit. Although this was a large area there were no people around to occupy any of the spaces. This looked as if it was waiting an influx of individuals to serve its purpose at some future date. Because my level of involvement concerned many different incidents, it's difficult to relate their proper place in the scale of events.

On another day within this month I had the privilege of revisiting Venice. This became a more relaxed form of sightseeing, which consisted of a gondola trip through the canals. My craft being operated by a young man dressed in period clothing. The journey was conducted with my presence encapsulated within a small cabin that appeared partially enclosed.

My viewing became limited to watching the scenery through a gap in some curtains. My host explained that no contact would be possible with the inhabitants of the city. Accepting his reasoning, it was never the less fascinating to see the architecture, which had no equals in the period. He gave little information away concerning the environment, and talked more of other matters. This seemed a wasted opportunity on my behalf, to relate the grandeur of the time. It becoming a chance of great significance passed up through being dazzled by the splendour of the occasion. If I could have written down in detail the positions of certain landmarks, in relation to other structures it would have been immensely important. This is one aspect of my time that holds certain regret, for you are only getting the most basic description.

It became one of two important events, which happened on that night. The second concerned a primary sense inherent within my physical being. This was touch. After returning to the centre of operations, my passage involved travelling down a corridor. At the end of this were some braids, which opened shortly before coming upon them. This led to an adjoining room in which a group of musicians were dressed as Gauchos, and playing South American tunes. It was possible to see the artists before entering their location. My thoughts were not however concerned with this. There appeared to have been an error in calculated distance between my alter ego, and the braids. I noticed it before coming upon them, and my brain patterns changed to a basic instinctive level. At the point of passing into the room I lunged at the objects in question and managed to grab them. This caused a feeling of real elation, to hold a physical object for the first time. To understand the sensation in more detail, it advanced my perceptions beyond vision, to that of touch.

This proved a real breakthrough and a caused a sense of exhilaration. In the past there never became a possibility of such an occurrence happening. I held on to these for dear life, and would not have parted with them for anything. The players who witnessed my actions came towards me, and began a new song. This consisted in the Latin American beat of an improvised verse, which suggested letting go of the braids. There was no chance of that.

The object held within my being felt exactly as it should have done under normal circumstances. This was too special an occasion to pass up, and my only course of action that appeared right involved returning to the physical world. I emerged from under the bed holding my bag of glue.

My reactions had been based on physical laws, which applied to the realities of normal existence. It appeared these were not appropriate to my alternate environment. This caused a sense of disappointment, and returning to the present situation nothing was mentioned about the previous incident. In expanding this particular subject it is necessary to relate another event that happened on a later date.

It proved similar to the previous conditions by its method of construction. It involved a setting in which a machine was hovering litter in a park. This was an intelligent device which had a personality incorporated into its circuits. The character of the machine was quite pushy, and it chanced its luck a little too far and came within my reach. My natural instincts were brought into action and I grabbed the device, which squealed like a pig after being picked up.

The same form of elation became felt as the previous occasion, and my response was to say 'Got you little bastard'. Emerging from under the bedclothes it appeared success had been achieved whilst holding the sheet in my hand. For a brief second in time I believed that a physical entity had returned with me through the passage, from the other place. It was a momentary sensation, until normal realities showed otherwise. The disappointment being felt deeply, it left me no option other than returning empty handed. The setting changed its theme, with the machine nowhere in sight; instead a young paperboy began shouting out latest editions.

He came over towards me and asked if I would like a paper. This was passed over, and it became possible to hold the object within my invisible hands. The sensation proved short lived, for the paper began to disintegrate soon afterwards. There appeared to be an incompatibility, which existed between both states of being. It seemed clear that some form of undefined principle came into operation, through the act of touch. Asking my guide if it was possible to hold objects, he replied "Perhaps one day". That was quite an interesting statement, which can be better understood from the present. What he meant was to reach this level required a separation of my soul, from its body. To achieve that status it would involve drastic actions, in other words dying. The principles, which governed my existence within an alternate state, had their restrictions.

The time spent within this framework was limited by conditions, which had different reasoning. One such factor concerned the damage that glues fumes caused within my brain. Since reaching this level of awareness, my hosts had shown the number of brain cells destroyed by a single inhalation. It was quite a staggering figure. To minimalism the risks they introduced a system that involved breathing from the bag once, every thirty seconds. This kept my attentions above the level required to sustain a connection. It did not take long to adopt this principal, without the aid of the green light, which switched on when the action was needed.

This system gave me the one and only chance of getting the better, of a higher intelligence. I actually managed to fool them for a brief period. This being achieved shortly after the green light arrangement began operating. The signal came on to inhale the fumes. This occurred during one of the sessions whilst in bed. Putting the bag to my nose I held the end tightly shut and began breathing deeply, which simulated taken in many times the fumes required.

It happened during one of the sets, and then after this action began alarm bells started ringing. Continuing with the bluff, my set expanded beyond its normal parameters. As an action it lasted about twenty seconds, when I revealed they had been tricked. I can honestly say this was a one off in pulling the wool over their eyes, and covered every occurrence from the first occasion, to the last. It gave me a little satisfaction to get the upper hand, if just once.

The visions, which appeared with the use of solvents, had at different times in my life found a way into normal situations. This is quite a rare occurrence, and when they have come it was usually in way to catch me off guard. One incident, which happened in the dormitory, typifies such an event. It was during the night through one of the weekdays. I had been sleeping quite comfortably, when something caused me to wake up suddenly. Above my head were three monks hovering in mid air. They were about seven inches in height, and had evil personas surrounding their presence. My reactions were to strike out at them shortly after seeing the vision. They were just out my reach, but the action caused them to disappear. This was not a dream, because they had a certain feeling unmistakably connected with my alternate existence. It did not frighten me, but it caused an initial shock, as does any incident of this nature.

The best one of all happened around three years later whilst walking along a country road on a misty night. I had stopped using glue long since then, and the circumstances were perfect to catch me out. This involved a journey from my new badminton club in Yarmouth, to the house in a small village, which had become my home at the time. It would have been in the early hours of the morning, and I was singing to myself whilst walking along the lane. There seemed no reason to expect anyone on the road, but an old man suddenly appeared. I was at first shocked after being caught out singing, more so than him showing up out of the blue. These initial reactions were overtaken after looking into his face. Like the monks it consisted of total evil. Between the embarrassment, and the shock I walked away, then ran about fifty-yards before stopping.

The source of his presence came from my alternate existence, and after considering the matter it generated a feeling of annoyance with my response. From that day onwards if such an incident were to happen, it would be met face on after the initial shock. Unfortunately I have not been given the chance to test my resolve. It was now the summer holidays in Eastmore, and they gave me an opportunity to visit Scotland for a week's vacation. The home issued me with a travel warrant and I went up by train, legally this time. The break turned out very well for a number of reasons. My friend's parents were on holiday, and they left one of the elder brothers in charge of the house. This turned into a perpetual party for the week, and proved heavy going. After the first night back, the rest of my time was spent there.

On one of these nights I came home to tell Jimmy my intentions of staying at Roy's. It was around midsummer time, and late in the evening. This night was exceptionally peaceful, with the sun about to wane. I looked out of our front window and saw an object flying towards the sea front. It would have been about one mile away in distance and moving very slowly. This seemed unusual for a number of factors, and my initial observations were no more than a curiosity.

I called Jimmy over to look at it, but he showed no interest. Going outside into the front garden there was little noise around, which should have enabled hearing the engines of this vehicle clearly. It emitted no sound, and it shape was indistinct because of the green and red colouring, which obscured any lines one could detect as an aircraft. I watched this for a good ten minutes before it left my line of vision. At the time my camera was at the home, which seemed a pity. I am not saying this was a UFO only it was unusual. At some point in most people's life they see something, which cannot easily be explained away. This was such an occasion.

The holiday passed in blur, due to the excessive drinking bouts. It proved good in its own way, as an experience. The one matter, which took me by surprise, happened after returning to the island. I embarked from the ferry and began walking towards the home. In the town there are a number of pubs situated close to the ferry terminal. On passing the first of these, there became a desire to have a drink. This had never happened to me before, and it showed how quickly that the alcohol bug could get to you. Walking by the establishment I consciously decided to give drinking on this scale a miss.

During the first week back my travels took me to the shops to acquire some glue. On the visit to Scotland no solvents had been used. In one of the stores, that operated as ship chandeliers I noticed they stocked a brand of glue remover. As it possessed the same name, this was taken to see if it could deliver similar effects as its baby brother. On that night my usage it conveyed the required effect, and more.

This involved the same format, but delivered with a higher intensity. The start of my trip became a free choice, as was normal under the circumstances. The feelings surrounding this trip were different to the norm, and being so I chose an alternate first setting. This was to see a naked woman. Its method of delivery proved spectacular. A female entered my visions, and ran towards me. She could only be viewed from the top half of her body, with each of her movements it became captured in freeze frame and that action remained as a picture until she reached me. In total there were twelve pictures that caught each response of her body in movement. She left my line of vision, and the pictures remained. My initial reasoning behind this had been sexual, but the class of its artistry had superseded them.

The sexual imperative wasn't pertinent to this environment, and had been dealt with by changing the perspective of the thought. Sex is a physical reaction relating to the flesh. This has no place within a higher consciousness, more the pity. If you can relate to my writings, and imagined what they could have produced given the abilities at hand. This also can be related to my own feelings during these times. It seemed an unimportant subject in the other state. In dealing with the essence of being it appears as a trivial matter.

The following setting involved joining a group of hippy characters that were gathered in a small room. My reaction was to participate in their discussions, which had a certain appeal to my way of thinking during that era. To one side of the group appeared an object, which could not easily be described. It was some form device of an unknown variety. This however did not lessen its appeal to my visual appreciations, with its colour scheme being purple and black. This offered a perfect co-ordination between both contrasts, and looked stunning. The object in question appeared as part of the decoration. It caused me to devote any attentions that would have been spent on the hippies towards it.

As the set ended and I was about to travel towards the next setting, but it occurred to me that this object seemed worth a second showing without any distractions. After asking to see device once again, I became pleasantly surprised when my request was granted. This was in response to giving the reasons behind my actions. The only other event worth a mention involved passing a shop, which had a number of televisions on display. They were very narrow in construction, compared to their bulky counterparts consisting of valves and transistors. I commented on this and after making the observation all of the sets fell forwards blocking out their pictures. As a session it was kept fairly short, because this substance had similarities akin to the shoe cleaner. It being too strong for my requirements and there seemed no point in upgrading the sensations at an unknown cost. My reasoning behind these ideas came from deep within, and was more instinctively based.

In the home glue sniffing had been brought to the attentions of the staff, because of the number of boys involved. This was a consequence of showing Derek, and the chain reaction, which followed. There could be no doubt as to where the source of their involvement came from. I had never been caught in the act, but it appeared obvious to those concerned the practice had been kept up after leaving Winchester. It was decided to send me to a psychiatrist during that summer for a discussion to see if the issue could be resolved. At the time it seemed an interesting prospect, to debate the subject with a professional who would have some understanding of my predicament.

The factor, which interested me the most, involved telling him about the set of events, experienced until that date. This created my first chance to talk freely with someone who could have an insight into the incredible circumstances surrounding my involvement. To my way of thinking it seemed a valuable opportunity, which should prove beneficial to us both. Reading the story so far will give an understanding of how this appeared to me, and why there became a need to discuss it. I decided beforehand to be as honest as possible, for there seemed no reason to withhold any information.

On the day in question, after being shown into his office we began talking. My intentions were to explain in detail how

events led up to a change in perception, from a basic understanding of the conception of hallucinations, to the form now
experienced. It became apparent shortly afterwards this individual had no real interested in the subject, by the way he directed his questions. They were basic, and had little relevance
to the matters at hand. He seemed more interested on what to
have for lunch. This was the impression that came over.

In total the meeting lasted fifteen minutes, and proved a
complete waste of time. The only utterance that warranted
any consideration, involved did I think it would be possible to
have an influence over physical objects. This was something
that had not been considered in the context of my alternate
environment. I reflected on the statement, and replied that
it may have been possible if the conditions were right. My
reasoning to his question was based on an expansion of the
principles in operation. The reason this line of thinking had
not occurred to me involved the way in which my dealings
took place. It had no concern with the outside world. All the
circumstances were generated inwardly, and my actions corresponded towards that idiom.

This was however an interesting prospect, which had not
occurred to date. In the context of out discussion we were
talking about the subject from different ends of the spectrum.
He viewed it as a young boy seeing pink elephants in the sky.
I had left those theories behind a long time since.

Leaving his office caused a sense of annoyance on two
fronts. It was like trying to explain the concept of vision; to a
man who had worn blinkers all his life. His ideas were pre-
ordained, and to expand beyond this premise was not within
his capabilities. I would have even settled for some form of
constructive argument, had he stated these were only delusions created by the substance. His reasoning seemed limited
to a basic understanding, and appeared simplistic in appraisal. I had not expected him to accept my viewpoint, only that
he may find the initial story interesting. The way, in which the

interview took place, did not even allow that to be presented right.

It changed the emphasis, and after making the statement concerning moving physical objects it was something that belonged within another context. I became angry with myself for saying this, because it involved a higher level of dealings, which had not been experienced yet. Making such a statement required an understanding of all the previous incidents. Within the context of this, it would not seem so incredible. If he chose to listen to me, rather than conducting himself in such a manor we both could have learned something.

After making my way back to the home, there followed a sense of resentment at a wasted opportunity. I had assumed a person in his position should have been more enlightened, and have a better capacity to listen. One of the factors that weren't apparent at the time involved the level of consciousness experienced and how rare it was. My assumption was based on the premise that he would have dealt with people who had gone through the same thing. In explaining this matter in depth, it would be more appropriate to evaluate the issue towards the end of the story.

There followed a set of circumstances that became intrinsically linked, by the question posed in the psychiatrists. He asked me was it possible to have an influence over material objects. When this had been raised, the answer should have been no, because it hadn't been tried. The timing involved in this incident, had it been one week earlier would have allowed me to answer the question with some conviction.

It transpired the following weekend had only two boys staying our dormitory. One of them was me and the other being a former inhabitant from Ashbourne Lodge. His name was Kevin, and during my spell in that home I had come to know him quite well. He was not a typical individual you would expect to find locked up for being unduly naughty. As a person he caused few problems to anyone, and remained quietly in the background without being timid. He possessed a pleasant deportment that was uncommon in such establishments.

As it was a Saturday night my attitude became more relaxed than normal. This was partly due to the dormitory being so quiet. With the conditions being thus, it caused me to do something out of character. This involved using glue in front of Kevin, with the lights on. Under normal circumstances this would not have been considered. My using glue is a private occasion, unless taken in conjunction with another person.

There were no problems in doing this with him watching, for he knew of my involvement since the times back at the lodge. Kevin was not the type of person who would consider using any form of drug. Having said this he was nevertheless interested as to the reasons behind it. We had been speaking for a little while as the effects were being generated around the room. Whilst these took place, he asked the reasons behind my actions. It became an unusual setting to discuss this, but he was giving a brief explanation from the early days to the present.

These actions were peculiar, because it changed the emphasis of my involvement to that of debating the subject, rather than concentrating the mind on witnessing the events. During the course of our conversation a thought formulated within my mind to see if I could find out anything about Kevin, through the medium of vision. This was only an idea, which had no guarantees of any success. After explaining to him of this possibility, he seemed quite enthusiastic. I stressed this was the first time of trying anything of this nature, and the outcome would be unknown. This would have to be conducted on a trial and error basis. Kevin suggested the first subject, which happened to be his parent's house in Southampton. I closed my eyes and viewed a building, of which its appearances were related to him. It transpired that my description fitted the place in which he lived. This action became appealing to us both, for different sets of reasons. Kevin's interests jumped dramatically, as would have been expected under the circumstances.

I was pleased at the initial success, but evaluated the revelation as basic knowing the forces being dealt with. Kevin then asked me if anything could be discovered about his family. He chose his grandmother, who had something wrong with her. Once again my eyes were closed and the visions corresponded with this line of questioning.

The way in which it became portrayed depicted an old woman that had fallen down the stairs, and caused injury to her leg. Marking the limb in red, similar to my own effigy with the defective areas showed this. I explained the vision to Kevin, and he said there was something wrong with his grandmother's legs, but this wasn't the information he required. The way in which it had been shown to me required analysis, which may not have been perceived to its full advantage. The other side did not give information away in an easily understood method, it usually being delivered in a cryptically form.

They have certain guidelines, which operate within a law structure that requires the participant's perception to make the best on offer. As far as this viewing went, it proved partially right which shouldn't be snivelled at. My feelings towards this situation were that it only scratched at the surface. There was more to be discovered, if the stakes were advanced to a higher level. The reasoning behind was instinctive, and no better evaluation can be given to its basis in logic. My partner in this viewed the whole situation as highly entertaining, and he willingly accepted my next suggestion with equal enthusiasm. I indicated that it was possible to affect his metabolism, if he agreed to go along with the experiment.

To his way of thinking this involved the same amusement aspect of the previous occasions, but this concept was soon to change. After studding him closely there became a link up between both our personalities. When this had been achieved I, or the agents whom operated through my body had the ability to alter certain of his functions. These actions were directed through my own brain, and it became possible to understand their effects in graphic detail.

This caused within me a certain feeling of dominance, which bordered on the sadistic. It became very gratifying and I knew Kevin was totally oblivious to this. After the connection had been made he appeared in a state of bewilderment. My following action involved reducing his body temperature. This proved a simple action, and it was possible to view the changes in awareness, to that which transpired within his being. The shock, which became apparent in his face, was plain to see. To have such control over an individual is a unique sensation and totally consuming. My level of control was only governed by an ethical code, which had been installed through the experiences of living.

To understand this statement better, one would have to comprehend both states of existence within the same context. Like Kevin I was consumed by a power, which engulfed my normal sense of values. At the time there was no comprehension what distress this caused him. My involvement became interlinked to that of his own, but with no consideration as to its effects. I understood his feelings to the same intensity, as he was experiencing, without the fear involved. There became a point in which this could have been taken beyond reproach, when Kevin shouted to me in order to stop these actions. This installed some form of normality. The link, which existed, was broken, and the next sequence of response came from Kevin.

He took a few seconds to compose himself, and then adopted a different persona. The words that came from his mouth did not correspond to the boy lying on the bed. He assumed a different personality, and spoke in concepts far in advance of his being. When he began talking it wasn't the words uttered that were so out of context, it being the tone of speech. This changed the emphasis from my having control over the situation, to him. He adopted a reverence, which surpassed any discussion I had ever witnessed.

The presence, which emanated from within him, was spiritual in essence. He said I would have to give this up soon. These words had a greater significance than their contextual meaning. It embodied more that a statement could ever offer. It appeared a warning that wasn't elaborated upon. At the time it took me by surprise, and its full meaning could not be understood. The reason I did not accept this at face value involved comprehending the effect glue was having within my body. There comes a point that cannot be passed, and this was rapidly drawing upon me. To think along these lines required giving up that which had become an intrinsic part of my life, and would explain why the matter wasn't considered at great length. This possibility had not really entered my conciseness, for how could one simply give up seeing a way of life beyond the concept of imagination. The experiment had proved very interesting, from both our understanding. There were no other dealings with Kevin throughout that night, and I continued with the familiar under the bedclothes.

The trip became conducted in routine manor, with nothing exceptional that can be recalled from it. They're being no mention of the incident, which had taken place and my efforts to find out any information proved useless.

On the following morning Kevin and I talked about what had transpired, through the previous night. This discussion offered a new twist that could not be easily explained. It turned out his memory of these incidents appeared incomplete. He recalled the parts concerning his house and grandmother, but not growing cold or making the statement. This seemed most odd, and I decided not to push him on the subject for it involved matters beyond my abilities to deal with, that were better left unresolved. That morning gave me time to reflect on the incidents that had been conducted in a different medium. It seemed very powerful and not good in essence. The source of my contact concerned the same entities, but the subject involved a different aspect.

To pursue this angle would have been rewarding, but fraught with many dangers. My reasoning behind leaving it alone was instinctive, and with the benefit of hindsight a correct choice. The structure of my normal dealings with the other side involved a simple format, which for a boy of my age proved quite sufficient. Another viewpoint may differ from these beliefs, and one could argue that any opportunity should have been exploited.

It was around that time I began to approach the subject of understanding the consciousness, from different perspectives. On one of my visits to Yarmouth whilst in the same shop that stocked the glue, I was looking at the book section of the store. This offered a good selection, and one of the covers caught my interest. It concerned the topic of yoga, and it showed a man adopting a pose in a complete state of relaxation. The picture related a level of comparison to that of my own situation, without the harmful side effects.

Looking at it just then did not depict as much information as described but there was an instinctive reasoning this was somehow right. The book was slipped inside my jacket and taken back to the home for study that evening. It described an approach to physical and mental control over the bodily functions. These were adopted and put into practice, within the dormitory on the same night. My actions caused a great deal of amusement to the other inhabitants, but this was of no concern as it held a certain appeal. I found the exercises quite difficult, due to certain inflexibility inherent in my physique. The aspect, which interested me more, involved the meditation. It became enlightening to dispel the rubbish, which flows through the mind at a constant rate. This is no easy matter to achieve, and it took many attempts before it was partially successful.

These actions found a way into my glue sniffing sessions, by two separate methods. The first is a comical observation that appeared before me in a trip. It consisted as an effigy of me sitting in a semi-lotus position. At the time a full lotus caused a great deal of discomfort, and it could only be managed for the briefest of periods because my right leg would not rest in this stance.

My representation had the same leg marked out in red to make the point, which by then did not require a graphic description. On seeing this it caused me to laugh. It was only on rare occasions when the other side chose to comment on an action, undertaken in the normal context of my life. In making this observation it did not need any words to describe the situation. The second involvement proved a great deal more significant. I had been practising meditation during different times of the day.

It was found that distractions could be put into their proper context, unless they were excessive. Attempting such matters were however, best left until late at night. This appeared to be an ideal time, and allowed a deeper insight into the processes involved. My mind had become a great deal more focussed than earlier occasions, and this one evening bore the fruits of these endeavours.

Sitting on the floor there followed a period that surpassed my longest attempt, by a good amount of time. It reached a point where the physical body became unimportant, and for the first occasion my thinking process came under control. These two actions brought forth a vision. It was the inside of train compartment. The carriage was similar to those in use during the time; only it belonged from a different era. My view would have been that of a person standing on the outside waiting to come in .It was comparable to looking at a subject created during a session with glue. The only detectable difference involved a level of clarity that appeared less sharp.

My time in this setting became limited, for the scene changed to that of a ship's cabin. This occupied a similar space, which would be relative to the train. The furnishings in this room also corresponded to a bygone age. My position in relation to this was also one step removed. I then altered to that of an aeroplane. All of these objects had a common reference to a given time. As an estimate it would belong in the 1930 era. My stay on the plane appeared to be shorter than the previous two, which allowed less time to study its settings. Returning back to the train, I found myself sitting on the floor of the carriage. This offered little chance to view my surroundings, because the object in question began to move forward.

This set of action shocked me, and brought the conditions, which existed, to an end. My eyes shot open to check normality still operated, on the same premise as before starting. It was, and the next discovery that became apparent involved my heart beating at a faster rate than could be previously recalled. If such an incident had taken place whilst using solvents, it would not have warranted any response. This however wasn't the case, as it presented a shock to the system. To draw a comparison it would be like changing your perception of something, which had always been accepted. Having attained a level comparable to that of solvents, allowed me to believe it could be continued in a similar manor with relative ease. This was not to be the case, for reason, which has never been clearly understood.

The meditation proved to be of interest, especially during the following weeks. I tried to reach the same level, which offered the visions, but never quite managed the final step, which takes you over the threshold. This became attempted at different times within the space of a day, and something happened during the early part of one evening. I was in the dormitory with the rest of the boys; before the lights were due to go off. Some of the people were reading the others taking, and one boy was playing his tape recorder. These distractions were not interfering with my efforts, which during that hour were only viewed as practice. My concentration became more in tune with the circumstances; it was possible to listen to all of these actions with a better clarity. Each of the sounds came to me in harmony with the surroundings, and they were viewed in an unattached sort of way. The tape recorder was especially prevalent, even though the music was not to my liking. As the sound came out of this, there followed the words 'to keep on meditating' enclosed within the lyrics of the song. After hearing this I went over to the machine and rewound the tape.

The last section was played twice, and there appeared no such words within the song, or anything like it. The boy who owned the recorder looked at me strangely, and was puzzled by my actions. I asked everyone in the room if they heard anything unusual coming from the tape, no one had. These words blended in with the song, which had been in the form of a ballad. It wasn't the sort of thing that could be discussed with those present, so it had to be left unanswered.

The length of time in which meditation became part of my routine lasted about a year, with a lessening form of conviction. I expected instant gratification, without the effort required. It wasn't futile, in the true sense of the word because anything of this nature is of benefit. There is one other important issue that can be classified within its spectrum, and that happened at a later date. From a present day position, this proved another wasted opportunity. By using the glue it had stimulated my brain in such a way, by overcoming various obstacles I had been allowed into the inner sanctum. By the same principles it created an equivalent route, which could have been used in meditation with a little more endeavours. It only required the effort of jumping from one ladder, to another.

The only excuse that has any bearing on my lack of conviction can be attributed to ignorance. I did not grasp the importance of my situation, and that which it could have been developed into. The fact glue achieved the same ends, with no effort seemed like a logical deterrent. When entering into certain possibilities, of what might have been you have to evaluate the normal course of life and the changes it would have caused. This branches into other subjects, and overall my choice of actions has not caused any regrets in the way they have been handled. Through the remaining part of the summer my habits were kept to a predictable routine. This consisted of going to the shops on Friday, stealing some glue and using it during weekend. My involvement at this level was coming to its end, though as a realisation not apparent at the time. This section offered more relevant occasions, which now seem so obvious.

During one of the sessions, whilst talking to Gong the conversation was interrupted by someone else. It wasn't possible to hear this individual's speech, only Gongs replies. He said "Protius you..." This referred to a prehistoric animal. The term was known to me, but on a remote level, it not being one of those in common usage. With the passage of time I have forgotten what he said. It also offered an insight into Gong's character; at least he had a sense of humour. In a similar vein 'Protius' being a word that was not unfamiliar. At the time this passed me by until brought into focus, many years later by two separate methods within a short space of one another. I bought a book with the same name by Morris West, from a second hand stall. Within the same week a question became asked on a game show on television as to who Protius was. The man answering the question failed to give the correct response, and he was given the explanation. It transpired he is a god of the sea in Greek mythology. At least it's something to have your conversation interrupted by an individual of such stature.

One other scale of comparison was that Gong spoke to him on an equal footing. In evaluating the capabilities of my benefactors, this description may not be too far removed from the truth.

On the same evening in question there was a part devoted to the subject of vandalism. That perhaps is too strong a description, it being more concerned with children writing slogans on certain walls. It was portrayed as a problem within the other society. They dealt with the graffiti by means of an automated machine, which located the areas in question, and removed it by the use of certain chemicals. This proved interesting because it paralleled a chemical substance, which had been on a science programme recently. Its counterpart was less effective than the superior technology demonstrated within this society.

The aspect of children had its introduction in connection with this set. As a theme it became further developed within the next situation of the programme. This meant going into a classroom where I was the guest of honour. My participation firstly concerned watching them at work. They would have been no older that six, judging from their appearance. After entering the room the teacher gathered them around, and I was asked to write my name on a piece of paper placed on the desk in front. The pencil had been provided, and left by the paper in question. This action involved mental co-ordination, as using my hands wasn't practical under the circumstances.

It appeared to be a simple task at first, but this proved to be very difficult. To create the correct actions required in writing one's name involved a great deal of dexterity. It seemed to be more than my abilities could muster, and the end result was no better than a scribble. This caused a sense of embarrassment, and I explained had my physical body been present this would have been easy. Leaving the classroom was a slight relief, because the children had been interested in my actions, which proved ineffectual. Travelling down the corridor a noise could be heard coming from one of the rooms, beyond the previous location. This attracted my attentions, and enquiring at to its nature my host said it was a classroom of children with gifted abilities. This involved IQ's in the three hundred-range groups.

His statement caused me to travel on the intended path, rather than making a bigger fool of myself in relation to the last exercise. The next setting is without doubt the most important circumstance in writing this story. It was a small room with no visible features. There appeared nowhere to go, and it left me staring at a blank wall.

At first nothing happened, which caused a certain amount of bewilderment. It was a brightly lit place that seemed to have no function. After this sensation had been installed in me, a new voice began speaking. He said 'Why don't you write of you experiences here'. The reply was fairly instant. "You have to be kidding, my English is very poor". No response was given to the deduction that proved totally accurate. My reasoning became ignored, and the room then offered an additional aspect, which had not been present a few seconds ago. It was a screen that blended into the features of the wall.

There followed four separate extracts of people who had been involved in writing, different aspects of the subject that concerned me. The first of these was Dennis Wheatly, who was depicted in the matter of black magic. Of the four candidates he was the only one known. The other three were portrayed in alternate guises concerning the supernatural. These people were given names, but obviously did not have such a high profile. Their themes were different and no less important in the overall framework of the subject.

When their profiles had been shown, the voice spoke again. "How do you think they got started"? This was his last utterance, and it left me speechless. The remark was put across in a strongly emphasised manor, which made quite an impression.

The setting changed and the impact of the occasion should not be underestimated. The situation returned to more normal guidelines, but my attentions were focused on the last incident. This caused me to finish my session earlier than normal, and get hold of a pencil and paper. Therein began a period of continuous writing covering one and a half pages. It being the first occasion in my life such an undertaking had been attempted. Through all the aspects of my education any writing that was required had only been copied, from the notes on display. It may sound odd, but the work before me proved the longest piece to come from within my own abilities. I never formed an interest in bettering these skills, which had not progressed in the slightest since beginning full time education.

The end result would have been no better than a five-year-old could have achieved. At the time I was quite pleased by the effort, which in its own way became a foundation stone. Reading through the material it seemed important for someone else to see this. The person chosen was a staff member, who read the jumbled mess. He kept a little smile on his face whilst reviewing my efforts, and suggested it should be taken to the headmaster and ask his opinion.

This seemed a good idea, because he was an intelligent person who to my why of thinking would be the ideal candidate. During the afternoon I went to see him, and explained in great detail why this had been written. He listened to me very closely, and did not condemn my reasoning as to its approach, or belief. It proved a relaxed occasion, which did not require going on the defensive, as might have been expected. This in reality became the first occasion of talking to someone at length, about my predicament. It felt good to be sharing the experiences in an adult format, and in its own way brought the matter into the open. The only real drawback was my level of expectation.

Looking at the issue from both sides of the coin, my presumptions were too high. For someone to comprehend the things that were happening, they would need a form of comparison. At the time my understanding of this dilemma, was not fully realised. It wasn't a run of the mill event that happened to those around me. The best example would be to describe Derek's involvement. If one were to examine this in comparison, it failed to advance as a line of progression, and remained in a simple format. This also happened to me throughout my early experiences, but there was a different emphasis between the methods of presentation. To understand this better, you have to be made aware how it is formatted. This depends on the individual, and not something that works for everyone. There are people who get no more than a buzz, which can leave them without co-ordination. I find it hard to reason their logic in carrying on this way, but some do.

The next group is able to have sound and vision, on a limited basis. This seldom amounts to a constructive pattern, and is abstract in its conception. Derek fell within this band and never had the chance, or abilities to advance beyond it. The reasons behind this could only be speculated on, and would come down to a point of view.

This account covers the vast amount of people who take drugs, and what they can expect out of them. The strength of the narcotic will establish its severity, and depending what you take will enhance your perception within one of these two parameters. In evaluating solvents, I am more able to understand how it works on the individual through personal experience. This being so gives me a platform to base any arguments put forward. To look at the issue it would be appropriate to compare the first two situations, within their understandings viewed by the current established opinions.

During my early experiences, that which had been shown to me was not viewed as originating beyond the concepts of my imagination. It is natural to accept the theories of the time without question, and this mirrored my evaluations to the events on display. When something occurred which could not easily be explained, I still followed this premise. When the time came in advancing between levels two and three, it became apparent shortly afterwards the thinking behind this was flawed. This offered a massive jump in understanding, which relatively few people have, the privilege to experience. It also explains why the established theories are directed between the first two levels. If you choose to evaluate a drug encounter within these initial boundaries, then it can be easily categorised. To my way of thinking this implies a limited effort, and complacency at the achieved results by the people who research such matters. There are however, other people who have reached the same conclusions as me. We are in the minority, and come from different walks of life.

These aspects have to be looked into in making a valid judgement; of something no one has a great deal of insight. In writing this story I challenge the concepts of the day and in doing so hope it can be viewed constructively. My reasoning is not egotistical, nor is it infallible. I have no benchmarks, or people who can be called on for an enhancement of my understanding. This has to be forwarded from experience.

When reading other works of a similar nature, they differ in approach because the author's dealings were handled from an alternate perspective. There are in fact, two books, which offer other insights into my own condition. One has been mentioned already. The second is a great deal more important, and holds a place within my own work. When this came into my possession, its timing was unfortunate because I had recently stopped using solvents. This book will be mentioned in due course, and its relevance signified.

There had been a new emphasis installed within my personality, created by the actions of last night. The factor, which wasn't so apparent, involved the amount of work it required. This encounter had planted little seeds, that one day would be called on to flourish. Considering that time, such an undertaking appeared completely impossible. After writing this small amount, no more was attempted because it seemed a daunting task. The idea however was not disregarded, and would have to wait until the circumstances were right.

This involved a three-year gap, when the first problem became tackled. My standard of English was appalling, and the only way to better this meant getting help. There were some adverts on television, which advised people with learning difficulties, to seek tuition. I followed this up and initially went to some evening classes. It became apparent this set up would not suit my requirements, and looking into the matter the educational people put me in contact with a personal tutor.

This was a retired gentleman, who taught me in his home for a few hours each week. The man's name was Mr Bolt, and in under an hour was able to join my letters. It proved quite an achievement considering all the time spent in the varying schools, which had amounted to nothing. This wasn't the fault of the educational system, it being a lack of effort on my behalf. There were a number of reasons for improving my English, but in essence its central purpose was to write this. Shortly after my lessons started I began its first draft. This was a personal matter in the early stages, and not even my girlfriend knew of its existence. When completed this comprised of seventy-two pages, and it showed me how difficult the task would be.

The initial part of this work proved fairly straightforward. I however found the end section hard to put into words, because it involved different levels of thought. At the time my abilities were not comparable to evaluate this, and relate the correct perspective. During that period I was quite pleased by my efforts, because it provided a basis. There was nothing else that could be done, and considering I was a semi-illiterate individual it seemed quite an achievement.

The writing became shelved for over a year, and it was brought out of the cupboard towards the end of 1981. This was a significant period in my life, for two important factors. The first of these involved loosing my employment, in rather a good firm. It was multinational company, who decided to relocate their business. This had been my longest period of employment, covering over two years. It proved quite a blow to the community in which I lived, because this was a large employer. It took away a certain amount of stability from my own life; as such an action has on most people. This however wasn't so important, because on balance my circumstances were fairly good.

The next action became a great deal more significant. My girlfriend informed me during the Christmas period of that year, which our engagement was off. This decision had nothing to do with loosing my job. It was more concerned with growing up, which she had reached before me. There is a vast difference between teenage romances, and the realities of adult life. These two actions left me at a bit of a loss. The only saving grace involved my sporting activities, and the friends associated with it. As these incidents occurred within a short space of one another, it left a considerable amount of free time.

During one of these days I began looking at my writings, and realised they could be much improved on. I set about this project, and doubled my previous attempts. The end result being the best I could do. This had reached a point were professional services would have to be called upon. The work had to be transferred from longhand, into typed manuscript. This involved finding someone who could be relied on to undertake an unusual request, with discretion. There were a number of people known to me who could type, but it required the services of a person who knew of my past before entering a respectable side of society.

During my spell at Eastmore, when the badminton club had taken off we formed set partners for the leagues. This being a mixed pairing, and my other half was Janet the headmaster's secretary. We played together for a number of years, until the policy makers shut down the home. Since that time she had taken a job in the county hall, it being a few minutes away from my accommodation. It was she who became chosen.

We met, and I explained the nature of the task to be undertaken. Janet came to my home and the work was handed over. She seemed surprised by the amount of writing involved. This was taken away and typed to her specifications. The end result reduced my work by half in typed transcript. It transformed my ideas into a readable format, and looking at the finished work it covered all that needed to be said at the time. I was quite pleased with this and decided the next stage of development could be undertaken.

I knew it wasn't long enough for publication, but there was a belief that it held something which should be of interest to someone in the publishing business. My reasoning went like this. It wasn't a normal story of the kind usually presented in their circles. The nature of the work involved a level of contact with higher form of life, and all the connotations associated with that. To have relayed this idea became my main goal, and within the writings there was hopefully enough information for the right person to investigate. My evaluations were not expected to be believed outright, it being more a case of finding someone in the business that had a certain understanding.

The next step involved going to the local library and looking through the addresses of relevant publishers. I chose five or six of these, and had someone type letters explaining the premise of the story. These were sent out; two at a time in the hope it might generate some interest. From these there only came a few replies. The nature of the responses took me by surprise. It was unfriendly in tone. I found this an unusual, because if one should condemn a person's action it would have been more appropriate to have the facts. They had prejudged my work without looking at it. This fails to make good business sense, from their point of view.

I could accept the difficulties involved and had someone said to me, we couldn't take this on for certain reasons that would have been understood. This caused a revaluation in approach, and other letters were sent which had a different structure. There was only one reply that could be considered half-decent, and it suggested trying a more specialised publisher. At the time my understanding of the intricacies of such an endeavour, were based on a simple approach. I could see the importance of these writings, and thought it would not be so difficult to make others think likewise. It proved fairly naive, but then I was dealing with an unknown factor. When you are younger sometimes life seems more straightforward, than it actually is.

The work was put away, and left for six years before seeing the light of day once again. This is from a writing aspect; it had been shown to a few selected people during that time for a point of discussion. I am glad this course of action was taken, for a number of reasons. The most important being it gave me time to understand the meanings of certain events that seemed unclear. Only with the passage of time was this possible. My story had to be further developed, and the issues gone into in a great more detail. This required a certain invention to come onto the market, and that was a word processor.

The next time of using glue presented a new experience in store. My concepts had moved away from the basic animated set routine, of a kind normally picked, to envelop more diverse subjects. As it became a free option, my thoughts revolved around aspects from our own history.

After giving this some consideration, the civilisation that held the greatest appeal was the Romans. It being my first request of this nature I explained the period in time to those listening, thereafter I was asked to make my way to an adjoining room. This being a large area, it housed a machine of a kind unlike anything known to me. My instructions were to stand in front of it, which by these actions caused a partial entry into its framework. It seemed an odd contraption, and whilst looking at the structure my environment changed instantaneously. The machine was gone, and I found myself sitting on a cobbled road in the countryside.

There were fields and trees surrounding me, with no other landmarks in sight. Ahead of this, about one hundred meters in distance were a group of people who were marching in formation, coming along the road towards my position. It appeared obvious they were soldiers, but only when reaching a little closer could the uniforms and regalia be fully recognised. It was Roman infantry units, who were living up to their reputation by the dignity emanating from the combined presence.

At first I treated the situation, as most other visions shown to me, thinking it was a generated image. In the past it had been possible to cause a change in action, by consciously directing the objects in question to alter their course. My attentions were focussed on this action, rather than studying that before me. I decided they could walk around my place on the road. This thought was sent forth, and it had no effect. It seemed quite strange not to have a reaction with something, which had become as a second nature. The soldiers were much closer now, and it became possible to study them in more detail.

It became apparent shortly afterwards these men held something, lacking in the others seen throughout my previous sightings. This was an air of reality. The initial realisation did not alter my belief that it would be them moving, and not me. It left little time before the soldiers would be upon my resting-place. I directed a serious of thoughts, with a great deal more effort than the first time, to bring this action into being, also failed to make any impression. The emphasis of the situation changed from one of an observer, to that of a person about to be trampled by a legion of troops, who seemed unaware of my presence.

My response was to scramble away from road, towards the grass verge. It being purely instinctive and this action brought me back inside the machine, a few yards away from the position I had started. It was in real terms; the equivalent distance travelled in the other setting. I felt quite stupid lying on the floor, acting like a dog that had been startled. Gaining some composure, the course of events carried on with no discussion as to the place, which had been shown to me. Only with reflection was it possible to understand this event, with some objective reasoning. It appeared quite different in presentation to anything seen before. You have to understand the level of graphics that could be generated in this place, was of the highest quality. There were however, differences between these and real objects. This feature became amplified when seeing people. The human quality is missing within such creations. This maybe intentional, in order to put some perspective into the situation. It allows a different awareness to that which is real, and the things that are not.

The soldiers possessed this quality, and it led me to believe a window in time had been created, for the purpose of showing me an actual event from the past. There were no confirmations of these beliefs, from the other side. It was left to my own conclusions, to make these judgements. As a setting it proved nothing extraordinary, and could have come from one of many places. I felt however this scene was close to home, albeit two thousand years apart.

This had been interesting, and on my next visit there became an opportunity to place a request for visiting another culture. I chose the Egyptians this time, which showed a great deal of imagination on my behalf. The conditions remained the same by going into the room with the large device. As before the setting changed and I found myself in a tomb, which housed many treasures. From these the most prominent objects were golden cacti that appeared directly in front of me. It seemed an unusual depiction of such a plant, with a thin stalk and heavy leaves. These went off in different directions, and appeared larger than a plant could support.

My knowledge of these matters is very basic, but it was unlike anything I have ever seen. It appeared to be made of pure gold, and there were others located in the tomb of a similar design. I took a dislike to its construction, and decided to alter this by changing its shape. These thoughts were directed forwards, and like the soldiers did not make the slightest difference. My time should have been spent looking around, but these actions took up most of my energies. It proved quite draining to prolong such a effort without gaining any result. The only other thing noticed before leaving involved the condition of the walls in this building. They appeared to be of a new construction. During 1986, a friend and I went to Egypt on holiday, and visited the pyramids in Cairo. We walked up the passage towards a chamber near the top. Its design was similar to that which had been seen with the aid of solvents. The main difference concerned the size of both rooms, with the one in the vision being slightly larger.

The session had not offered anything outstanding, apart from the inability to use my normal powers. After leaving the tomb and returning to the machine, I asked a very significant question to my guide. It was a requested to witness the most important event known to, me within our own history. This was the crucifixion of Jesus Christ. I am not a religious person and do not believe in the literal translation of the Bible, but it certainly is a fascinating subject. My guide replied this would not be permitted. At the time it was only a simple request, but if one were to look at this in more detail it had connotations beyond my understanding at the time. If they had shown me the event in question, it would have caused a major reaction, if not then at some point in my life. Our understanding of this situation is largely based on speculation. It's not something, which could be portrayed in the visualisation of the penultimate act. This could be very misleading and taken totally out of context.

I could not see this at the time, and viewed it as a missed opportunity. It was lucky in a way there were no inherent beliefs within my person. The momentum continued and developed into another set. This involved a contrast in conditions, presented to discover a wide variation in my emotions. It proved very clever, the way this was achieved. It began by creating a set, which involved a comical situation. This appeared very funny, and it caused me to laugh at its presentation. This developed into the funniest part of the sketch, and then changed to a setting in Africa.

From seeing one thing I now found myself placed in a straw hut, where babies and young children were suffering. They either had malnutrition, or were inflicted by horrifying wounds. The blood covered the floor, and its effect on me became instantaneous. This generated the two extremes, from one emotion to another. I felt the full force of both changes within my personality. These were not real children, but its effect became no less diminished by the lack of a fundamental difference. The sight of suffering can be dealt with from my inner self, but it still leaves it mark as it would to most people. The purpose of the exercises was to determine this, and achieved the desired results.

It was around this period when the topic on offer, took a change in direction. This involved the subject of UFO's. My first encounter with these concerned a blank map of the United Kingdom. I was asked to pinpoint a number of different cities, which the speaker reeled off. This involved locating the area he mentioned, and placing a mark on the sites to the best of my knowledge. This proved trickier than had been imagined. My efforts were not very accurate, as became pointed out after the exercise. Its purpose was intended to show possible landing sights for the said crafts. After this, the situation developed to a more localised region. This was the South West of England. It transpired that a fleet of flying saucers would come from the west, on a cloudy moonlit night. I viewed this from an aerial position, and could see the Isle of Wight below. The reasons behind these actions were unknown, but I hoped some would land on the Island. It seemed a really exciting prospect, of which I would have been one of the first on sight.

The theme of space travel was further developed, within that evening. This meant going outside the atmosphere and walking in the void beyond its confines. To keep with the occasion I became encapsulated within a suit, of a kind astronauts wear. This appeared to be only for effect, because my inner presence would not require such a device. These subjects were at the heart of many young boys' ambitions, and they may have been created for effect. The only way it could bare any relevance on realities was if it were to happen. From the present this has not occurred, so we can only wait and hope for such a possibility.

My involvement took a new twist by the method in which my glue sniffing took place. By changing groups, from D to C there were different bathing arrangements. My new section had two showers, and a small bath. This being a pity because is was nice to wallow in the larger bathrooms of my former group. I decided to have a bath in D group, and by chance had some glue stashed away in the dormitory at the same time. The thought of combining both occasions seemed quite interesting, and it involved no unforeseen problems. After running the bath the glue was poured into the bag, and therein began an interesting experience. At first the light was kept on, and any situations were viewed with my eyes opened. The visions offered an aspect within the water that had only been gained through difficult circumstances. In the water I could see fish swimming about, and they were touching my skin. It became apparent this was an illusion created by the conditions, but who wanted to get technical.

These circumstances were better than had been imagined, and there seemed one way to improve on it. This involved switching the light off. The setting changed to that of the ice station. I returned to the sleeping quarters, and found myself lying on the bed with the criss-cross bedding arrangement. This was placed over my alter ego and its purpose explained.

My guide said this where I would have to lie here until the ice began thawing, then along with the others my survival would depend on consequential actions. His reasoning did not surprise me and accepting this description requires no further explanation. Lying down on the bed, my invisible arms were crossed in the position, which seem natural.

When this had been done there followed a current, generated by the arrangement, which covered me. It proved a relaxing sensation, and resting in there allowed a period of reflection as to the purpose of this building. It was some form of storage unit, which reduced bodily functions to a minimum, commonly known as suspended animation. The size of the complex would house thousands of people, to repopulate a planet after an ice age. As a concept this sounds fascinating, almost science fictional based. It would have to be established if the place in question was the Earth.

This detail was left out in the explanations. Presuming it was, this is not so fantastic as first appeared. There are periods in which dramatic climatic changes take place. In understanding why they come about man's knowledge is rather limited. A second possibility could involve nuclear winter. This realisation became known to the scientific community not so long ago, and after the conditions had been shown to me.

In total the time spent lying on this bed would have been around ten minutes. After that I became kited out with the clothing set aside, and ventured outside on to the ice pack. This was to face a condition that may happen in such a place. The speaker asked how I would deal with a polar bear attack. My response was rather light hearted, and evaluating the situation suggested it would be combated with the large knife provided. He found my attitude lacking conviction, and told me to be serious. This became the first time a level of annoyance had been directed towards me by one of its personal. When the stint on the ice station ended, I returned to the place most of my activities were conducted.

Towards the end of this session, something happened which caused a level of understanding concerning my relevance within their society. It involved an old film clip, which depicted Roy Rodgers and Trigger. This became like reviewing something from my own past, and it offered a parallel between that time and my own. Whilst looking into this simple portrayal, it made me realise that I could be contemplated in a similar light. We both existed within a period of time, seen from a higher plain. This developed into a conclusion that perhaps my time was in the past and studied as a lesson from a page in history. It proved a sobering thought that left me; concerned for the society in which I live.

If memory serves me well, this session took place on a Friday night. The rest of the week did not involve any more usage, and seven days had passed with nothing-eventful happening. On the following Friday afternoon it seemed particularly quiet in the building, because most of the boys in our section had been allowed home for the weekend. I had an arrangement with one of the staff members, to clean his car every so often. For this service he would give me twenty pence, which for its time seemed quite reasonable.

During that afternoon it was exceptionally warm. Combining the two factors of heat and quietness, it caused a certain lethargic approach to the day. They're being no rush to complete the job, which he wanted for that evening.

After wandering about the building looking for something to amuse myself, I was unable to find anything that caught my interest. It being around two o'clock I thought it would be a good idea to have a little sleep, in the dormitory. It seemed impractical to mess my own bed up, so one of the others was chosen to lie on. This would save making my own. I could not get off to sleep as had been intended, and in truth there was a feeling of restlessness, which had been effecting me for a couple of hours. After changing position a number of times, I settled on my front whilst resting the head on the pillows. This seemed the best option, and after a little while any agitation there had been appeared to go away. I wasn't tired in the slightest and the time became spent thinking about a number of matters.

There followed the sensation of drifting away, as happens before one goes to sleep. What made this so unusual was its detachment from my consciousness, which held a normal level of awareness. The sensation had drifted in and appeared separate from my own identity. At first this seemed no more than slightly bewildering, and offered no form of concern. That soon changed after attempting to open my eyes. It proved very difficult to achieve the simplest of actions. At that point my body defence systems jumped into action to counter, an unknown condition. I held each side of the bed and pushed upwards with all my strength. This enabled the top half of my body to raise a few inches from its original position. It proved to be ineffective, and slumping back towards the bed I lay there completely lifeless. The factor, which caused the most concern, involved my mental capacities that remained intact. It could be likened to the process of anaesthesia, in reverse.

There appeared only blackness surrounding me, and it was possible to see this in detail. That, which had been darkness, now changed its complexion and altered it's setting to that of a vision. It was a room with a small pool, in which a group of people were sitting around the edges, or in the water. The first person to catch my attention looked similar to a girl I met during that summer. There were however striking differences between them both. This female was a lot more attractive. The situation did not require any niceties, and my main concern involved that which had taken over the bodily functions. My first reaction was to say loudly "I must be dreaming". These words were not spoken from the mouth, for it became an inanimate object on the bed with the rest of my body.

The girl informed me that she and her sister were to show me around. The other girl stood up and looked very attractive. Under normal conditions the girls would have received my full attentions, but the concerns over this situation were no better understood. I stressed the point once again, about this being a dream. Shortly afterwards I regained partial command over my functions, and was able to open my eyes with great difficulty for a few seconds. In this time it allowed me to raise my head a fraction from the pillow, before the control became lost. It proved a brief interlude before returning to the previous location. The girl said, "Oh you are back". My resistance to the situation was soon forgotten, and after following them any thoughts to my well being were left behind. After this became established it appeared similar to a dream in many respects, but its hold over me was much stronger.

Following these girls I travelled down a corridor, which differed in construction from the type in a glue sniffing experience. It appeared much brighter, as was the whole setting. This led into a room in which a solitary woman was standing. Looking at this person she appeared familiar, having a similar face to that of an older woman from a previous establishment. It was very odd the way she appeared to me, and only by following the contour of her body, did each section become fully visible. The face being my first point of reference and then looking downwards I could see that she was naked.

At first everything was as it should be. The breasts were fairly standard, and my attentions were directed to the area of the vagina. This is what should have been in place, but there was a penis instead. It being partially erect, and seeing this altered my conception of the human physiology. It proved quite a shock and something beyond normal understanding, at the time. This one action certainly left an impression, above all the other events of that day.

My memory from that point onwards is a blank, until waking up almost two hours afterwards. It felt quite strange to know something could take over my functions, with relative ease. I lay on the bed and tried to remember as much as possible about the incident. Unfortunately there were no other factors, which came to mind. These efforts caused me to forget the little job, which had been planed, but it proved a fair exchange. The purpose of this exercise was unclear. I tried to make a connection between this and other circumstances within the spectrum of the overall picture. The only conclusion that could be drawn related to the men who were pregnant, in a loose sort of way. That matter had never been understood either.

On the following day I went to Yarmouth and got some glue, specifically to learn something about the incident. When the connection had been made, it proved impossible to get any information. The subject was approached in a number of different ways, but my hosts were able to deal with these enquires, and brush them aside. During that period, towards the end of the summer I came across a book on hypnotism. After reading the introduction it seemed quite an interesting subject. My initial enthusiasm had to be put into practice, and like anything of this nature it was dived into before reading the whole book. This involved a subject, or victim depending on your point of view. My choice being Derek, and like myself he was game to try something new.

The book described different ways in which this could be achieved. Some of the methods required certain implements, or settings to gain the best results. These seemed quite technical to my way of thinking, and I opted for a more direct approach it was the eye-to-eye, method.

We sat on the floor and began staring into a specific pupil, whilst trying to push inwards with our thoughts. I found this quite similar to meditation, and by concentrating on a fixed point it caused a distortion in Derek's face. This was quite interesting, but viewed more so as a distraction of the original purpose. The object of the exercise being to gain a hold over

Derek's will, with his reasoning more based on the amusement angle. Our efforts lasted twenty minutes or so, before a tear came down from one of his eyes. This also happened to me shortly afterwards, and it broke the level of concentration. We finished our first session after this, and discussed the changes, which had taken place. It transpired the differences in my face had been a great deal more varied than Derek's.

The most interesting aspect involved my eye, which seemed to drift towards the forehead. It had not been successful as far as hypnotism went, but it was difficult to know how long these things took. We had not been disappointed by our first outing, and repeated the exercises during the coming weeks at different times. With each attempt, it seemed slightly better than the last. The breakthrough came one afternoon, when Derek's eyes finally closed after a struggle. This had been hard earned, and the only way to check its validity concerned the lack of pain the state is meant to initial. I read this in the book, without passing the information on beforehand. In my cupboard was a large needle, which seemed as good an object to test this theory as any. Derek remained motionless for a few minutes by then. The needle was brought over, and slowly placed in the back of his hand. I watched the expressions of his face whilst doing this, and they never changed. This went in about half an inch, and left there until he awakened. It took about five minutes for this to happen, and Derek had been unaware of the time, which passed. I had a smug grin on my face, whilst telling him to look at the back of his hand. It proved quite funny to see the expression of shock, which came over him, at this revelation. The needle was pulled out, without any pain.

Like the meditation I had believed it would become gradually easier, to achieve the same state. This failed to be the case, and part of the reason behind this concerned my action with the needle. Of the following attempts, only two held some form of success. I managed to put him under on the first of these, for short while. This required a lot of effort, as part of him began fighting the action. The next event proved more significant, and slightly worrying. After going under, he appeared not to be coming out of it. This stasis lasted around thirty minutes.

I had read in the book some people get stuck in a trance, and need professional help to bring them around. It would not have been wise to try normal methods to wake him, for these can be dangerous. His recovery came at an opportune moment, because if he remained like it much longer, I would have been forced to tell someone. For Derek no time had passed, and the only thing he could remember was the letter D, and the number 6. This seemed quite interesting, because of my recent involvement with the glue concerning flying saucers. Derek visions with solvents were generated by the same source as my own, albeit at a lesser level. I know this through experience, although current thinking would tend to differ. It wasn't inconceivable the source would use him to relay a message, delivered in their usual style.

His words could have meant many things, but the most obvious conclusion became December the sixth. The only way to see if this theory was correct involved, watching the skies on that night. This was about four months away, and it seemed worth spending a little time to see if it was right.

The hypnotism became used on a number of people within the home, but none of them produced the same results as Derek. It is a subject that causes a certain amount of concern, and apprehension. The most unusual aspect of my attempts, where the changes in my own face some these people witnessed. I did not find the same level of variation. There proved one exception to this, and it concerned a boy slightly older than me. Looking into his eyes I could see a change, which showed an elder man, and it presented certain evilness about it.

The person in question did not see any great difference in my expressions and nothing more was attempted in order to delve further into the matter. It became a subject that held most of its interests in Eastmore. I used it throughout the next five years, only on rare occasions if the topic was brought up.

There became one other time during 1986, when my interest became renewed. It involved a fellow squash player at my club on the island. He owned a shop, and run a sideline business as a professional hypnotist. I arranged to play him in a friendly match, more for the purpose of learning of his experiences. After the game we talked about the matter, and I told him of my early attempts. He invited me to his home for a demonstration, on the following week. During the course of the discussion it transpired his interests were more broadly based, to include aspects of the supernatural. Because this discussion had gone so well, and it covered two of the subjects close to my heart I briefly told him about my story on this matter. It created the opportunity to let him know certain aspects, from my own dealings.

The writings were taken to his house on the following day, so he may have the chance to understand them better before our meeting. I did not believe his attempts to hypnotise me would be successful, because of a natural urge to counteract it. My reasoning went something like this. I assumed he should try to put me under, by a similar method that had been used on Derek. By these actions it would have generated a conflict in interest, and caused me to fight against them. It would have helped me understand the subject better, had the book in my possession been read until the end. My own attempts were conducted by an inefficient method, and this became understood in a simple demonstration.

On the day he asked me to lie on a couch then tense, and relax different parts of my body. During this procedure he was speaking the whole time. I complied with the requests, and felt no difference within my consciousness. This went on for no more than five minutes, when he asked me to imagine a sunny beach on a warm relaxing day. The next suggestion being that a pretty girl would come along and place a balloon around my wrist, and then it should slowly rise upwards. I smiled when he said this, and would have betted a lot of money against it becoming a reality. When my arm began to lift from its resting position, my astonishment knew no bounds. I was able to discuss this with him, whilst lying there. He reversed the procedure, and the reasoning as to how it worked was explained to me.

This proved very useful because it helped me understand how my dealings with the other side, had been quite so potent. In a way it bruised me ego to think I could be manipulated so easily. It was however a valuable lesson which offered a potential, which had not occurred before. This method could be used as a back door entry, towards my sessions with glue. I realised this during the course of our discussion, and assumed that Den would have come to the same conclusions.

He had only read part of the story when this took place, so it would have seemed appropriate to let him finish and see if the same deduction would be reached. There appeared something unusual about these circumstances, which did not seem so relevant at the time. This concerned Den's responses at achieving what he set out to do.

It had gone very well, better than I had imagined. I would have assumed this should have pleased him, but these were not the signals that came across. In his face there became a recognisable tension, or apprehension. I saw this quite clearly; even though his words seemed normal there was something wrong. As this appeared out of context for the conditions, I chose to ignore the matter and wait for events to develop. This did not go according to plan. He kept the story for longer than imagined, and after a few weeks asked him if he had finished it. He said that it should not take much longer, which seemed odd considering it could be read in two hours.

This dragged on for over a month, when he asked me to his house in order to pick up the manuscript. I thought it would be an interesting prospect, which had some potential. At no time in this discussion was my opinion, directed with any amount of conviction. I wanted to treat it in a casual manor, answering any questions he may have raised concerning the whole subject. These were few and far between. I found this most unusual, given the circumstances. He had a woman working in his household that assisted in various duties. She also indicated an interest in the supernatural, and Den let her read my story. It became through her that any meaningful conversation took place.

This was unexpected, and in its own way conciliation prize. She seemed prepared to discuss that which Den would not. Her opinions were positive, and whilst leaving the house I felt slightly puzzled. It was something that left me unsure how to evaluate the situation. During that time Den was one of a handful of people, who had read my story. I became selective as to those who should do this. To my way of thinking he seemed the ideal person, because of his skills. It is slightly bemusing to have something; you have considered carefully turn out differently. At the time my understanding of how this would be reacted to, was based on simplistic principles. Only through experience can one learn how others see a controversial subject, and the reactions that can be expected. Through the years this has followed a consistent pattern, and I have a much deeper understanding as to its approach.

Returning to the events within the story, it was coming to the end of our summer holidays. I began using glue more than normal, because of the excess free time during the last few weeks, before returning to the departments. There became a reference in one of the trips, to my involvement with hypnotism. It was constructed in a light-hearted vein, and being portrayed in this way I did not take it too seriously. This involved having surgery to open my third eye. At the time this term did not mean anything, and being so it was construed as a comical observation to that which other people had seen. About one year latter I came across a book, with this title. The story was very unusual, and its interpretations were somewhat odd this being par for the course, because people who write of experiences with the other side, tend to use abstract explanations.

I can never understand why someone portrays his or her dealings this way. All it requires is a simple description that Mr Average can comprehend. These people seem to lose sight of the objectives, and direct their work beyond normal explanation, by alienate the reader, and confuse what they are trying to say. This sort of talk should be kept to an intellectual circle, and a two level approach directed towards the subject. I am not stupid, but when you lose the tract of a sentence, with three unknown words the point is lost.

On a continuation with the same trip, I had some more dealings with the ice station. This part is quite vague, and not worth speculation on a memory which is unclear. There followed a meeting with King Henry VIII. This was a cartoon delegation, which more resembled the real configuration than an animation. It proved quite interesting to see the representation on show, because it was portrayed from the other sides understanding, and not my own. He was escorted by a group of servants who catered to his needs. The purpose of this set became explained, being to gauge my knowledge of the customs, from a bygone age.

I tried to imagine such a meeting, and how one would respond to a personage of his importance. In evaluating this problem, my reactions were based on the given time, and the way you approach the situation. My first action was to bow, which is totally out of character. After greeting the King I began speaking to him. He did not reply to any of these questions. Instead of speaking to me, his responses were reiterated through a servant. Our discussion had certain inaccuracies, which seemed out of context for the period. I pointed these out to my guide and mentioned the most striking difference.

From my limited knowledge, the King would not have chosen a subservient to direct his question.

The set ended, and it had been amusing in its own way. Whilst travelling between locations my guide made an interesting observation. He said I was a 'rebel without a cause'. This is a well-used phrase and its meaning is understood now without reservation, however just then James Dean's most prominent handle, had not come into my vocabulary. I asked him to repeat the statement, more than once. This did not go down too well. The speaker raised his voice and rebuked me for not listening. There was severity in tone of a kind never experienced in my life. It wasn't something that could be argued with, and by irratating him held witness to another aspect of their being

On one of these nights, which if memory serves well was a Sunday? I had an acquired a tin on that weekend, which allowed more, goes than normal. It was late in the evening whilst bringing it out from its hiding place. After starting which took place under the sheets, I emerged from the bedclothes to look around the dormitory. This would have been for a final check of the room, before devoting all my attentions to the matters in hand. There was only one visual difference to the surroundings, and that concerned my bed. This now appeared to have assumed the guise of a bath. It wasn't the best of depictions, but as it occupied my immediate visualisation to hand, this proved quite amusing. There appeared a lot of foam about, which added to the illusion. Being able to knock this about it offered a duality between the sense of sight, and my own natural instincts.

It felt quite strange to encompass both perceptions. I became carried along by its simplicity, and allowed myself to forget the realities of the situation. In this bath there came to hand an object, which looked, and felt like a sponge. I held it aloft to see if any water could be squeezed out. The action was completed and a stream of liquid came forth. This looked odd by the slowness of the movement, and it seemed like a good idea to run this over my face to feel it splashing against the skin. As this made contact, my first response being to think how unusual it was to feel something. The liquid ran down my face close to the mouth, and it seemed only natural to taste it. For a split second I believed the circumstances before my eyes. This concept changed when my taste buds told me otherwise. It was glue, which ended up being spat out on the counterpane.

I became really annoyed with myself for being taken in so easily. In the past there had been similar conditions, which if acted on face value would have caused some form of injury. When looking at a given situation, you have to be aware of potential dangers. These are created like everything else, to test a reaction. If you happen to fall down, there is no one to blame but yourself. The bulk of the mess was wiped up with the counterpane, to limit any more damage to the bedding. The trip continued on a normal footing, with no mention of the incident.

I watched a sketch that depicted a park setting. There followed a machine that spread rubbish around the area. Behind this a similar device cleaned up that which had been created. It would appear to be a pointless exercise. The only conclusions, which could be drawn, involved technologically reaching an impasse. I had come to learn their society, had taken innovation full circle. If the need to strive has gone, what challenges is there left. This could have been a reflection of their culture, or perhaps it involved our own expectations. Either way not a pleasant thought, I for one would not like to live in such a society. In some respects if you look at man's aims this is the ultimate goal, but as with most things in life there is a price to be paid.

One other part of the evening's entertainment involved a woodland setting. This place would be some kind of nature reserve, and it held many different species of animal. It being cartoon based, but this did not lessen its emotional level within my consciousness. The animals were very friendly and came over to see me. This created a good feeling, because it touched a part of my soul, which has empathy towards the animal kingdom. I can never understand mankind's desire to kill creatures, of any denomination without due cause. It is something, which caused distress to be aware of. My host chose a good subject to gain a response.

Their followed a weeks break before the glue was used again. On the Sunday afternoon, my tube was brought out from its hiding place. The reason for using it in the afternoon was more to do with an inability to find anything else that would amuse me. The conditions were fairly safe because we only had one staff member in the group, due to some activity taking the others out of the home. I lay on top of my bed fully clothed watching both environments, with half my attentions directed towards the door.

The tube became partially used without interruption, but it gave no enjoyment because it was one of those days in which nothing would have pleased me. This is quite rare, as my personality is usually contained within a stable band. The bag was taken outside and disposed of in a safe area. The holidays were coming to an end on this day, and the thought of returning to the departments seemed appealing. There was nothing else to do apart from watch the television in the common room, with the remaining boys. This wasn't my ideal choice, but it seemed the only alternative at the time. The sequence of events, which followed, is without doubt the most astounding in all my dealings with this other culture.

I sat there, and watched the last part of a programme on Southern television. It held no interest for me what so ever, it being more of a case of excess boredom. At that point I lay slouching on the chair, when my attentions were caught by something, which happened on the television. The programme had just finished, and there was a break in the continuity.

On this commercial station you normally expected someone to explain what was coming on next, or the advertisements. The screen went blank for a few seconds, and then a title appeared which stated the makers of the following programme. It was Stella Tec Productions. This is the area I dealt with pertaining to space studies. It wasn't mentioned before this point, because it was only a name. My interests lay in the end result, not the title. This heading stayed on the screen for around five seconds, which proved ample time to gain my attention. The subject of this cartoon concerned an alien living on this planet. He was depicted in a form similar to those witnessed, in my dealings with the other side. The one major difference was his height, in comparison to the humans within the film. He appeared much taller. The setting for this was a city in America, probably New York. As a backdrop it conformed to its structural design.

When the cartoon began it had the alien standing on the sidewalk, whilst the other people were going about their business. As he started walking the people avoided him, as they seemed frightened by the prospect of confronting someone so different. If a person came upon him by chance, they ran away in a hysterical manor. The alien had difficulty in comprehending their actions, and tried to be as natural as possible. He continued along the pavement until reaching a museum. This housed a display of Egyptian artefacts. There were people already in the building, who did not see him arrive as they were looking at a mummy's tomb. It appeared these individuals would like to see inside the coffin, so the alien lifted the lid off to assist their desires. This caused more panic and the people ran away. They interpreted his actions as a threat, and it left him feeling unhappy, because all he wanted to do was help.

After this he left the building, trying to understand why people reacted this way towards him. They're being a certain amount of sadness conveyed by the situation, and the only bright point of the story came when a small individual walked over and took his hand. This was portrayed differently to the other people, who were stereotypes. There followed the only narration of film. "At least somebody loves him". In the background hovering above the buildings was a flying saucer. This was the final part of the film. It ended the same way in which it had begun, by showing a blank screen for a few seconds. There were no credits as to the makers, and when the normal picture returned it involved a man speaking about certain programs that day. This took place in mid sentence, instead of the full description. I stood up and went into the corridor to evaluate the context of this film. It had been put on for my benefit, and contained a message of hope for the future.

In making such a statement, which sounds crazy, it has to put within the context of my life then, and incorporating the present date. With the passing of time this animation has shown me different situations that were yet to come, and its structure encompassed issues beyond my comprehension for many years, until their proper time.

Looking at the situation logically, one could argue the title and subject were no more than a coincidence. This factor compounded by a glue sniffing session, in which I wasn't in the happiest frame of mind. It is reasonable to assume these conditions could have swayed my judgement, or ultimately there is a need from within to believe something, beyond the point where reason becomes clouded. If one accepts this, then the deduction must be that I am taking pieces of information and making it fit my aspirations.

As said this is a logical deduction, and if you hold certain beliefs it is the only conclusion. This would depend on how you interpret the writings so far. My involvement with this culture had allowed an understanding of their capabilities, it being well within their means to override the television signal. The issue, which requires more attention, involves the subject matter of the film. In examining this it can only be portrayed in segments of time, in which the points become relevant. The alien was a representation of me depicted, from their point of view. As with most information given one should not take the translation literally. This requires an in depth analysis, and once again only with the passage of time do I now have an understanding of this.

Through the years this matter became something, which caused a great deal of thought, from many different angles. The most obvious is to believe that somehow or other my connection with this place had deeper roots than the mind games, which occurred during a set period. It wasn't possible to understand the depiction of the alien within the film, until the early nineties.

I rewrote my story, with the aid of a word processor and showed it to different people who had an interest, for one reason or another. The first person was Mr Crosbie. He was given the initial draught, which although technically not worded very well, held most of the relevant points. I wanted him to be the first to see this, because he was there when the events took place. It also held more prominence through the discussion-taking place in his house. By that time I had come to realise the dangers a story of this nature could cause, had it gone into print. My approach was to seek out the people, who would have to deal with these problems had the writings made an impact. I looked on this issue as the overriding concern, in any actions that may result from pursuing the matter.

With the information at hand it offered him the set of events, in enough detail to have an in-depth discussion of all its connotations. I left this at his new workplace, and allowed ample time for it to be digested. Our meeting took place in Yarmouth, close to where Eastmore once held us both in different capacities. The talks had similarities with that of another conversation, with Den the hypnotist. Mr Crosbie did not really commit himself on any of the issues. The only point he seemed prepared to agree with concerned my conclusion it was dangerous to pursue the matter further. I could relate

to his viewpoint, but having said that there were other important issues not brought out into the open. It appeared unusual
to see him react this way, because from the people I have been
associated with, throughout different times he should have
approached the subject more constructively.

He gave the name of a man who runs the drug co-ordination centre in Southampton, and his suggestion was this
person would be more appropriate to discuss the matter with.
He indicated that during the coming week he would arrange
a meeting. This allowed the time to correct the grammatical
errors in the story, and present him with a clearer version.
When my work had been sorted out, I drove to the centre of
the city and gave him the Revised Version. It transpired that
he also took a long time to read this. For someone in his position, he would have been in contact with drug users of every
conceivable kind. Given this experience, it presented an opportunity to have a broader based perspective of the overall
picture.

Our discussion proved fairly brief, and once again the issues were not really covered. This approach was beginning to
annoy me.

The part, which proved most frustrating, concerned his
knowledge of the subject. Having read similar works of this
nature before, he gave me a story on a comparable matter.
This was all well and good, but it did not bring me any closer
to resolving my own situation. All I wanted was to speak to
someone who could express their opinions, on the varying
issues. This was tuning out to be a Chinese puzzle. In reality
these approaches proved no better than a dead end. This appeared quite sad because in one light it is these people who
deal with the result of drugs themselves.

My actions required a change of course. During that time I
was living in Portsmouth, and fairly close to my accommodation was a psychic foundation. It seemed quite funny it had
never come to my attentions. The building wasn't the sort of

place that you would have given a second glance to. It was run down and in my travels it had been passed hundreds of times. This housed different people, who were interested in the broader aspects of the supernatural.

I explained briefly my reason for coming, and left the story for the person in charge. He was elsewhere during my visit, but one of the members said they would pass it on. A woman told me his phone number, and I gave him a call a few days after. At least this was not a drawn out process, as he read the story by the following weekend. He found it interesting, and suggested more work would have to be done to give a better explanation. This of course was correct, but I felt disappointed he would not elaborate on specific issues. Our discussion only lasted a few minutes, and I found it difficult to understand why these people failed to notice the importance of the matters at hand. Walking back home caused me to think of the different times in which my work had been presented, and reacted to in a similar sort of way. I felt really despondent to think the issues involved, where being passed over as if they did not warrant a mention.

The following days were spent analysing the matter and it seemed difficult to see why the right sort of interest had not come from one of the quarters. During that period my thoughts returned to the time in Eastmore, when the cartoon had been shown on Television. The understanding behind its purpose was now dawning on me. That, which had been portrayed as an alien, had a double meaning. It being a representation of the action my story would have on those around me. The alien, who was the subject, covered my involvement and the way in which I related the experiences on paper. The people were depicted as representatives of the information, and how it would be reacted to. When the programme had been shown to me, this did not have a relevance to that given time. Only through my actions did this come into prominence, it seemed a very clever piece of scripting.

That version holds within an accurate picture of how I perceived its various meanings, with one exception. The alien held a small persons hand towards the end. I believed this represented my first girlfriend, of whom I had a long relationship. This may have been a misunderstanding on my behalf, because it is out of sequence with the run of events and how I looked on the cartoon from a simple viewpoint with my initial dealings with people and there reactions.

When I did the major rewrite of this story in 1992 I believed that on balance this work was too dangerous to enter the public domain, and downgraded the meaning of the cartoon. The fact that these sequences took place in America suggested, it take's place in America. I now understand that will involve a rather large jump on my behalf, and all the consequences that goes with it. The events mentioned were a necessary jump forward, within the tract of the story to explain this incident. It is better to portray it as a whole, rather than depicting the different issues throughout the years.

I stood in the corridor and tried to understand that which had been shown. My first action involved going into the adjoining group and asking if they had seen the same programme. This had also been relayed through their television. It seemed a pity I did not have any money on me, because the best way to validate its source would have been to telephone the station. There was nothing else that could be done. My glue, which had been thrown away earlier, was by then of no use. It would have to wait until the following day, when the shops reopened. We returned to the departments on the Monday, and life carried on as normal. During the dinner hour I went to Yarmouth and got hold of a tube of glue. The reason behind my actions was to try and find out the meaning of the cartoon.

As time appeared limited it was used in a toilet, located between the home, and village. Dispensing with the normal formalities, I asked the meaning behind this programme. They did not give me any answer to this, as had been expected. With it being an important issue, this caused me to ask other moral questions. I wondered about my purpose in relation to this existence, and was it my first life. To the second question they gave an answer. "This is your first life". It surprised me to be given such a straightforward reply. The number one was then placed on the door in large lettering accompanied this.

My questions came to an end, and the scenery changed to that of a mine. This occupied both sets of perceptions. It being visible either with my eyes opened, or closed. This had a large machine, which began cutting the rock shortly afterwards. It created dust that covered the environments within both settings. My natural reactions generated in the brain combated the experience by coughing to protect the bodily functions. Because these conditions did not exist within my physical space, I believed it was stupid to react this way. It created a situation where my capacity for reason, had to override that which the brain deemed as a threat. By concentrating I tried to convince the area of the mind, which deals which such matters, it was an illusion. My efforts got me nowhere, and the coughing continued. It proved an interesting aspect of the power of illusion, which could generate the conditions to react in such a way. This only lasted long enough to make a point, and then changed the subject matter. I did not spend much longer in the toilet, because time was limited and the whole event caused me to be late in returning.

Because life had resumed to a set pattern, with the holidays over I went back to the routine of using glue at the weekend. The next occasion would have been on a Saturday night, when the conditions were better suited. There appeared something different about this trip, which became apparent shortly after beginning. The way in which I reached the other level always followed a set pattern. It took around thirty seconds before the changes became visible, and during that period my consciousness altered the direction in which it flowed.

As a method this presented something, which had not received much attention, because it offered nothing of real interest. This night began by changing the framework. I could see the sky above me on a cloudy night. The part of me, which occupied the other existence, travelled from the body, and rose upward from its resting place. There appeared a break in the clouds, which formed the shape of a circle. This became illuminated and I was drawn towards it. After going through the barrier, it caused me to reach the other side. It was certainly a more interesting way to travel, and I hoped it would be adopted from now on.

The trip became like many others visiting certain departments and taking part in experiments, relating to their section's interests. I had grown used to this unless something out of the ordinary happened. The first part of this evening became devoted to size. That is whatever part of me occupied their space. I will call this the soul, for it's the nearest comparison that could be classified in terms of an understanding.

My hosts said the object in question occupied a great deal of space. This being demonstrated by explaining they had to create large settings to hold the essence of my being. There followed a transformation in scenery, in which I found myself seated on the floor of a large empty building. In the opposite corner a warrior stood with battle-axe in hand. The voice that spoke these words made a comical observation. "Don't think you're too big to handle". It was delivered with a tinge of humour, which seemed out of character to their normal approach. They obviously thought it important for me to understand part of myself, which came to their environment. It being only on rare occasions that information was imparted, and reasons behind such offerings did not always seem to have relevance.

Towards the end of this session, shortly before intending going to sleep, the setting changed. I found myself placed on a little island that became separated from two mainland's, on either side by a narrow waterway. This being part of a small planet which had no atmosphere and it was possible to see the heavens, although set in darkness the most prominent object was a sun which burned brightly. This appeared close to the planet. On each of the mainland's there were numerous flags blowing in the breeze. I had ample time to study the various features, before Gong spoke to me. He said, "You will have to stop coming here soon". This revelation is something I had not seriously considered, and as a statement not very welcome. Leaping straight on the defensive, my reply was instant, asking why I should want to do this.

From it's beginning to that particular time, my involvements had been full of interest and not something you would want to end a relationship with. I became so busy giving reasons to defend this position, that my attentions had been diverted away from the set. Its relevance came to me in clarity, those words had no place in. The sun was a representation of what would happen if I chose to continue. In other words burn up. The flags were standards of others that stood before me, and carried on. My position had reached the point of no return; it was the boundary that should not be crossed.

This may sound like drawing conclusions from limited information, but there was no mistaking its meaning. Some people call this premonition, or sixth sense. You can choose any one from a number of metaphors, and reach the same conclusion.

When this had been installed in me, the setting changed. I found myself in a room, with a plain yellow backing. In front of the wall were a number of metal rods that were bent at the top, to make a right angle. As my attentions became focussed on them, they began to move. It was a gentle swaying movement, which caused them to pass each other. In total there would have been around thirty rods. After the movement began, a light came forth from each of the tips. This continued for about five minutes, until I finished the proceedings for the night. My bag was put under the bed, and went to sleep. In the morning it involved a time of deep soul searching. I found it hard to believe the bubble could now be burst. They had given me a warning, which in reality, should not be ignored. It seemed very difficult to accept that my good times had come to an end.

During the next week there was no compulsion to use solvents at all. This seemed very strange because, it felt the need to have it as part of me had just gone away. Glue sniffing was never an addiction, in the true sense of the word. It would be better described as treat element, to look forward to on certain days. This began to play on my mind, and by the following Sunday I got some glue for the hell of it. This had been a difficult choice, given all the factors to be taken into consideration. It was an impulsive decision that morning, shortly before the shops closed. I went to Yarmouth and lifted a single tube. There became an opportunity to use the glue in my dormitory, and I did this whilst lying on top of the bed fully clothed. The concerns about being caught were of secondary interest, in comparison to that which might happen.

It began in a normal way and continued with the same format as countless times before. There was however one slight difference. Thought the following sets there were innuendoes, given ever so often. The characters would say, "Oh you're still here or, isn't it time you left us" .I chose to ignore these remarks, and hoped by doing so everything would carry on as normal. My actions did not alter the course of events, and finding myself back in the setting I became confronted by the circumstances, which offered only one option. This time no words were spoken, and the only visible difference being, that of the sun which, now appeared closer than the last time.

To be at the point of no return causes changes within a person, and it proved a solitary occasion. My future lay in the next choice made. The previous time had generated different emotions and my perception had been clouded by the thought of losing something, special to me. This was different because, now only the realisation mattered. Standing alone I decided to call it a day. It was either that, or to have my standard elevated for the next person to see, whilst standing in my place.

The setting changed and had me in the room with the flashing lights. There was no need to continue with this, and called a halt to the proceedings. Informing Gong of my decision, it seemed fitting he should be the one to hear me, rather than another being. I said goodbye, and he concluded our dealings by saying "Goodbye William". My bag of glue was folded over, and walking down to the nautical department I threw it into the sea. This action created mixed emotions from within. There was a feeling of sadness, because in its own way this seemed like loosing a good friend. On the positive side it ensured a normal life from a health perspective. It became a very important day for me, and returning to the building met one of the staff from my group. I told him that from today onwards I was giving up glue sniffing.

These accounts cover most of my times, with this level of involvement, however as with some changes in life it brought forth a new sense of direction. About one month after taking the pledge, the nautical department organised a trip to HMS Vernon in Portsmouth. This navel base housed a fire fighting school, and part of our course concerned the fundamentals of dealing with a fire on board ship. It being the first time any of us had been involved in training of this sort, the outing was looked forward to by all concerned, and our expectations were matched by the excitement of the occasion. We spent the whole day in the base, then after finishing one of the drivers took us back to Portsmouth harbour. This is where the ferry terminal is located, for the return journey to the Island.

There became a little delay at the ticket counter, whilst Mr Thompson sorted out the travel arrangements; I hung about with some of the other boys in the entrance, as he was dealing with these matters, it being a fairly small building which at the time had only limited facilities. In the opposite corner there stood a wooden table, which I imagine had been used earlier in the day for selling newspapers. It was something that you wouldn't give a second glance on entering the room. I must have spent a few minutes there before turning my attentions that way once again. In the centre of this table, there now appeared a solitary book stood upright. My curiosity became aroused, because I could not remember seeing it previously. Walking over to the table and looking at this more closely, the title was laid out in bold lettering. This concerned a biography of Uri Geller, by Andrija Puharich.

The whole situation felt slightly unusual, because I assumed the owner of this stall would have been around somewhere. Checking the immediate vicinity there appeared no one, who fitted that description. The book was picked up and looked at more closely. It proved a new title, which caused a disregard of my first theory. This concerned the possibility of a second hand book that had been left behind. Circumstances did not allow more time to act in an indifferent manor, as Mr Thompson had finished his business, and began rounding up the boys to make our way to the ferry. This only gave me a few seconds whilst he turned his back. The book was slipped inside my jacket with some trepidation, because I could not see everything going on around me.

Through my years of shoplifting, you build up an instinct of how to approach the subject with care. This wasn't it. I trusted to luck, and as good fortune would have it my actions was not detected. We boarded the ferry that offered a chance to look at the story in more detail. It was around that time when Uri Geller had come into prominence, and he interested me as with many other people. My only knowledge of his attributes, where learned from the television. This was limited to bending spoons, and the like. The journey only allowed a brief glance at the introduction, as the crossing took around thirty minutes. The conditions were not appropriate to study this in detail, and it became apparent shortly afterwards this book would require a great deal of attention. After leaving the ferry, there was a short train ride along the pier. Mr Thompson phoned Eastmore after reaching the other side, to arrange our transport back.

During this interval I went to one of the kiosks, and attempted to steel some sweets. At the point of lifting them, the woman who worked behind the counter turned around and caught me. My actions could not be construed as anything else, and it left me in a difficult position, because there seemed no possibility of explaining the situation away.

The commotion, which followed, attracted Mr Thompson's attentions. As events turned out it was quite lucky she decided against pressing charges. This entailed some severe grovelling, in which we both apologised to her. My instructor took me to one side gave me a right blocking. It proved quite rare when he became agitated, but this managed to get him upset. He believed my actions, could have affected my entry into the merchant navy, explaining the headmaster would be told and any outcome lay in his hands.

The factor, which annoyed me, the most involved being caught. I had shoplifted by then, for over five years. During that time, which had been a successful carrier my failure rate proved minimal. From memory I had only been caught three, or four times. It was a double blow to my ego, with this being a petty item.

We arrived back in the home and it took three baths to cleanse the smoke accumulated on my skin, during the fire-fighting course. It was the dirtiest experiences any of us had come across in our lives. That night did not offer much chance to make a start on this book, and it involved something that required no interruptions. On the following morning I reported sick, this being the first time since coming to Eastmore, circumstances had caused me pull that particular stroke. It allowed the time in my room to begin reading this story. I lay in my bed and examined over a hundred pages, which far exceeded any research throughout my whole life. There were similarities in our conditions of involvement, concerning dealings with external forces that I could relate to. This opened my mind beyond the limited understanding, which had previously been known.

This was the first occasion that a comprehension of my own dealings was put into perspective. Until that point I had not come across anyone who dealt with circumstances, on a similar footing. It is worth stressing that although our contacts came from the same place, they had different objectives.

Uri and Andrija were subject to the highest form of involvement anyone, could hope for. You have to understand this other society is based on a collection of beings, which are superhuman, by our understanding. People like me who where induced at a lower level, had only minimal insight to the reasoning and purposes behind their actions. There is a system in place, which deals with people, in different grading. As far as I was concerned my interest to them seemed fairly basic. This is meant as no insult to Gong, or his counterparts on either side. It became a privilege to experience the conditions shown, throughout my own time. However we are not talking about me on this occasion.

The more I read of the book it created a semblance of meaning to my own involvement, by portraying a society which has a great deal of interest in mankind's development. These beings chose certain people to act on their behalf, in a variety of ways. To understand this beyond its limited confines would require knowledge of our own existence, which is not available. The one part of the story, which held most relevance on a personal basis, involved a setting in which Uri and Andrija both had to undergo a certain test. This lasted for a period of days, and drained their strength.

The author's description of this matched my own ordeal, whilst in Ashbourne Lodge. It described to me in detail the conditions and feelings, which formed a unique occurrence within my life. This one section of the story could not be explained, unless they had gone through it themselves, and gave me a validation beyond any reasonable doubt; the author was telling the truth. The purpose of this test seemed to evaluate my capabilities in a given situation, in the future. Unlike Uri there must have been something lacking which did not allow this to be developed. It caused me to think what might have happened, if my own criteria had been accepted. The possibilities were quite phenomenal.

If one looked into Uri's background, according to the book there was a serious of incidents, which made him different to those around him. In talking of this I do not include bending spoons and other similar events; however these are the aspects which people focus on, and the situation creates a difficulty, which shall not be resolved easily.

How can one authenticate actions of this nature? They originate beyond the spectrum of man's development, and the being's that grant them only wish an indication of their existence. At this stage in our development the capacity to deal with such realisations is very limited. People are governed by a given set of beliefs, which if challenged in too strong a manor would cause an adverse reaction. The beings that operate throughout a different plain, realise this implicitly, and chose their methods of contact with care. All that people from this time will get are certain accounts of dealings, such as this one. The experts who wear blinkers will rubbish it, and in the end result it boils down to a personal opinion.

The book in my possession is the only one I have come across, which makes sense. The others are written from a different perspective, and whom they are directed to eludes me. The way in which Andria's book is presented conforms to a format, which I had to deal with, and being party to these events gave a good comparison. Had the story come into my possession whilst still using glue, my dealings with them would have been very different. This of course was never meant to be. Its purpose was to make me understand, after the event. I even thought of getting hold of some glue and carefully wording a serious of questions that seemed very important at the time. This was decided against, with some reluctance. If one evaluated the possibility of such a book coming into my possession, by sheer chance the odds would have to be very long indeed. It being an important story in many aspects and under the circumstances its delivery came by an unnatural method.

I cannot prove this in any way, but it would not have been the first time a manipulation of my environment had taken place. There was the television programme, and the message from the tape recorder. The whole thing can be brought down to a simple set of principles. You either believe that which has been written as a possibility, or it is not. Each of us has their own convictions, and reading such material offers an insight to one group of people. For the others they would evaluate it very differently. I will explore both positions towards the end of the story, and represent their various interests.

As a footnote to the collected works on Uri Geller, some years later I came across another book written about him The subject of this story followed a simple premise, it concerned making money: hobnobbing with well-known people, and making money. In his recollections of the dealings with Andrija Puharich he pays him warm regards, but suggests the subjects of that particular story were a combination of an active imagination, whilst under hypnosis.

Having read that particular story a number of times, the contents far exceed an active imagination. This statement is more designed to distance him from these involvements, whilst make money, and hobnobbing in a comfortable atmosphere, which people accept. I partially understand his reasoning behind doing this, but it reduces his abilities to that of a circus performer, which belittles the purpose behind it.

After reading Uri's biography it caused me to have a renewed interest in mediation, and hypnotism. It seemed my only chance of making contact in a way that offered a safety net. My attempts did not produce any results worth mentioning, and because the initial enthusiasm gave way with the passage of time, returned to a more stable outlook.

Life in the home trundled on quite pleasantly and I concentrated on fundamental issues. Towards the end of that summer one of the boys introduced a new game, to the rest of the members of the dormitory. It involved breathing deeply whilst bending over, then standing up and holding your breath. The next part concerned someone squeezing you, which caused that person to pass out. We found it to be very amusing, as the time you were unconscious seemed much longer that it actually was. The first occasion it happened to me caused an extra sensation the others did not experience. This being a noise, which sounded like, barbers clippers coming from my right ear. On subsequent attempts this grew louder, until it induced an unusual condition.

This consumed my whole personality, and after falling to the ground it appeared similar to having one's entire memories taken away for good. On the point of coming around I had no recollection of my physical existence. It proved a very strange experience, which left me feeling naked, even though fully clothed. This sensation wasn't unpleasant, and it contained within something of purity. My first recollection of the environment concerned the room, and the partially opened window that was only a few feet away. Whilst looking at this, it brought me to realise I had stopped breathing. This action appeared not to belong in this other condition, but my brain had other ideas and caused a reactions required to bring about its most precious commodity. I opened the window and stuck my head outside, then took what seemed like my first ever breathe. As a sensation it was quite staggering. When the respiration returned to normal, my attentions were drawn to the courtyard and surrounding landscape. It appeared like witnessing something I had never seen before.

The whole experience proved quite beautiful. My identity still meant nothing, and turning around saw people who were at first unfamiliar. This being the point my memories started returning, and the transformation from nothingness happened before my eyes. It's a strange sensation to have one's identity restored in this way, being able to feel this realisation gain in momentum, and deliver a personality forthwith.

After the incident it became possible to reflect on the various actions. This was a deeper routed sensation; even more intense than anything was that had taken place whilst using glue. It went beyond a point in which my consciousness became separated from the essence of being. For a brief period I believe this would be like returning to the cycle of life conception, and felt what it was like to experience an event from a given moment in time.

This became quite special, and I believe it could be compared to the point where we are born, or leave this earthly plain for whatever comes next. It appears that under these circumstances all the actions one has accumulated, in life is left behind with the shell. I have to say this only a personal deduction, from something well beyond the reach of my understanding. It was quite lucky that shortly afterwards one of the staff members found out what we were doing. He had some knowledge of medical procedures, and informed us this was very dangerous. He explained the reasons why, and we stopped doing it thereafter.

During November one of the boy's left D group, and his room was in my opinion about the best in the home. I asked for a transfer back to a single room, to continue with my meditation. It was important to have no interruptions in furthering these attempts. The only drawback involved leaving a group I had become fond of, but my goals outweighed this minor consideration. Shortly after moving an incident occurred, which I believe should not have taken place.

This came about by an unusual set of circumstances. It was late at night and, a very peaceful evening. The contrasts between this room, and the dormitory were quite different by the lack of noise. I had been lying in my bed for some time; face buried in the pillow and remained motionless. During this period I did not feel tired, and through the early stages my mind began contemplating the usual rubbish that circulates. There reached a point when my thinking eased up, and all that could be seen involved the blackness in front. This wasn't a conscious choice; it just happened and proved to be similar to meditation without going through the formalities. That which had been darkness changed to red. Under normal circumstances this would have caused a reaction, but something within me indicated it should not be responded to. I complied which proved somewhat difficult.

This was achieved by looking beyond the change, as if it held no significance. When you encounter something out of the ordinary, the brain reacts in ways, which are difficult to counteract. My only option seemed to play down its interest. The red colour turned out to be a corridor, which had at its top a television set. This was at first shown from a side angle. As it began turning around to reveal the picture, my excitement began reaching the point where it could no longer be controlled. This caused a certain amount of frustration, which also generated signals, something was wrong. The television was still turning, and at the point where the picture would have been revealed.

My actions obviously alerted someone, because a large white hand blocked out all scenery, and everything returned to the normal darkness that should have been there. I banged my fist against the pillow, and swore at the same time. It became an interesting experience, which had been aided by an outside influence. They probably got their arse kicked for doing so. This is difficult to classify, because it could fall under a number of headings. A fine dividing line closely links the subjects of dreams and meditation. All paths lead to the same place, and dreams have proved to reveal things beyond a logical explanation. I could write another story on them, but it would cause too much of a diversion.

These are a great deal more complicated, and to understand them properly in any way is beyond my abilities. Throughout my years I have seen many things, which became a reality with the passing of time. These on the whole relate to me specifically, not world events.

A good example concerns an incident, which proved important in the early eighties. It was shortly before the Christmas holidays, when my girlfriend was due back on the island for her vacation. This dream proved quite potent and involved her lying on top of me, with the engagement ring being placed in my mouth. This held a poison that became administered by her, and I was unable to do anything. This dream was particularly significant, because she informed me; a few days afterwards our engagement was off. I did not have the slightest indication there was any problems in our relationship. However this is not the main point. About three years later I took my O Levels in English at the local technical college. We had to read a number of stories for this, and one of them was called the Withered Arm this story concerned the involvement around a dream. It was of a ring of poison being placed in the mouth, and the significant actions, which followed.

From my own dreams I chose this one because it offers a three way split. You have the dream, the events, which became a reality, and the story, which mirrored the circumstances. All of these were to form part of my life, in different times. Although it is not the best one, which could be chosen, this offers a different aspect in depth because of the circumstances. As a subject it often proves inaccurate, and not something to base decisions on, having said that I still pay attention to that which is shown to me.

November had now passed into December, and the sixth day had come about. This concerned my interpretation of Derek's D 6 during hypnosis. I waited until after midnight, and then went onto the roof from an access point in my room. During the set created whilst using glue it had been a cloudy night, with a full moon. Tonight did not match these circumstances. I watched the heavens for a good three hours, and nothing appeared which related to the vision. This opportunity did however, depicted something special in its own way. It allowed a perspective of how small I was in comparison, to the universe. Under normal circumstances this form of evaluation, would not have come about. It presented a chance to see myself within a different light.

The following year concerned a transformation into adulthood. This began without recognition, until a remark became passed. I had finished my course in the nautical department, and awaited a placement on a ship. During that February I was offered a job in a local factory, in advance of their holiday period. They were very busy, and the amount of people having a vacation would affect their workload. One of our staff members played golf with the managing director, and they arranged a transfer of labour on the course. One of the three jobs became offered to me. This was only meant to last a week, but each of us performed our tasks well, and the firm offered us longer-term placements. As with most companies the wages were paid one week later. We were called to the offices to get these, and the cashier called me Mr Stead. This being the first time an emphasis had changed in recognition, from the boy to a man.

My stay in this place lasted over three months, and on one of the days a rumour began circulating going around the factory that a ship had come for me. On returning to the home I went to Mr Thompson's house where the details were explained. He said a placement had been found on Royal Fleet Auxiliary vessel. This left me one week on the Island.

My remaining time was spent at work until Friday, when I had a weekend free to enjoy myself before a total change in life. Those few days were exceptionally good, and spending the time with friends outside the home, made me realised how much it would be missed. On the Monday after saying I went with Mr Thompson, for registration In Southampton. When this became completed we parted company, and the next journey was made alone. It involved a train ride to Portsmouth. This took around one hour, but in that time one and a half years had passed me by.

After finding the ship, it transpired a computer error had place one too many deck boys. As I was the last to arrive, the captain gave me a travel warrant for the Island. He said to contact the shipping pool, and they'd sort out the problem. I returned to Eastmore much to everyone's surprise, and my relief. Mr Thompson phoned up the agencies, and was informed the next available ship would be mine. This only took a few days to sort out, and we visited a shipping agent in Southampton. They offered me a place on a ship bound for Central America. The man, who described his companies operations, made it sound very good. By then some of my apprehensions became eased with the time allowed to make an adjustment. These anguishes had not been mentioned to anyone, and looking back they were only natural. I had become very fond of the island, and considered it my home.

These reactions are common to many people at the point of leaving, something they are attached to. It was lucky my ship stayed in port for over a week before making its journey. This allowed time to accustom myself with its conditions. We departed Southampton, and sailed passed the island. I could see Eastmore house and the nautical department from the ship. It proved a strange experience, as if some form of magnet began drawing me towards it. This soon passed and we travelled across the Atlantic, towards Panama. This was the first port of call, to take on supplies. It was very exciting to behold the lights of the city, in the early hours of the morning. This being my first time abroad and after we had tied up the ship it allowed a chance to visit the town. The differences were quite varied from anything I could have imagined.

The sailors headed to one of the bars in the town, and I accompanied them. This turned out to have a dual purpose, as it was a brothel as well. This proved quite funny because during one of my lessons in Eastmore, Mr Thompson told us to beware of the 'Panama Pussies'. From the way he described this it presented a picture of sailors practising fidelity, this wasn't the case. I went with a prostitute, as did a number of others. The whole occasion was good fun. In the morning one of the boys, and me were the last to leave. We walked through the town, which offered contrasts of a kind never seen before. In one part that could only be described as a shantytown, between the city and docks I noticed we were the only white people. This drew some attention from the locals, and made me realised what a black person must feel like in narrowminded communities.

We stayed in Crystabel for one day, and then joined the queue to get through the canal. That proved quite an experience as well, it being a stop start affair with the ship being towed by locomotives part of the way. At one of the lock gates a workman asked me if I would like to buy some grass from him. Initially it took me by surprise; because this was the first occasion such a propositioned had ever been made to me.

By then it was roughly a year since giving up glue sniffing. I bought a small bag that proved inexpensive, and hid it in my cabin. It gave me time through the rest of the day, debating whether to use it or not.

During the years of being involved with solvents, the opportunities to try anything of this kind had not existed. The only person known to me who took real drugs was Steven, from my beginnings in Scotland. It was something that did not gain a foothold in teenage groups, of my generation. I had a basic understanding of this substance, therefore to the best of my knowledge it would not have produced the same effects as solvents. This factor swayed the argument, and during that evening my cabin door became locked and I made a small joint. The effects did not turn out the way they had been imagined. It began by creating wavy lines that were mingled with the darkness of the room. These were similar to interference you sometimes get on television. Watching this for a few minutes, I felt the need to use the toilet. As first this seemed a natural desire, but it proved impossible to go. This sensation intensified and created severe stomach pains. All that could be done was to lie on the bunk and put up with these. It lasted quite some time, before lessening in severity. This allowed me to urinate, which proved a great relief. As things returned too normal I opened the porthole and threw the bag away.

My little experiment turned out quite unpleasant, and the reasoning behind it did not receive much thought. Everything appeared fine the following day, when we reached the Pacific Ocean. Our ship went to Costa Rica for its cargo of bananas, then sailing to Albany New York. The list of destinations had been pinned on a notice board, but for America it just stated Albany. I had not known where this was till after our departure, and it created an opportunity to meet someone who interested me a great deal. This was my actual mother. She had sent me present from her home, whilst shopping in New York during the early years of my life.

My adopted parents had explained the situation by then, and in reality it caused me to wonder what she was like. I did not feel any resentment towards her, it being more a curiosity. The ship stayed in Albany for about a week, and my plans revolved around hitching into the city and try to locate her through the records departments. We worked a system on the ship that allowed any free time as your own, after a certain amount of hours. I planed to rough it during these attempts, which is something that had not been tried for a few years. After my intentions were made known, this did not go down very well. The crew said New York wasn't a good place to do this in. They more or less stated I could end up dead in the attempt. Everyone concerned reiterated this advice, even after telling them of my times in London. There appeared to be a vast difference in the safety levels of both cities.

Their arguments worked on that occasion, and the ship went south for another cargo of bananas. On the return voyage the boiler blew up, and we limped back to New York. The ship was put into dry dock for repairs, and we were given the options of flying to Miami and transferring to a sister ship, or go home. The majority of the crew chose the later, and we left for England on the following day. This would have given me a two-week break before returning to the shipping agents. There had been tension on this voyage between certain of the elder crewmembers, and looking at the overall picture I did not feel my future lay in this job. This experience had taught me a great deal about life, in more ways that one.

My decision wasn't final, and in truth had I not chosen to go back, the future remained uncertain. These actions would have to wait until the holiday was over. This was spent back on the Island, in Eastmore house. They say absence makes the heart grow fonder; well in this case it certainly became true.

Shortly after arriving I went to see Mr Thompson in his house. He was going to collect a small boat from the estuary in Yarmouth, then sail it along the sea front. I went along for the ride, and it proved a good opportunity to tell him about my first voyage. This being an exceptionally pleasant evening and you could not have picked a better setting for a talk. There were no intentions of explaining the apprehensions about the job, or the possibility of not going back in the future.

We took a small outboard motor from the car, and connected it to the craft. It was of a lesser output than the larger ones used in the nautical department. When fired up, it created a bridge for music to be played within my mind. This happened almost instantly, and changed the emphasis of our meeting. It would be better to explain this in more detail. Ever since my early use with solvents, I had the ability to create music from within. This initially only took place during a session, but as time progressed it became known certain kinds of engine noises allowed a lesser version of this. My abilities were affected by the different tones, which usually came from industrial engines. An example would be a bus running at certain revs. This symbiotic relationship only lasted as long as the frequency was maintained. When it changed the tunes could still be played, but at a lesser level. I used these times to amuse myself, and throughout the years certain songs have become established favourites for the conditions.

This however was quite different. It brought me much closer to a perfect balance. This engine generating about six hp and its revs were fairly high. If there had been a radio in the boat, it could not have produced a clearer sound. The only problem with the situation concerned someone being in the boat with me. It did not allow my total attention, which should have been devoted to one subject. It created no problem talking to him, as I could incorporate both issues quite easily. However this wasn't the point. The tunes flowing through my mind were only an obstacle, if with a little time and practise it would have been possible to have a direct speaking link.

The journey lasted around twenty minutes, and towards the end one song emerged from the others. This was Amazing Grace, the instrumental version with a few of my own lyrics thrown in. It repeated on its self-a number of times, without any mental efforts to break the loop. I tried a number of times to contact Gong, but could not reach beyond the songs. These mental efforts were interrupted when my instructor spoke to me. In the end it was pointless fighting the inevitable, and just listened until the boat pulled up at the jetty. When the engine became switched off, the link, which existed, was broken at the same instant. This particular aspect is something I paid little attention to, as it only interested me during the said times, and soon forgotten.

This is nevertheless an interesting phenomenon that occurs within other people. You don't generally here about it unless it is taken to the other extreme. Some years afterwards this was brought to my attentions, by articles in the newspapers, which concerned a certain Peter Sutcliffe, who became responsible for killing a number of prostitutes. I only have limited knowledge of the man's behaviour, relayed by the media. He said that voices instructed him to commit these actions, and the name giving these orders was 'God'. It must have created an enormous conflict within his person, to receive a message of this nature from the Supreme Being. How is it possible to question the reasoning, of such a command? I am not saying for one minute that it was the almighty, but somebody used his name in vain, and got away with it. You have to understand that if the same conditions were imposed on twenty people at random, at least a few would comply with any instructions given.

This man had natural receptive capacities, beyond that of my own. There was no build up or introductions, someone went straight for his jugular, and got him when it suited. There are many sides to the other level of consciousness, and not everything that comes to a person is of a beneficial nature. Those who are involved in dealings with the other level should be made aware of this fact.

My two weeks holiday passed, and the point had come to make a decision. To buy some time I arranged a transfer of ports, to Leith in Scotland. This got me out of one difficult situation, and into another. There was a belief that I could fit back into the lifestyle here, to way it used to be before leaving. It seemed a bad error of judgement, and the following months were not the best of times. I had no one to blame for this, apart from myself. All the things, which had become important to me, were left behind with the move. I did not go the port to await another ship, and my life became reduced to watching the television.

On one of these days, whilst feeling particularly sorry with myself a notion came into my head, and it involved an old friend for whom contact had been lost. This being glue and it seemed a good alternative from the present position. My line of thinking did not include the problems associated, with such an action. It being similar to having a rush of blood to the head, and leaving the house I walked to the shop and bought a tube. I went to the primary school and seated myself in the same spot the police had caught me, some time before. It being well over a year since my last attempt, the smell took me by surprise. This became stronger than had been remembered.

When it took effect this offered a different setting, than any of my other experiences. Something appeared, but it held no visible shape or context. The best description would be to say it was a hazy vision. This did not seem close to my location, and my attentions could not be directed towards it, because a voice spoke from the distance. It was Gong and the only words he said were "Can't you take a warning". This sentence brought a semblance of perspective about the situation. Throwing the bag away I went home and felt silly for acting on impulse.

Staying in Kennoway for around six months, gave me enough time to realise this wasn't the place to build a future. At the beginning of the following year I left Scotland and returned to the Isle of Wight.

Packing a few belongings with limited money hitched south, and turned up on the door of Eastmore. My predicament required a little help, and explaining this to Mr Crosbie he let me stay in the home until a job and alternate accommodation were found.

It proved quite lucky both of these came within a few weeks. It became a funny stage in my life, and everything fitted back into place fairly quickly. Our badminton team did particularly well, and on the whole I appeared reasonably happy. This lasted until the following autumn, when a vacancy existed through the nautical department. It involved a contact Mr Thompson had developed with a company sailing under the Liberian flag. He sent two boys with them already, and during that time no one in the department had finished the course. The agents asked him to supply a deck boy, and the only person he could think about was me. It proved a second chance, and after some reflection, I believed it held the best prospects on offer. Part of the reason, which helped in this decision, became the location. It concerned working in the Bahamas. The opportunity for going to such place was something that could not be turned down.

We visited the shipping agents on the mainland, and he arranged for a flight on the following week. I became carried along by the splendour of the situation, and it did not sink in how much the Island would be missed, until the plane landed in Miami. It seems quite funny, looking back at these emotions from the present day. The job and location proved quite good, but my homesickness remained. There were two ships operating in the Bahamas, and we carried water from Andross to Nassau. It being a continual procedure, with most time spent in the capital. This is where the water was pumped out and it took twice as long, because it is easier to get something into a ship, than out.

As a result all of the free time became spent in Nassau. This proved the best of both options, as the main island had most facilities and places of interest. The only opportunity we had to spend time on Andross came about by a mechanical problem in the pumping station. The captain gave us the day off, and it allowed an opportunity to visit a beach only seen from the distance. I went alone and discovered a little piece of paradise, all to myself. It was quite a special occasion, and stripping naked went swimming then lay on the sands.

This lasted a few hours, and no one disturbed me. In the evening we went to a bar by taxi, taking the cook and stewardess, who were both local girls. The little township was a few miles away, and very different from its counterparts in Nassau. Before entering the bar a man asked me if I would like to buy some grass from him. My first reaction was to say no, then join the others in our drinking session. After a few beers I thought back to the last occasion, and wondered if perhaps too much gear had been used for a novice like myself. The reaction it caused seemed out of place, and if the amount became reduced this should not happen again. That was my logical basis in rationality, beer assisted.

Going outside I found the man and did a little haggling. A bag of Colombian red was purchased for a few dollars, and going back inside I made a roll-up with only a little grass as a compliment. We were seated around a single table, which had only one support to hold it. The locals were playing dominoes at the other end on a larger table, and the passion this game generated became astounding.

My joint was smoked, and it did not draw any attention. This appeared to have no effect, and it caused me to think the allocation had been insufficient. At this point the stewardess looked over in my direction, and she gave a little smile. Returning this gesture, I found the grin that came on to my face would not go away.

This felt rather perplexing because, my mental capacities seemed unaltered. It was really odd, and no amount of effort on my behalf to change this had any effect. This situation must have appeared funny to the girl, who watched the conflicting emotions within my face. She did not understand what was happening and acted as most people would. It caused her to laugh at me. This action triggered a signal to bring about a physical and mental demise of my own body.

I started laughing hysterically, which attracted everyone's attention. This appeared the least of my concerns, because it felt like something had completely overtaken me. I stood up and leaned against the table that was not designed for a person's weight. It broke and sent all the drinks crashing to the floor. Even though my control became lost, I knew an effort had to be made to regain this. The people and circumstances were a distraction, and the only place which offered a semblance of normality, seemed outside in the dark. Sitting against a wall, my eyes were closed in order to gain some composure. This action brought a return to something I thought had been lost forever. My visions returned, but not in any format ever presented before. I was one step removed from them, and they were going through my head at a phenomenal rate. Many of my past dealings were shown to me, and because of the speed I could not interact in any way. It was like trying to board a roundabout, which is travelling so fast you efforts are repelled.

My capacity to attempt this became limited by the conditions. These finally overwhelmed my reason, which had been the last function remaining intact. From then on I only had partial awareness of my conditions. It ended our evening out, and some of the crew carried me into a taxi and we returned to the ship. My consciousness became locked in a condition, which had total control over it. I woke up the following day and completely missed one of our voyages. We had landed in Nassau, pumped the water out and were on the way back to Andross. There were no adverse effects, and the factor that puzzled me the most concerned the capabilities of this drug.

I had learned through speaking to others, what could have been expected. From their responses it should not have brought about this kind of reaction. This argument could be further developed, by considering the small amount taken. It seemed a pity that common sense did not prevail, and if a little thought had been used its meaning would have been understood. I continued to try this on the following two nights in my cabin. The initial one of these proved similar to the first. I prepared myself for this eventuality, and the peacefulness of the cabin took away a number of the problems. It allowed me to be in a static position and pay attention to the visions, rather than my conditions. These preparations helped my cause, but did not change the outcome.

It was still impossible to have a real grasp within this field of activity. There was however, one difference. Towards the end before sleep overtook me, I began having difficulty in breathing. This caused me to salivate, and became slightly uncomfortable.

As it appeared no more than an inconvenience, the significance wasn't grasped to the full extent. Stupidity is difficult to quantify, but my disregard for the obvious proved quite astounding. There are occasions, as my mother said many years ago 'You will have to learn the hard way'. This became such a time. My lack of concern was due the way in which these events had been presented. No one told me off; in fact it had only been visualisations. Tonight was no exception, apart from one aspect. My attentions were focussed on the visions, until my breathing problems returned. This time it wasn't a minor difficulty it became a major problem. It started in a simple enough way causing slight discomfort. This built up to draw my attentions away from the sights, to that involving the most important function the body can provide.

What should have been causing this was unknown. It reached a point at which panic, almost overtook me. For some reason or other, not enough oxygen was getting into my body. This is a horrible feeling, and the only factor, which allowed me to ride it out, involved the early condition of being an asthmatic. During childhood I had been accustomed to attacks of this nature. Unless you have experienced one, it is difficult to describe the sensations it causes. This proved worse than anything did from my childhood.

I knew from within that a battle would have to be fought against it. There being no one to help me, and if my emotions were to get the better, that would be it. I was kept in this state for well over an hour, before it began to ease up. This being gradual and it let me off the hook in stages. Towards the end of this a final vision appeared it showed the planet and flags facing the sun. I was given a practical demonstration how this would come about, and it proved powerful enough to show that it wasn't any kind of loose threat.

My condition had passed, and it allowed a few hours sleep before the duties began in the morning. I took the remainder of the grass and gave it to one of our sailors. This voyage lasted another two months, and the opportunity came about to go home. It was taken and therein followed the bleakest period of my life to date. I ended up homeless, and the only place of refuge became a staff member from Eastmore's boat in Yarmouth harbour. This was through, the autumn and winter. There were a number of factors that made life difficult, in comparison to the easy times that had been enjoyed.

On one of these days I took a tube of glue from the shops, and returned to the yacht. A feeling of self-pity that consumed the moment outweighed my concerns for that which may happen. Laying on the bunk this tube was used, and it yielded no results. All that surrounded me was an emptiness, which offered nothing. I came to my senses and threw it away. This proved a futile action, and it helped me look inwards to that which I had become. In most peoples life there is a low point that teaches us experiences at different times. This was my own, and from it came a new beginning. These circumstances taught me more about living, than many other events put together. Hardship can be beneficial, although it is not possible to see this at the time. My life changed for the better afterwards, and this nadir became the basis for a new outlook.

This is an ending to one part of the story, and the start of another, although the relevant points are less frequent. The following years were on the whole quite good. I lived what can be described, as a comfortable existence. This stage lasted nine years,

During the early part of 1986, there became a period of discontentment in the direction my life was heading. This had been building up over a number of years, but as with all things they have to be balanced against the positive aspects. It boiled down to this. The Island had been a great place to grow up in, but my childhood days had gone and that which lay before me wasn't so appealing any more.

This line of thinking created a problem, which involved leaving the familiar behind. This proved quite different from my teenage years, when a form of homesickness overtook the rational approach to changing any circumstances. These conditions had more to do with practical considerations, as the pattern of my life had developed. This wasn't an easy decision, and if circumstances had not altered, I would not have embarked on a choice of the heart, not the head. My ideas changed then, and it created the necessary push to break away from a lifestyle, which in reality could no longer be continued. It's quite funny looking back to this, and my actions were designed to force the conditions prevalent for change.

During that period I had taken part in a bodyguard, self-defence demonstration that was shown on local television. The man running this was a former staff member from East-more, who ended up as the head doorman in a nightclub. This became broadcast through the Southern region, and seen by one of the old boys from the home. He came from Portsmouth, and we lost contact through both changing addresses some years before. It transpired these two met shortly afterwards, and my phone number was given to him during their conversation.

My friend Michael came over to the island and stayed for the weekend, where we reminisced about the times in the home. Michael wanted to alter his circumstances, and go travelling to see different parts of the world. He wondered if I held the same sort of ideals. This seemed an interesting prospect that offered a certain amount of appeal. When he posed this question, I wasn't ready to make the change, but a few months afterwards the conditions were right, and the time had come to leave. Our plan involved travelling To Israel, and working on a kibbutz. This we did but neither of us liked the set-up that much. After three weeks we left, and spent a little time looking around the country. From there our travels took us to Egypt. This involved a package holiday to Cairo, and taking in the sights.

The air ticket, which brought us to Israel, was a return, and it had a month's grace before expiry. We intended using it one way, and then sell the return to someone cheaply. Because our initial plans had not worked out, the best option available concerned returning home. This was more to do with financial considerations, than anything else was. I viewed it as a temporary hiccup, but it caused Michael to end his ideals. After coming home my stay proved longer than intended, because another friend needed someone to help in his work. He was shop fitting, and this was his first job. I could not turn down the offer as it paid a good deal of money.

It was November before setting off again, and my destination became India. This time I travelled alone, and had a route planed out to avoid similar circumstances happening again. My travels took me from Bombay, to the northern part of the country by train. My destination was Kathmandu in Nepal. The reason for going there was to walk in the mountains.

The scenery proved quite spectacular, and after choosing which trek seemed best for me, set off. The first part of the journey involved a bus ride to a village settlement. There were a number of tourists on this, and we were dropped at the start of this walk. The first night was spent in the village, living in basic accommodation. I went outside to use the toilet, and was taken aback by the clarity in which the heavens appeared before me. It became possible to see the Milky Way, in all its glory. Being high up and a clear night offered something that was really spectacular. I stood there for some time watching this, which proved the highlight of the trip. The walk itself became very hard due to the lack of oxygen, and I went as far as possible without specialised mountaineering equipment. In its own way this offered a little challenge, the return walk proved also difficult, because of the terrain.

There was a bus that left the village on the same day, bound for Kathmandu, but it went back by a different route. There were a number of tourists onboard, and we broke the journey by stopping at some town for the night. This having electricity, we found accommodation between two boarding houses. It offered a chance of exchanging views on our trip. There must have been ten of us in the one room, talking to one another. As we became acquainted one of the girls asked if we would like a joint. This grows wild on the mountains, and she had bought some from one of the locals. It wasn't grass, but the resin, which is the other constituent of the plant.

As she made this I wondered if the same conditions, applied as before. It allowed a little time to evaluate the risks. This being a different substance than grass and its properties were unknown, having said that my last occasion pushed me into very dangerous territory. When it reached me I looked at it for a few seconds then inhaled. It was quite strong and taking three drags passed it on. This created an interesting situation, and I decided to go outside and look at the scenery. My reasoning was that if I had to depart with this life, it would be better to have a pleasant view before going.

The differences that occurred were less dramatic than had been imagined. It caused a slight change to the perception, with no visions or sounds. The effects lasted an, hour or so. At least the same form of danger wasn't present. Returning to the capital on the following day checked out the best prices and bought a ticket to Thailand. A few days afterwards I left Nepal, and flew to Bangkok. It being mid December, the cultural and climatic differences were quite diverse.

The city proved interesting, but as it was coming up to Christmas I wanted a relaxing holiday, rather than keeping on the move. The place chosen being an island in the south called Ko Samui. It appeared a good choice, because it did not have the tourist mentality associated with more established resorts. During my stay I met a Swedish couple called Anders, and Eva. These were to become very good friends. It was one of those occasions where you hit it off right away. There were a number of Swedish people on the island, and they celebrated Christmas a day earlier according to their tradition.

I was accepted into the group that involved smoking grass on frequent occasions. This is plentiful on the island, which is a home to many travellers. At first there became some trepidation involved in doing this, but it didn't bring about any serious consequences. I did not smoke to the same level as them, because an uncertainty was still inherent about the situation.

The holiday lasted two weeks, and then travelling south by bus went into Malaysia and Singapore. My intended destination was Australia, where a distant relative lived in Adelaide. When you move around there are places you visit, and some that are for working. These are the more industrial countries, and this became an opportunity to earn some money.

My first intention was to work in the city, but it proved difficult to get a job. There is a region, some seventy kilometres away, which makes wine, and is the largest area in the country. This is where a job became found, after a little wait. I stayed in a motel on the outskirts of Nuriootpa, and worked for a firm called Penfolds. Before leaving Thailand I arranged with Anders, and Eva to get in contact with me through a phone number. When they came to Australia, it became possible to get them a job within the firm. They moved into the same motel with me.

My stay in this country was longer than theirs, and during this time one of the supervisors in the winery, and myself had become friendly. We were invited to a party in the town, and it proved quite an experience. The hostess supplied some grass for this occasion, it being stronger than anything taken before did. It caused a disturbing reaction, which involved a surge from within that felt like my soul was being dragged out of the body. This became totally overpowering, and something beyond a simple description words could offer. I kept a grasp within my environment by talking to someone from Penfolds, who was boring at the best of times. This sensation lasted a little while, and then returned to relative normality.

It left behind a feeling of being put through the treadmill, and I felt quite drained. There followed an intense hunger, which in popular terms in called the 'munchies'. It seemed lucky a barbecue was on the go to counteract this. We left shortly afterwards and cycled back to the motel. It became a strange sensation, and the journey appeared very difficult under the circumstances.

On the following week, my friend who worked in the winery said it would be cheaper to move into the house he shared with four other people. This seemed economic sense and his offer was taken up. It changed my aspects of life from living fairly quietly, to one of going out most nights. If you are well connected it offers different outlook. The house was on some farmland and one the boys who lived there also worked in the same firm. His name being Phil, and following the summer he intended walking across the Australian deserts with some camels in tow. His concept had been well publicised, and he asked me if I would like to come along. This was a long venture, well over a year. I declined on a financial basis, plus all the other considerations. It seemed a pity, because opportunities like that do not come along every day.

My initial plans after the six months were up in Australia, had involved going to New Zealand, then America. That was before meeting my Swedish friends. Anders had offered me a job in his parent's restaurant, in Northern Sweden.

This being during their summer and it was located beyond the Arctic Circle. I flew back to England for a change of clothing, and then travelled by different routes until reaching Jockmook. Eva was there to greet me at the station. The reason for going for going they're over the Southern Hemisphere, well why not. Most places are only a day's travel, and it offered a different opportunity with people I liked.

The restaurant was a pizzeria in a small town that had few places to amuse you. This being the case it proved quite popular with the younger members of the community, to have a drink and a central area for people to meet. Our stay was brightened up when four of the seeds from the Marijuana plant from Thailand, began growing. The conditions were ideal in Northern Sweden, because during the summer there is hardly any darkness. It was quite something watching this little plant begin to blossom. It proved to be the eternal fruit, for after picking the leave a replacement would be along in a few days time. This wasn't as strong as its counterparts in Thailand, but it proved sufficient to keep us amused. The sessions were milder in comparison, and it did not have the strength to push me towards dangerous liaisons. In a similar vein after returning to England, there have been times when this substance was taken a little too often. This was due to my conditions of living with others that used drugs frequently.

The sensations it offers are limited, and because of this nine-year gap I have reduced my connectable levels, which is a good thing. In this period the only sensations that are worth a mention concerned half visions. These were stronger than thoughts, but did not have the power to encompass the whole visualisation. These images relate back to my childhood, and concern ornaments my mother used to keep in the house. They had religious connotations, such as the Lords prayer. In a way it offered a warning suggesting it would be foolish to continue. They all used the theme of dying, and how it should be faced. This may sound slightly obscure, but it came through clearly enough.

I can now look on these sensations from an experience point of view, from the present day. The more you use something the lesser it becomes. In the case of cannabis this offers no more, than a slight altercation of the personality. I still use this and its chances of achieving anything worth a mention are quite limited. I have come full circle and started of with nothing where I began. There is not much more I can say about the events which have taken place, apart from some kind of evaluation, which hopefully should bringing it all together.

The writing of my story is a relatively easy task in comparison to giving it a definitive explanation, because there are alternate avenues to look at when forming an opinion to that which I say. This is the fourth time of setting about a major rewrite, and through the years I have come to understand the importance of putting more effort in to this section in order to give this perspective, it seems only right to break this down into relevant sections.

I will start with the drug issue, of which solvent abuse is categorised under. To my knowledge not a great deal of research has been undertaken in this field, which I find surprising, considering the resources at the so called experts hands.

Drugs have been around for a long time, and when you look at their various properties, it seems important to understand with equal devotion the specific effects they cause. I believe my own experiences are relevant towards understanding this issue. It is also with equal importance that my motives are made clear. Drug abuse today is more widespread, than when I began in the early seventies. The approach various authorities take has been on the whole ineffective, and will continue to be so because a need exists. This need will not go away.

I write my story from a factual base, which happened to me, not a theory, nor an opinion. In order to understand something like solvents it is important to explain the sequences, and stages, which happen to the individual. I do not personally know of anyone who has experienced these circumstances to the same level that I have, not that these people don't exist; I just haven't met them yet. It is also not my intentions to moralise on drugs, one way or the other. Narcotics of any description are bad for the health, but people use them.

There is no other way to explain this set of events, other than tell it like it happened and deal with the issues when they arise. I have an interest in drug related matters that began shortly after giving up glue sniffing, and throughout the years have come to understand that very little is known about the effects side. This is quite funny because it was one of the reasons that stopped me doing something with this before.

I watched a program on television some years ago about three boys, who had dropped out of society. They lived in squat and used solvents whenever they could, to extremes. I looked on these people and saw the down side of something, which to me was a rewarding experience. This is the other end of the spectrum and it helped form an understanding into another condition, that of the victim. In my time of using solvents I had never known anyone to abuse a stimulant to the level they did. In life there are people who fail through personal choice; this can be drug related, alcohol, or circumstances. These boys decided solvents was a good enough block on reality, and pursued their aims beyond any reasonable consideration to the body. From their accounts none of them experienced anything interesting, other than numbness through excessive use. I find their way of thinking to be very destructive, and the only hope for people like this is through a change of heart.

The drugs question is a very big issue, and it would be quite easy to divert away from my own experiences to encompass other aspects, but I believe my comments should be restricted to that which relates to my own circumstances. In describing these it is important to explain what they are, and why they happened. Looking back with hindsight, it gives me time to have a deeper understanding of the events, which lead to my entry into the third level of consciousness. I believe the stages are threefold. The first of these is a change to the perception, which happens on taking solvents, or any chemical, which has similar properties.

This seems to be a universal principle, and most stimulants bring about this result. For some reason or other certain people get stuck in this cycle, and do not advance on to the next stage. I have no idea why this should not be so, nor do I understand why they continue doing something which can't be that enjoyable. I did not experience this and after the change to my own perception, came the first stage of part two. This is sound effects. These are abstract and emanate from within. It is the first major altercation to one's own environment.

By concentrating it became possible to change these sounds, and in doing this allows you link with something else. I believe this one action is of the highest importance and part of the reasons why I got as far as I did. With time it is possible to train your mind to interact within this field of activity.

My writings are a personal account of a particular drug experience, and their broader implications. I believe this is important in a number of different ways, of which the first of these concerns how the establishment views the current opinion on stimulants. The drugs issue is tackled from the negative side of its properties, and when it is discussed little mention is given to the sensation the drug causes. I understand this line of thinking and believe it to correct, but only to a point. If your job is dealing with drugs in society, then it only seems fair to have a good understanding of the other part of your work.

There appears to be a narrow minded approach to drug sensations in professional circles. One thing that brought this into focus with me concerned a television program called "Sacred Weeds" on channel 4. This was an attempt to comprehend different drug effects on a group of volunteers. It made me realise how little is known about the whole subject; by the way it was conducted. This was set up in a controlled environment, and the people who participated were given their particular stimulants. The volunteers in turn explained how the drug altered their perception at different stages in its life cycle. Monitoring this was the usual group of professional bodies, and others who were interested in the results.

The one thing that stuck out about this experiment, were the debates, which followed. I listened to the people's accounts, and understood the sensations they had experienced. The discussions, which ensued, broke down into two basic lines of argument. The presenter followed one line of thought by interpretation the volunteer's accounts of their actions. The range of viewpoints was quite diverse, and the one's that I found most interesting were the anti drug effects brigade. I have a special name for people with this type of opinion. "The flat earth society". These groups of people are so narrow minded, and hold back progress into bettering an understanding of this matter. Their basic argument is all form of drug sensations is no more than a serious of delusions, in one way or another.

These beliefs are incorrect in many ways. The aspects of this I find most disappointing are the potential they have squandered at their own hands. In order to research something it helps if your viewpoint is not bigoted. I believe the whole package to understanding stimulants should be looked at in with a fresh approach, and if this is done in the right way it will bring about results. Where these results take you is another question.

It would be quite easy to go off in many directions as you discuss drug issues, but I will keep these opinions rather limited. The reason behind this is the enormity of the subject. When people express their particular views they tend to argue a case in one way or another. The difference between having an opinion and the contents of this story are substantial. This is an account, not an opinion. It has a start, middle and an end. It also depends on how you look on these writings, and how much validity you think they have.

My story has three possibilities in real terms. The first of these is it's a lie created for the benefit of fame and fortune. People come out with all sorts of tales for one reason or another, with little or no evidence to back their claims up. In my case the contents, places, times and individuals are quite easy to verify. I used solvents, and within the context of my memory these accounts are fairly accurate. It could also be said that a different picture is being presented of these circumstances, in order to change the emphasis of this story. In other words, make out it is more than it actually was. My line on the serious of events that happened has never changed, a better understanding has. I do not want to waste too much time on the lie issue, because it can be removed from the equation without a great deal of difficulty.

I look on the presentation of this story, and the particular forms of attack it will receive. It would be better to dispense with lies, and concentrate on the next form of condemnation. This is delusions, and grand delusions. As a subject for discussion this is the one that will receive most attention. In the beginning I used glue and began something, which took me into another state of awareness. To be in this third level is a special condition. I can compare it to sitting here writing this story with all the sensations going around me. If I were to explain all of these circumstances to justify my life and give it some perspective, I would argue a case to define my existence.

This other perception is no different, and just as real, only in an alternate way. I understand the concept of a delusion, and if I had not reached this level if would be quite easy to fobbed off, by the conventional line of thought. A drug experience like my own should be compared to other peoples accounts, and when you find the right one's there will be a number of similarities that cant be ignored. I believe if enough searching is undertaken in this field, the results will be astounding. The validation principle is very important, and in order to get some way towards this you should look at these individuals and listen carefully.

This approach is the first stage to understanding a conception that has enormous implications. At the end of the day there are only two possible outcomes, it's either right or wrong. The people, who say drugs are only delusional, have a limited form of argument to say otherwise, because the truth is always waiting to be discovered. It is quite simple to achieve a comparable set of results as my own under the right conditions, if protocol will allow it.

There are many avenues to look at when forming an opinion into drug experiences, and this version presents an alternate viewpoint. The currant way of thinking on this subject is wrong in its approach, and understanding. I have looked on this from many different angles, and find it difficult to see why someone has not worked it out yet.

As said the drug issue is a quagmire and I will have to leave the various debates, and go on to the next segment of information. This subject will cover my dealings with the other side, and what does it mean, it's a big question with a number of possible answers. Through the years I have given a great deal of thought to this, and feel the time is ready to share it with someone.

In the beginning my views on the effects of solvents had little substance to them. They were events, which happened, and did not receive much attention. As time moved on and situations became more developed, I began to question the beliefs that I once held. It can be compared to a large puzzle that needs unravelling. You have life here, a middle ground and the other side. In crossing over from one to the other, sets of tasks are presented to the individual, which have to be undertaken. I did this without any real understanding of the events on display. The first and most important is an interaction of the mind with a serious of sound effects. This enables speech to be developed in the future, and without use of this option it limits one's ability to understand the big picture.

I believe people who take drugs of a hallucinogenic nature, and manage to trip will see events, but not communicate, or interact with the displays around them, if they did not attempt to link up with this facility. I think it is one of reasons, why a better understanding of drug effects has not been realised. Had my experiences only been visual, they would have meant nothing. I can also see why this one factor has limited professional studies from being advanced, in comprehending what drugs actually do.

The willingness to explore these events with the mind is a natural ability, and it sets the conditions of any future dealings you will encounter. All of these circumstances are governed by a set of principles, which have to be followed. In my case I got there in the end, which shows how it can be achieved. This is nothing more than a set of tests, or initiations that allow access to the third level. If my writings can be understood, I hope to explain the importance of using one's mind in order to do this right. Experiences should be looked at inwardly, because they are the most direct paths to the other level of perception.

The last paragraphs contain the information on how to reach the other side. I will now attempt to explain the meanings, and methods that were depicted during final section of my program. Having advanced into level three I realised this was in no way, any form of delusion. To be in this condition is very structured and makes the word seem irrelevant, so I will ignore this line of thinking and concentrate on its explanation.

When looking at the events as a whole, I form an opinion as to the overall reasoning behind my involvement. The society, which dealt with me, is superhuman by our standards, and does everything for a purpose. I want to talk about some of the more important purposes. The way events were presented is rarely explained, and it is up to me to get as much information out of this as possible. These individuals know everything about our society, and when they choose to tell me something it is put over in an unusual method. I will give a good example of this. Shortly after reaching level three Gong spoke to me about the subject of music, more specifically the Osmands.

He emphasised how popular the band was with all of his people, and became enthusiastic. This was out of character from any discussions we ever had, which includes all the times afterwards. I do not believe for one second he was talking about the musical ability of the band. What he was saying is from all the individuals who are known that their way of spiritual and ethical belief is the correct one.

He used the Osmands as a shinning example of how to conduct one's life. This piece of information was intended as imparted knowledge, for you the reader. I am not a religious person, but if I were this form of ethics would be chosen. Gong and his compatriots have a thousand times the insight into all forms of beliefs, and a better understanding as to what they represent. He gave this to me, to give to you.

I understand the significance of such a statement, and realise its implications. These revelations are of singular subjects, and another good example is the time I was informed that communism as practised in Russia was based on evil. In saying this they give an insight into a system of ethics, which on face value is rather interesting this was delivered as a powerful statement, which made me wonder as to its purpose over the years.

When the communist era came to an end I thought it was a final act in the demise of a political system, but instability would cause the ice age scenario to take place as a result of a nuclear war between the super powers. This although not quite eliminated from the equation is not correct, even with the collective wisdom of our political leaders. This is how it was envisaged throughout the nineties when the last rewrite was completed. As I give an account of these events it belongs in a process of evaluation

When my last rewrite was completed then, I made a couple of fundamental mistakes regarding the end section of this story. The first one is not enough work to explain the meanings behind my own involvement, and still do. It is not intended as definitive understanding; more block analysis in different sections. All of the subjects I have only limited insight, and I came to see that a lot more effort would be required, in this field. The story is an explanation of my life and times, which at the end of the day is only reciting a serious of events. It is much more difficult to incorporate other thought processes along with my story, and marry them up.

This is not helped by the fact that the other sides are very good at guarding their opinions. Having said that, there is another set of principals, which can be used in this other conception. I discovered it was possible to understand various situations presented to me, without being told what they actually were. This goes much further than forming an opinion or a supposition into the events on display. I believe this sense is part of our make up, which in the spiritual context comes into use. It is particularly noticeable during times of danger, or having information relayed to you without infringing on a law structure.

During my time in the third level it was only or rare occasions that I received a direct explanation, into certain events that were shown. I came to understand visual perceptions could be explained alternatively by the use of another capability, which is emotionally driven. This function is perhaps; linked to a human stage of development that has not kicked in yet. We have only limited understanding in any of these fields of activity, because the technologies do not exists to monitor the brain well enough yet. I am no form of expert in anything, what my experiences should be classified under is that of a witness, having said that my opinions should be looked at in their contextual meanings, because I experienced these conditions from a different angle.

How information is presented comes under different headings. I gave two examples earlier about the Osmands, and Communism. It may seem obscure to the reader, but to the participant it is not. That is one form of the learning process the next is slightly different.

In the third level I was introduced to themes, in which my participation became involved. The ice station is the most prevalent, because it was used more than any other was subject was. I looked on this as an important revelation, purely in terms of quantity. This analysis took on a new meaning, and I tried to build up a picture round it by incorporating other parts of my experience with this theme.

I came to the conclusion my interpretation of events would be very off putting because of their connotations, and decided to leave the opinion open to the reader. This is one way to put it across, but over the years I believe the correct method is to say its contextual meaning as shown, and interoperate the feelings associated with the time. To advance this one more stage I would have to have to give my overall analysis to the bigger picture seen from the present day. The visions about the ice age that were shown to me have three possibilities, as I understand them. Unlike the Osmands or Communism, which were statements, these have no such contextual meanings. It could be no more than a theme to get my attention within a field of activity. That is a very plausible explanation, and I hope that for the sake of everyone here it is the case.

The second is a set of events that will destroy the fabric of society, as we currently understand it. The third is some part of my life, which is yet to come, and takes me on to experience similar circumstances to that shown in the visions. I must admit this whole concept slightly concerns me, just in case it's the second possibility I looked on the ice scenario as a result of a nuclear war, and the winter that follows on from such a conflict. But other forms of evidence suggest otherwise. Only time will tell the proper outcome, and I am interested to see how events develop. In a way it would be quite pleasing to have read this one completely wrong.

I want to now discuss which is to me, the singular most interesting aspect of all my involvements with the other side. During my dealings in the third level I came to understand that within their culture a division of beliefs existed. This does not require a lengthy explanation; they are good and evil. After becoming aware of this factor I told Gong about the reluctance in being involved in something, which made me feel uncomfortable. He answered the question by presenting a visual description, which helped to explain his societies, values. The message depicted two aliens in conflict over their individual principles. As the information developed, it became clear this battle of ideals was over me.

These images were very powerful and relayed more information than a simple message of its nature would have, under normal circumstances. This aspect presents a meaning, incorporated within its visual imagery that is emotionally enhanced. The point is then made clear to you the individual. At various times this facility has been used on me and I find it difficult to express this concept, because of the unusual sensations associated with it.

I believe the nearest comparison would be precognition. In this case the message is delivered, which is an insight into good and evil as seen from an advanced society's way of thinking.

This aspect fascinates me more than any other, because of its implications. I find it hard to believe that a race of beings could develop to the form, which they have, only to derive purpose from malevolence. During my various encounters I entered this conceptions domain, and the range of feelings, which bombarded me, were very specific. I never met any of these individuals, or spoke to them directly whilst taking part in these experiments, but I certainly felt its conceptual foundations. Through the years I have considered this possibility, and look at why such a conception exists. There are two separate reasons according to my way of thinking.

The first is my involvement could be considered in the same way a scientist, would deal with a chimpanzee. The difference between both our levels of intelligence can be compared along these terms, if I choose to flatter myself within our comparative statures. Although I don't believe this is way things are done, you have to accept its possibility and understand the reasons behind it. I concede an advanced form of life would treat every aspect of my personality with equal devotion, than includes fears and the darker side of nature. To confront these brings out a reaction, and like the scientist, the end results are all that matters. It can also be argued that a different set of values override any derogatory consequences to me.

I also have to consider these outcomes are intended to do exactly that. I offer this set of conjecture to explain a monkey, scientist type scenario. Although this is possible I believe the next description at hand is more accurate. During my time on the other side Gong was my mediator, and guide through many varied experiences. He is a good individual and I feel his intentions are honourable. The development of his race is demonstrated by the technologies that they had on display, which show abilities far in advance of mankind, at this stage. I believe their interest in us offers the insight into both capabilities, and purposes. I have often thought what the end result of an evolution, such as his would amount to. Taking he is good, what if someone else developed along the same lines, but his ethical code was bad.

My conjecture can be looked at as life stands today. Take two famous people from both ends of the spectrum, Mother Theresa and Saddam Hussan. Both of them affect our opinions, and we view their actions according to a good bad principle. Saddam craved power; Mother Theresa had only noble intentions. At the end of the day when all the conditions have disappeared for suffering and material aspirations have gone you are left with an ethical code to pursue your particular values. I assume the development of a race would evolve along these lines. I believe these are the principles of this particular society, and a division has grown between them both. I felt this, although how sure one is in the strength of these beliefs is uncertain.

What these beings ultimate aims are can only be guessed at, but I know one thing they have a great deal of interests in mankind. It was my intention to speculate what they actually are, but these guesses can be no better than a stab in the dark. When looking at these individuals it seems more appropriate to understand what they do, and the methods used in achieving their aims.

I will now offer my own reasons for writing this story, and the ultimate purpose behind my objective. A good way to start this evaluation is to begin from a simple premise, and work outwardly in terms of complexion as it develops. To start of with I have always felt a need to explain the set of events, which took place under the influence of solvents.

This at first was relayed as the spoken word, and told in sequence, albeit rather a shorter version. My choice of people who were told of these events became selective, and this trend continued with the various writings. Having read the story so far will give you an understanding of the conditions surrounding my dealings, and why such a need arises to explain an event of its nature, to the best of my abilities. The use of the spoken word has its limitations, and during my younger days this was the only option open to me, because my educational abilities were none existent. As time moved on I began to see this problem would require assistance, and I decided to learn English in order to make a start.

There were many problems to overcome in reaching this level of competence, or the lack of depending on viewpoint. The important factor is in the beginning I was almost illiterate, and in order to write an account of this length required a total overhaul of every concept, from basics to complicated principles. That was quite a challenge, and on balance the end result justifies all these efforts.

My initial understanding in presentation of the story was based on simple principles. I knew the events that were witnessed came from beyond the concepts of my imagination, and they held within their structure important messages. The simplest way to express this was writing, and I believed if these suppositions were put across well enough the meanings would be grasped, and someone or other could develop a working relationship within this other society.

I did not understand at the time, quite how difficult a set of ideas would be to get across. I found much to my surprise reluctance, even in accepting this subject as a point discussion. Through the years this aspect has caused a certain amount of bewilderment, but I now recognise the approach and reason behind the attitudes concerned. Drugs are a taboo subject and when the line is not taken it disturbs quite a number of people, because to change a perception that is commonly held is not welcome. The explanation that I have presented certainly does that, and it bothers me there is no easy way around this problem.

At one time I placed too much emphasis on the negative aspects of this account, and came to the conclusion it was on balance better to leave it alone. I remember the day clearly going into that room, when I was told to write this story. That was a defining moment in my life and it has altered the purpose and reasons to my way of thinking, as well as the meanings, which govern these thought processes. I was afraid that a work of this nature would encourage an increase in the use of drugs, more specifically solvents. It's not a pleasant prospect to see this story taken the wrong way and abused, but I am afraid certain individual will do just that. It follows on that given this will happen, some could die. I came to realise this factor, and through the years of developing the story I have given this one aspect top billing as the single most important reason, why nothing was ever taken beyond a limited discussion point. The victim became a stop point, and I unloaded many of my own negative fears in with this concept. A good example went like this.

I viewed the writing of this book as on the whole a bad thing, because of its potential use in the wrong sort of way. This can be looked at in percentage terms, and my best comparison would be to compare at all the people I personally know who used solvents. None of these individuals have died through it, or become some sort of deranged madman. Included me they used glue for a time then stopped.

This is also the same for most class B drugs; it's when someone abuses there given properties, such as the dropouts in Brighton you run into problems. The authorities tend to focus their campaigns on the extremes, and forget about the vast majority whom for drugs is recreational. If you choose to examine these events from the extremes, then all work must stop and my evaluations cannot be developed. I believe the way ahead shouldn't be viewed from this principle, because it only forms a kind of denial about the whole subject. This one factor should not restrict a form of understanding from being undertaken, no more than my fears associated with the problems a book of this nature would cause.

I focussed on what the results in both good and bad terms my writings could bring about and I came to the conclusion that the voice, which said to write this, must have been from the darker side. Once again no one said this, and I let my concerns about its effects change my opinions towards these statements. Many years ago after being directed into a brightly lit room an individual suggested, I should write of my experiences. He knew full well the implications of such a statement; although at the time it seemed a complete unfeasibility because it reached beyond any capabilities I possessed, or could ever imagine being part of me. This character knew otherwise, and he installed a sense of purpose to make it happen. This driving force has never left my personality, In order for this to happen it will require a number of initiatives, on my behalf to bring this out into the open.

There is one other important factor, which needs a more detailed explanation. This involves the cartoon on the television. I believe my analysis on this was on the right lines, but too limited in substance. It depicted a scenario yet to come on how this story will be responded to. I looked on this at one time being more localised and not where it was set, in America. My first reactions to this were based on the initial impressions, which came across on presentation of my story and the kind of responses it would receive.

Taking this on a bigger scale the United States, it was intended to show me how this story would develop, even before it was written. I understand why something of this nature would receive such a reaction, and look at these revelations as what will be. It could be argued that if this is the eventual outcome, then why bother. I look on success and failure as both being comparative, because one day all of this will be understood. My promotion of this story is intended as a guide to reaching the other side, what you will experience and some of the meanings behind these actions.

Armed with this information you will achieve a great deal more than I did. I know the capabilities on display, and if these are used correctly the sky's the limit. Taking drugs as one issue, I found they can start you on the right path, but meditation should take over. I failed to grasp the significance of these actions when presented with the opportunity. Don't make the same mistake. I could go on to develop many other points, but that would just be rattling on. Instead I will leave you with two separate pieces of information. The first is why I have chosen to do something with the story after all these years.

What motivated me to upgrade the versions has usually been proceeded by times of trouble in my life, and I find it channels these particular energies into a creative direction. This particular interpretation is completely different to that. It began as before by getting a bottle of wine, and reminiscing through a little read of my last rewrite. This happens, every so often and it's like reviewing one's life in microcosm. On the last occasion this sensation did not go away, and I kept reading it over and over again. This began to bother me, because there was no obvious reason for doing this. It was the equivalent of relentless pressure, without an outcome. I could not understand why this was happening, and it reached a point where the only logical course was to rewrite and do something with it. This was a profound experience, unlike anything I have ever encountered. Without any rhyme or reason it caused me to change my thought patterns, and how I had decided to deal with this story over a relatively short period of time.

I know me quite well and this is not an easy thing to achieve. Something had overtaken my values, altered them, and reconstructed my life with the greatest of ease. It caused me to disregard any thoughts I had over this subject, and advance it to the next level. Two days after making the complete change of course I was watching the news, when they announced Roy Rodgers had died. He was a focal point in my learning curve, and through him I understood the interest this society has in us.

There is one very important aspect of his death. You have to understand the way information is given from little pieces, to major announcements. The word that was missing is "Trigger". From this other society point of view, this is how information is relayed. It was indeed a trigger, without any question of doubt. I now have to present this as it was, without stupid analogies, or consideration to my personal opinion. The big picture is more important than any regard I have to my views or that which I think is relevant. At the end of the day I am nothing, and my views count for little more. What I have to do is relay all this information to you the general public, and wait for the feedback. Good or bad.

That is my job and is part of a learning process for you. Life advances and as technologies improve these events which became part of my life can be portrayed in easy stages to comprehend, and with a bit of effort you will go part of the way to understanding them. It is quite lucky the society I had the pleasure to be involved with is totally switched on, and can deal with all aspects of humanity, from any angle. I look on the big picture and see the whole subject from two basic viewpoints. They either take place, or the various encounters were designed to gain my responses in a given situation. Either way I am interested to see the outcome, and look at both objectives with interest.

Any opinions I have written are no more than my understanding to a serious of events as I saw them through different ages. This of course could be wrong in a number of ways, but having the benefit of first hand knowledge allows me to express them as I see fit. The conditions took place, and it is to these you should pay more attention to rather than my evaluations. There are other relevant pieces of information I choose to leave aside, because they are of a personal nature. In one aspect I have to use the wait and see approach, to verify some of these conditions. Time will only tell, and my understanding over certain matters will come about as it meant to, when they are meant to.

The last piece of information is only a little thing, but quite important. On a trip to Australia I befriended this boy who was travelling around the country, much the same as me. We ended up together and after a few days the subject of drugs was brought up. I told him about some of my dealings in this activity, when the name Gong was mentioned.

He said there is a Rock band of the same name, which sings of drug experiences, relayed through the medium of song. I have never heard their music, but the chances of this being coincidental are quite slim. It depends on how you look at facts of this nature, and choose to interpret them. There is a simpler way, go to the people who wrote these songs and ask them what they mean. If a basic approach can yield results with one person, imagine this factor being multiplied many times over. I think this is way ahead, and it will help to put everything in its proper place. The rewards that will come about by fair impartial work will be nothing short of astounding. You do not have to be the brightest person in the world to understand that. I believe my story will help to bring these conditions around, and hopefully be of benefit. It will not be easy to achieve this, but I believe in the ultimate goal. This is the reason for all that I have done, and it's eventual outcome.

There is not much more to say, it is now the time to act on my beliefs. I only hope that on balance these writings are more beneficial than harmful, and it helps to change some wrong attitudes.

As I read my story from the present day there is a little piece of information missing. On one of my trips towards the end section I was in a room and talking to someone from the other side. I was permitted to see the left hand side of my soul. It is luminescent and incorporates a basic shape of human form. This would explain how I could grab various objects at different times. In size it is about a quarter the length of your body, like a compact form of humanity, as an embryo. At the time I never looked on this as any importance because I operated this vehicle thought my time in the third level. I now know what a special event this was, but then it was just a thing. It's funny. I have seen an alien, and my soul but for different reason I did study either. In a way its nice to know you have one and in a way it should make you think about the many things we do in life, it's a buy now pay later scheme I chose to leave certain events out of the story for personal reasons this is one such circumstance. During 1978 I was working in a small holiday camp in Brighstone on the Island. This journey involved cycling along the coastline on my return trip. One evening in the late summer I was heading home as it was starting to get darker, and came to a junction opposite a small petrol station that was closed. I noticed some lights on the horizon, out to sea. The first thought was these were some sort of flares, but as I watched they did not move or burn out. In total there were five lights glimmering away. As it was getting darker I watched these intently for some time until they disappeared, as an estimation half an hour, would have passed ,every possibility was considered, and the only option left was UFO,S. I tried communicating telepathically, but there was no response, nor did they come closer. I saw no people around, to share this with, or noticed any cars during this time, it was unusually quiet. Over the years I have only told a few people about this, and never written it down, keeping it separate from every thing, what makes this especially unusual is that it happened again 21 years apart in the exact same location.

During April 1999 my wife had a new car to test drive, and I borrowed this to do some business I was driving by this same location in the evening, before it was dark, once again and the circumstances were similar, apart from the month. They were there again, only eight this time. I stopped the car and stood in the same spot and witnessed a re enactment, no closer but the same. Most people would be happy to see this, but I wanted more, it wasn't good enough. I went before they did.

These events together have caused me to wonder why such a commitment was made to show me this; one could have been a coincidence, but not two. Some years later I was watching a program on TV, about UFO, s flying over a city in America being filmed. This is the same vehicles in both my experiences. The effort of showing me these sightings has to be for a reason, and that is some form of hope, in that they have some form of belief in me to do what I must.

Printed in the United Kingdom by
Lightning Source UK Ltd., Milton Keynes
140862UK00001B/69/P